Cook's Corner

Presented by

The Fayetteville Observer

Acknowledgments

A heartfelt thanks to all the cooks who have shared their recipes with us over the years, especially those who graciously brought us dishes so we could photograph them for this cookbook. Also, thanks to the *Fayetteville Observer* staff members who worked to compile, photograph and edit the recipes, especially editor John Rains, librarian Daisy maxwell and photographers Cindy Burnham, Rachel Santillan, Marc Hall and Raul Rubiera.

 • ISBN: 1-59725-081-3

Published by Pediment Publishing, a division of The Pediment Group, Inc. www.pediment.com Printed in Canada.

Foreword

On Wednesday, Nov. 8, 1995, a column for local recipes, *Cook's Corner,* was introduced in *The Fayetteville Observer-Times'* Food section. In the first column, Carolyn Sublett of Fayetteville shared her favorite recipe – low-fat broccoli and chicken casserole from a cookbook at Sublett's church, Village Drive Baptist Church. "This is delicious," She said. "You don't realize you're using low-fat ingredients."

Over the past 11 years, the column has had various writers, the Food section has undergone several redesigns, the newspaper has even changed its name, but *Cook's Corner* has continued to be one of the paper's most popular features. It has also been a real reflection of Fayetteville's diversity. We've helped people make Japanese sushi, Chinese fried rice, German onion pie, Filipino noodles, African rice and fried plantains. And it has helped keep alive some strong Southern – and family – traditions, such as Carolina oven-fried chicken, liver pudding, bread dressing and Chapel Hill cake.

We've selected some of our favorite recipes for this cookbook, along with the columns about the cooks, as they appeared in the newspaper. We tried to give you a large selection and a variety of dishes. We hope you enjoy trying out some new recipes, and along the way, learn a few things about your neighbors. Happy cooking!

Nutrition a Staple in Underwood's Household

February 23, 2005

Candy Underwood

Candy Underwood grew up knowing how good fresh food and excellent cooking can be. Her father grew up on a farm and was used to fresh food straight from the garden, cooked the old-fashioned way.

Underwood learned to cook that way, and the first things she learned to cook were country-style steak, mashed potatoes and string beans.

While attending Campbell University, she studied home economics and education. Part of the curriculum required that she stay in the Home Management House and cook meals on a rotating basis with fellow students.

After college, she went on to earn a master's degree from N.C. Central University. Today she works as a family and consumer science agent for the North Carolina Cooperative Extension.

Her job is to counsel people on food, nutrition, housing, clothing and human development. So good nutrition is close to her heart.

Candy is careful what her 12-year-old son, Ted, eats. Like most youths, she says, he doesn't like to eat everything that is put before him. Her husband, Mark, has a rule that Ted must at least take a taste of everything that they eat, even if it's only one bite.

She says children will learn to like a new food if they taste it between 10 and 20 times. Underwood jokes that she is well on her way to learning to like goat and alligator meat as a way of practicing what she preaches.

Her motto is "eat smart and move more," and she insists that children need to watch less television, play fewer computer and video games, and engage in more sports and outdoor activities.

It is hard to watch your nutrition when you are eating out a lot like many families do because of their busy schedules, she says, but she believes it is possible if you learn to avoid fatty foods.

Underwood's mother, Mary Ellen Creech of Laurinburg, helps supply her family with nutritional meals by canning and freezing vegetables such as fresh creamed corn when it is plentiful.

In preparing meals, Underwood loves to use the recipes that have come down to her through her family. One of her favorites is a squash casserole that she inherited from her father's mother, Rena Creech of Smithfield. The pecan pie recipe came from her Great-Grandmother Prevatte of Robeson County. The lemon icebox pie recipe belonged to her husband's great-great-aunt, Jesse Green of Cedar Creek.

"These recipes have great sentimental value to me," she says. "Just to know my great-grandmother made this pie. When Jesse Green died, I asked for her recipes and cookbook, and it was given to me."

– *Melissa Clement*

Squash Casserole

2 cups of cooked squash
1 cup bread crumbs
1 cup milk
3 tablespoons butter
½ medium onion, grated
2 eggs beaten
2 tablespoons sugar
1 cup grated cheese
Salt and pepper to taste

Drain and mash cooked squash and mix with all ingredients. Place in a greased casserole dish and bake 30-45 minutes in a 325-degree oven.

Icebox Lemon Pie

1 (15-ounce) can Eagle brand condensed milk
½ cup lemon juice
1 teaspoon grated lemon rind
2 egg yolks
Cookie-crumb crust
Meringue

Put Eagle brand milk, lemon juice, lemon rind and egg yolks into a mixing bowl. Stir until mixture thickens. Pour filling into a prepared vanilla-wafer crust. Top with meringue, made with a standard meringue recipe.

Cookie-Crumb Crust

33 vanilla wafers
6 tablespoons butter or margarine, melted
¼ cup sugar

Place vanilla wafers in a plastic bag or between 2 sheets of waxed paper. Crush into fine crumbs; measure 11/4 cups crumbs. Place crumbs in a medium bowl; stir in sugar. Melt butter or margarine; add to crumb mixture. Mix well.

Turn the crumb-butter mixture into a 9-inch pie pan.

Spread evenly in the pie pan; pat onto the sides and bottom to form a firm, even crust.

Grandmother Prevatte's Pecan Pie

1½ cups light-brown sugar
½ stick margarine or butter
2 tablespoons milk
2 eggs
1 tablespoon flour
1 tablespoon vanilla
Unbaked pie shell
1 cup pecans

Melt margarine or butter. Stir sugar and flour into butter. Put in eggs one at a time and stir. Add milk and vanilla. Pour into unbaked pie shell. Place pecans on top.

Bake slowly in a 300- to 325-degree oven until done.

Mom Combines Beans, Pasta in Salads

May 1, 2002

Eileen Rettig

Eileen Rettig and her 11-year-old daughter, Katie, like to make salads that are hearty enough for main dishes.

"We don't eat much meat," Eileen says. "Maybe once a month we will eat chicken. We eat a lot of beans, rice and cheese."

One of their favorite summertime meals is taco salad, made without ground beef. They shred lettuce and add grated cheese, sliced onions, olives, cooked kidney beans, tomatoes and diced red and green peppers. Just before serving, Eileen adds crushed tortilla chips, and Catalina or Russian dressing and mixes it like a tossed salad. She serves it with salsa and sour cream.

"In the winter we like a lot of bean soups and stews," she says. "I like black beans, pinto beans, kidney beans and the mix of 15 different beans. I like any kind of bean."

Eileen soaks beans overnight. Then she drains them and does the quick-boil method from directions on the bag. She says using both the long and quick softening aids in digesting the beans. For some salads, she uses canned, cooked beans.

"I used to make homemade breads, but I have discovered Great Harvest bakery and don't make as much now. I do a lot of baking around holidays, like Easter breads."

Eileen says Katie never had a taste for meat and would refuse to eat it when she was a toddler.

They bypassed the fast-food hamburger phase when Katie was young. "If we go out for fast food, we go to Chick Filet or Katie will eat a waffle at the Waffle House," Eileen says.

Eileen homeschools Katie about three hours a day. Katie goes to enrichment activities on Wednesdays at The Church of the Open Door.

Eileen says the homeschooling schedule works well with her home business. She has been an independent contractor for a scrapbooking company since getting a divorce and moving back to her hometown five years ago. She earns money from the supplies she sells to create scrapbooks of family pictures and memorabilia.

Recently, Eileen prepared lunch, snacks and desserts for 90 women who attended an all-day

Black Bean Salsa/Salad

- 2 16-ounce cans black beans, drained (you can use more)
- 2 16-ounce packages frozen shoepeg corn, not cooked
- 2 cups diced red onion
- 2 cups diced red pepper
- ⅓ cup dried jalapeno pepper or fresh jalapenos to taste
- ½ cup chopped cilantro (or more if desired)

DRESSING:

- ½ cup balsamic vinegar
- ⅓ cup olive oil
- 2 tablespoons Dijon mustard

Serve with Frito Scoops or tortilla chips

scrapbooking convention in Fayetteville. She says the women paid $30 each for the workshop to cover supplies and cost of the food.

Eileen baked banana nut bread, coffee cakes, brownies and toffee chip cookies in advance and froze them for snacks and desserts.

The day before the workshop she made pasta salad with vegetables, chicken salad with mini-shell macaroni and black bean/salsa salad with frozen shoepeg corn. The black bean salad recipe came from Ann Hedgecoe Smith.

Catering the workshop was a major undertaking.

"One lady did a little dicing for me," she says.

Eileen also makes desserts for monthly workshops. She says the women like to get together to work on their scrapbooks and socialize, like women used to do at quilting bees.

She looks for new recipes in her favorite food magazine, *Taste of Home.* That's where she found her recipe for the crispy, toffee chip cookies.

– Alice Thrasher

Sinful Brownies

- 4 ounces unsweetened chocolate
- 10 tablespoons plus 2 teaspoons butter
- 4 eggs
- 2 cups sugar
- 1 teaspoon vanilla
- 1 cup chopped nuts
- 1⅓ cups flour
- 8 ounces chocolate chips
- 4 teaspoons chocolate syrup

Melt the chocolate and butter together. Cool.

Beat the eggs until thick. Beat in sugar gradually. Add chocolate/butter mixture. Add vanilla and flour. Mix in chocolate syrup. Fold in nuts and chips.

Turn into a greased 9-by-13-inch pan. Bake at 325 degrees for 25 to 30 minutes. Cool.

Banana Nut Bread

- ½ cup shortening or 1 stick of butter
- 1 teaspoon baking soda
- 1 cup mashed bananas
- 1½ cup all-purpose flour
- ½ to 1 cup chopped nuts
- ¼ teaspoon salt (optional)
- ½ cup brown sugar
- ½ cup granulated sugar
- 2 eggs

Cream the shortening and the sugars. Beat in the eggs and bananas. Add the dry ingredients. This doubles well for two loaves.

You can also bake these in muffin tins. Bake the loaf at 350 degrees for about 60 minutes. The muffins take less time. Just peek at them every so often starting at about 20 minutes.

Cinnamon Swirl Coffee Cake

- 2 cups all-purpose flour
- 1 teaspoon baking powder
- ½ teaspoon salt
- 1 cup sour cream
- 1 cup butter
- 2 cups sugar
- 2 eggs
- 1 teaspoon vanilla

FILLING:

- ½ cup brown sugar
- 1 cup chopped nuts
- 2 teaspoons cinnamon

Mix filling with a fork. Cream the butter and the sugar. Add eggs, vanilla and sour cream.

Add the dry ingredients.

Grease and flour a bundt pan. Pour half the batter in the pan.

Add the filling. Spread the remaining batter over the filling.

Bake at 350 degrees for about 55 minutes. Cool on a wire rack.

Pasta Salad

1 package of any size, shape, style pasta (12 to 16 ounces)

2.26-ounce bottle of Salad Supreme (Eileen Rettig uses only ½ to ⅓ of the jar.)

1 16-ounce bottle zesty Italian salad dressing

Vegetables, such as chopped seeded cucumbers, onions, olives and tomatoes.

Cook the pasta according to package directions. Add the Salad Supreme, Italian dressing and the vegetables. Refrigerate several hours or overnight. Stir or shake occasionally.

Note: The original recipe calls for 16 ounces of pasta and an entire jar of Salad Supreme and a large (16 ounce) bottle of Italian salad dressing. Adjust to desired consistency.

Chicken Salad Supreme

2 to 3 cups of cooked, diced chicken breasts

Dash of salt

1 cup chopped celery

1 cup cooked mini-shell macaroni

½ cup chopped onion

1 can mandarin oranges, drained

1 cup seedless white/ green grapes (halved)

½ cup toasted slivered almonds

Optional: minced parsley

½ cup Miracle Whip

½ cup mayonnaise (more or less, depending on the consistency you desire)

½ cup heavy whipping cream, whipped

Combine the chicken, onion, celery, and salt. Refrigerate several hours or overnight. Add macaroni, oranges, grapes, and parsley. Mix with mayonnaise and Miracle Whip and refrigerate until ready to serve.

Fold in the whipped cream and almonds just before serving.

Note: This is a very forgiving recipe. You can vary the ingredients and the amounts and still have a delicious salad.

Toffee Chip Cookies

See photo in center of book

1 cup butter, softened

½ cup vegetable oil

1 cup sugar

1 cup packed brown sugar

1 teaspoon vanilla extract

3½ cups all-purpose flour

1 teaspoon cream of tartar

2 eggs

1 teaspoon baking soda

1 teaspoon salt

3 cups crisp rice cereal

1 cup quick cooking oats

1 cup flaked coconut

1 cup chopped pecans

1 cup toffee bits or almond brickle chips

In a large bowl cream the butter, oil, sugars and vanilla. Add eggs, one at a time, beating well after each addition.

Combine the flour, cream of tartar, baking soda and salt. Add to creamed mixture. Stir in remaining ingredients.

Drop by tablespoonsful, 2 inches apart, onto ungreased baking sheets. Bake at 350 degrees for 10 to 12 minutes or until lightly browned. Remove to wire racks to cool.

Preparing Meals Is Part of Family Life

August 25, 2004

Selena Kimsey

Selena Kimsey has always enjoyed doing things with her family.

So when she started her own family, the 26-year-old Orange County California native included cooking in her family affairs.

"I first remember cooking when I was 7," she said. "My parents owned a diving and fishing business. Mom stayed at home. One night I helped prepare spaghetti."

On weekends growing up, Kimsey and her brother, Anthony Draves, would stay with their grandparents in San Pedro.

"Dad would try to catch tuna since we are Philippine-Portuguese Americans. I was in charge of cleaning and making rice," she said. "We ate rice so much, one day Anthony ate mashed potatoes and didn't know what it was."

These days Kimsey likes to plan the meals for her husband, Andy, and their 5-year-old son, Vincent. Another one is on the way.

Andy is a 33-year-old submariner in the Navy and is currently on shore duty stationed at Fort Bragg.

Being an officer in the Navy is stressful for Andy, Selena Kimsey said, so she wants him to come home, eat and relax. "Some nights is an easy night with stew prepared in a crock pot," she said. "Other nights, it is more complex."

When Andy cooks, he gets out the grill.

"Andy is a passionate guy," his wife said. "He picks up the cooking slack when I do not feel good due to the pregnancy."

Being a housewife, Kimsey says, is no cakewalk. So on weekends, the family makes meals that are more complex. A few of the dishes that are prepared on the weekends are Chicken Cordon Bleu, Chicken Adobo or Chinook Plank Salmon and Seafood Alfredo.

Vincent has even started to help prepare meals, just like Kimsey did as a child. Vincent helps with the spaghetti, shucks corn, cleans the dishes and hands his dad spices while Andy is grilling.

"People who are pretty good cooks get started from a young age," Selena Kimsey said. "And it starts with the family."

– Ealer S. Wadlington III

Chicken Cordon Bleu

- 4 boneless skinless chicken breasts
- Fine bread crumbs (I use the ones in the tin cans)
- 2 to 3 eggs beaten
- Honey Ham
- Swiss Cheese

Slit chicken breast in half and fold out to where you have a flat chicken breast with two equal sides. Tenderize the breast to about ¼ in thickness.

Place ham and cheese in the center and then fold over one side of the breast to make a sort of sandwich look.

Then place chicken breast with ham and cheese in eggs. Then place in bread crumbs and cover entire breast on both sides with crumbs.

Bake in a glass baking pan at 350 degrees for about 45 minutes or until chicken is cooked to 180 degrees. This dish goes very well with garlic mashed potatoes and fresh steamed carrots or broccoli.

Chicken Adobo (Filipino Version)

- 1 whole chicken (cut into eighths)
- 1 whole garlic (chopped)
- olive oil or vegetable/ corn oil
- 1 teaspoon ground black pepper
- 4 whole black pepper cloves
- 3 dried bay leaves
- 1 cup soy sauce
- 1 cup vinegar
- 7Up or Sprite
- 1 whole lemon (cut into 4 parts)

Cook's note: This is a very salty recipe so if you are on a low-salt diet this may not be a good dish for you. But it is so yummy!

Remember to wash your chicken very well. I recommend using the lemon (in ingredients) to scrub all over the chicken parts and rub some salt into it as well.

Heat oil and add all of the garlic, and cook until garlic is lightly browned. Add chicken and saute until the chicken is beginning to tenderize.

Add ground black pepper, whole black pepper cloves, soy sauce, and vinegar, and let simmer for 25 to 35 minutes or until chicken is done.

Make sure to add more vinegar or soy sauce until it suits your taste (should be a bit tangy). When chicken is tender, add some 7Up if you want a sweeter taste, and let simmer for 5 more minutes.

Serve over rice.

Chinook Plank Salmon

1 2-pound fillet of fresh salmon

1½ tablespoons olive oil

Dillweed

Salt to taste

Season (with olive oil) and preheat the plank to 350 degrees.

Season the fish with salt and dillweed and place the fish into the oval of the preheated plank. Brush olive oil over the fish. Bake for 20 to 30 minutes or until done.

Seafood Alfredo

¼ pound of raw peeled and de-veined shrimp

¼ pound of large scallops

Alfredo sauce

Basil

Fresh garlic

Oregano

Olive oil

Saute garlic in frying pan with olive oil. Combine basil, oregano with garlic. Cook scallops and shrimp until done.

Pour in Alfredo sauce (I use a jar from the store, nothing special, such as Prego) and season to your liking with Italian spices (oregano and basil) and of course garlic.

Cook fettucini noodles to al dente.

Serve with salmon fillet over noodles and pour sauce over fillet with shrimp and scallops.

Make sure to pour freshly grated Parmesan cheese over your dish and add any spices that you wish.

Serves 4

Cook's Note: This is great with fresh steamed broccoli.

A Talent for Barbecue Leads to Many Requests

April 30, 2003

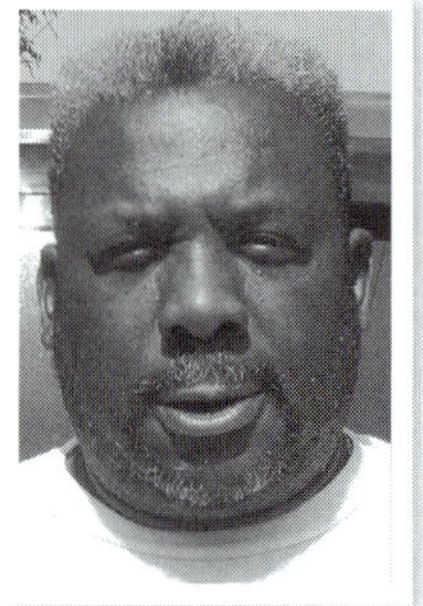

Delton Burnett

Delton Burnett was no stranger to cooking while growing up. He came from a long line of cooks who would prepare huge meals for family get-togethers or neighborhood gatherings in their back yard on Deep Creek Road.

But Burnett was 38 when he discovered that he too had the gift for cooking. It was then that Burnett, now 53, barbecued his first hog. The results and comments were so favorable, cooking became his favorite hobby.

Now it's not unusual to see Burnett's grill going full blast on any given weekend cooking up ribs, chicken or barbecue. In fact, word has spread around Fayetteville about his cooking talents. He is often asked to prepare meat items for other people's events.

"What really got me about cooking that first hog was not that I thought it was good, but other people were telling me how good it was," Burnett said.

Yielding a tasty barbecue involves making sure the temperature is just right and having a good sauce, Burnett said.

"You have to have a good sauce after you get it cooked," he said. "If you don't, it's nothing. It's just like having fresh pork."

Burnett gets his sauce from Bobby Thornton of Roseboro. Thornton makes the sauce himself and distributes it all over the state.

After the hog is cooked, it must be finely chopped. Burnett said he chops his the old-fashioned way — with a meat cleaver.

Cooking the hog takes six to eight hours, depending on its size, Burnett said. Most of his hogs weigh 70 to 100 pounds. If the temperature outside is cold, cooking could take longer.

A cooked hog is just one of Burnett's specialties. He also enjoys cooking ribs and chicken over the grill. He prefers cooking what he calls Carolina–or Colorado-style–ribs the full rib that hasn't been cut. Baby back—center cut ribs—are OK for feeding small groups. But Burnett is accustomed to cooking for big gatherings, so he prefers the larger ribs.

On one occasion he cooked at a family reunion in Virginia for more than 1,000 people. He grilled 350 pounds of chicken, fried 350 pounds of fish, and made a couple of hundred pounds of ribs and 300 pounds of barbecue. Cooking the food took three days.

When cooking ribs, the temperature is important. Burnett said the ribs must be cooked slowly so they will be tender. Good seasoning is also important. He prefers a mixture of Louisiana Cajun and Soul seasonings.

Burnett likes cooking over gas.

"I'm a gas man," he said. "A lot of people use coal and wood because they like that flavor. I like the gas flavor. I'm strictly a gas man. You can get your temperature just right, and you don't have to continuously watch it."

– Jeffery Womble

Chopped Barbecue

70 to 100 pound hog that has been cleaned

250 to 300 gallon cooking grill

Louisiana Cajun Seasoning

Soul Seasoning

Barbecue Sauce

Place hog on grill. Depending on the size, cook the hog for six to eight hours. When meat is fully cooked, pull from skin and chop with cleaver.

Add Louisiana Cajun, Soul and other seasonings if desired and barbecue sauce.

Barbecue Ribs

Choice of Carolina/Colorado or Babyback ribs (Amount varies depending on the number of people being served)

Soul Seasoning

Louisiana Cajun Seasoning

Barbecue Sauce

Season ribs with Soul and Louisiana Cajun seasonings. Place ribs on grill, turning occasionally.

When ribs are almost done, brush with barbecue sauce. Cook until tender for about two or three hours, depending on size of ribs.

Barbecue Chicken

Chicken parts (Amount varies depending on the number of people being served)

Soul Seasoning

Louisiana Cajun Seasoning

Barbecue Sauce

Season chicken with Soul and Louisiana Cajun seasonings. Place chicken on grill, turning occasionally.

Cook slowly for about 1½ hours or until well done. When chicken is almost ready to take off grill, brush with barbecue sauce.

Military Life Includes Culinary Adventures

September 1, 2004

Maria Chavez

Maria Chavez loves to cook. She makes a point of using sea salt — "It's not as harsh," she says — and she uses a convection oven for baking, calling it "the Cadillac of ovens." As she skins a whole chicken and chops fresh ginger, garlic and onion for a marinade, she keeps up a running commentary on the dish she is making, the dishes and pans she has collected in various places, the importance of composting and her experiences with cooking.

A little while later, with the chicken safely in the refrigerator marinating for the next day, she explains that she was not always so proficient in the kitchen.

Growing up in the Schwaben region in the state of Bavaria in Germany, she did not have access to many ingredients and recipes. Wartime limited the food that was available, and the recipes she learned were bland.

"I did not know how to cook anything but what my mom made," she said. When she met and married Juan Chavez, an American soldier, "I literally did not know how to cook."

Her husband, who is of Mexican descent, taught her to make a few dishes — pinto beans, rice and stew.

The couple left Germany and moved to Fort Bragg. The year was 1959, and Maria Chavez was 20 years old. It would be the first of many moves that would take them around the world.

One day her husband told her he was bringing his boss, a major, home for dinner.

"He goes, 'Don't worry; just make whatever you can,'" she says and laughs. "I cooked the only three things I knew how!"

She says the officer complimented her meal of pinto beans, rice and stew.

"It must have given me a little bit of confidence," she says.

After that, Chavez started expanding her cooking abilities.

When the family moved to Japan, she had an opportunity to take a Chinese cooking class from Nancy Chih Ma, a cookbook author.

"She asked me to be her assistant," she says. So Chavez got to shop for the ingredients for the class as well as participate in hands-on cooking.

Later, back in the United States, Chavez had the opportunity to learn from her mother-in-law, who taught her how to make many Mexican dishes but without using exact measurements.

Chavez still makes some things from recipes and some things without measuring, like her mother-in-law

Maria's Apfelkuchen

- 1 stick butter
- ¾ cup sugar
- 3 eggs
- ¼ teaspoon lemon extract
- 2 cups flour, unbleached
- 2 teaspoons baking powder
- 6 tablespoon milk, or a little more
- Apples, peeled, cored and sliced (⅛ inch slices)
- Powdered sugar

Combine butter, sugar, eggs, lemon extract, flour, baking powder and milk in that order and whip until dough is smooth and creamy. Place in a greased springform pan and top with apple slices. Bake in a preheated 350-degree oven about 50 minutes. It should get a little brown on top. After baking, allow it to cool. Sprinkle with powdered sugar and serve with fresh whipped cream.

taught her. She also has the confidence to adjust recipes herself, substituting one ingredient for another.

Chavez has many stories to tell of the places she lived while her husband was in the military.

Chavez's husband, who started off enlisted in the Army, became an officer after 10 years and eventually retired as a colonel. Altogether, he was in the Army for 37 years, and Maria Chavez was married to him for 35 of those years.

The years brought some interesting adventures, like the time she was in charge of making enough apfelkuchen, or apple cake, to feed 650 people for a bazaar. She got five people to volunteer to help her and asked her neighbors to let her use their kitchens. The bakers set up an assembly line and went to work.

"I'm telling you, within five hours we had enough apfelkuchen for 650 people," she says.

Chavez's family has reaped the benefits of her interest. When her children were young, she made them breakfast each day, she says.

Now her three children are grown, and she has seven grandchildren. "And I teach everybody to cook."

– Cathryne Meeks

Delicious Lemon Cheesecake

CRUST:

½ cup unsalted butter, softened

¼ cup light brown sugar

1 cup flour

½ cup regular oats

½ cup pecans, finely chopped

FILLING:

3 8-ounce packages cream cheese

¾ cup sugar

1 teaspoon lemon rind, grated

2 tablespoons lemon juice

1½ teaspoon vanilla extract

3 eggs

TOPPING:

1½ cups sour cream

2 tablespoons sugar

½ teaspoon lemon rind, grated

1 teaspoon lemon juice

Combine all the crust ingredients. Mix well and press into a 10-inch springform pan. Combine the ingredients for the filling. Mix until smooth and creamy. Pour into crust and bake at 335 degrees for 55 minutes, or until set. Combine ingredients for filling.

Spoon evenly over cheesecake and bake an additional 10 minutes, until brown on top. Cool several hours in the refrigerator before serving.

Cream Cheese Tart

2 8-ounce packages cream cheese, softened

1 cup sugar

1 teaspoon pure vanilla extract

2 heaping tablespoons sour cream

½ teaspoon grated lemon rind

2 eggs

12 vanilla wafers

1 21-ounce can cherry or blueberry pie filling

Preheat oven to 350 degrees. Place a paper cupcake liner in each cup of a muffin pan. Beat cream cheese with a mixer until fluffy. Add sugar, vanilla, sour cream and lemon rind, beating well. Add eggs, one at a time, beating well after each addition. Lay a vanilla wafer, flat side down, in each muffin cup. Spoon cream cheese mixture over wafers. Bake 20 minutes. Allow tarts to cool completely. Serve with cherry or blueberry filling on top, or pie filling of your choice.

Cooking Has Been a Lifelong Interest

October 27, 2004

Kelly Denny

Kelly Denny started helping in her grandmother's kitchen when she was about 5 years old. Now the resident of Raeford cooks a variety of foods for herself and her husband, and she is always experimenting with new flavors.

As a child, Denny said, she spent the summers on her grandparents' 280-acre farm. She would pull up a chair to stand on and help her grandmother cook. They made everything from homemade sauerkraut and jellies to casseroles and pies.

"And I don't use measuring cups or measuring spoons.... That's another thing she taught me," she said. Instead, she measures ingredients by how they look and feel.

Now Denny cooks something every day, often trying something new.

"We rarely eat the same thing more than once in a month," she said.

Her favorite recipe is for a Greek chicken pita, and her husband's favorite is a pot roast she makes with cloves of garlic inserted into the meat.

Denny also likes to bake, especially pies. She always makes a dessert on the weekend.

Sometimes she makes creme brulee, which she said is easier than people might think.

"It's really easy to make; I don't know why the restaurants charge so much for it," she said. It can be made ahead of time and the top braised just before serving, for a dessert to serve company, she said.

Denny said the people in her neighborhood often get together for cookouts, and this year they are planning a neighborhood Christmas party. Denny and a neighbor plan to make a lot of cookies to give out, and they'll have hot cider. Denny said she buys apple cider, then simmers it on the stove with cinnamon sticks and cloves, for a warm, satisfying drink that is also a Christmas tradition.

– Cathryne Meeks

Chicken and Salad with Pita Bread

3 chicken breasts, cut into bite-size pieces

1 handful fresh parsley

1 head Romaine lettuce

1 red onion

1 cucumber (Denny uses the seedless variety)

Herbed feta cheese

1 handful fresh cilantro

½ cup olive oil

3 tablespoons red wine vinegar

Juice of 1 lemon

2 to 3 tomatoes

2 garlic cloves

Pitas

Chop lettuce, onion, cucumber, tomatoes and parsley into small pieces. Combine and set aside.

In a small bowl, whisk olive oil, red wine vinegar and lemon juice. Add chopped garlic cloves and chopped cilantro to dressing mixture. Pour ¼ of dressing mixture over chicken pieces and fry in a hot skillet until thoroughly cooked (approximately 10 minutes).

Combine salad, chicken, cheese and remaining dressing and serve with warm pitas.

Serving suggestion: This is great with a side of hummus and flat bread.

The Hubby Will Love It Pot Roast

1 boneless beef chuck roast

8 to 10 garlic cloves (halved)

1 cup carrots

1 cup celery

1 cup onion

Salt and pepper

1 tablespoon olive oil

Note: 1 cup of potatoes can be substituted for any of the vegetables.

Cut 10 small slits on each side of the roast, and stuff half of a garlic clove into each slit. Salt and pepper both sides of the roast, and fry it in the olive oil in a pot until dark brown on all sides. Add vegetables and ⅔ cup water to the pot and lower the temperature. Cook for approximately 3 hours or until tender.

Serving suggestion: Serve with homemade mashed potatoes and rolls.

Her Cooking Butters up Her Guests

November 17, 2004

Mary Frederick

Butter her up; she won't mind.

The first commandment of Mary Frederick: Thou shalt use butter.

She's got lots of suggestions for anyone who would like to learn a thing or two about cooking, but only one law: If the recipe says butter, use butter.

"There's no sense in trying something else," said the 83-year-old grandmother as she put finishing touches on a sinfully delicious caramel cake. She'll make two more just like it for the Haymount United Methodist Church bake sale this afternoon.

While the church has lots of delicious fare on sale in the annual fund-raiser, Frederick's wares are among the first to go — heady praise for a lady who started cooking mainly to beat boredom.

"I didn't really do much cooking until my husband and I were in Europe," Frederick said. Her husband, Chuck, served in the Army in three wars.

"There wasn't much to do at the time," she said. "So I bought my first cookbook and started trying it."

She was a natural, especially at baking. Soon, guests were dropping by for coffee and sweets.

"Chuck did love his sweets," she said. "Now he's gone, and it's frustrating cooking for one."

Especially with the number of cookbooks, Frederick said.

From that first book in Germany, she's gathered a collection of hundreds of books from the usual Betty Crocker to a rare White House cookbook with William Taft's wife on the inside cover.

"I've still got a lot of these recipes to try," she said.

When she's not in the kitchen, Frederick likes to read. "When the girls were growing up, instead of toys we'd buy books," she said. "The only problem is now we've got so many books, I don't know what to do with them.

"I guess I should say I really like the Food Channel, too," she said with a grin. "I could watch that all day, except then I'd miss 'CSI.' "

Her preference is to cook traditionally, with lard and butter when called for. "It's in the recipe for a reason," she said. "It tastes better. People can experiment, but when it comes down to it, you cannot improve on the flavor and texture of butter. It's made for cooking. Nothing can take its place."

– Chick Jacobs

Chili Con Carne

- 1 pound ground beef
- 1 cup chopped onion
- 1 can (2 cups) broken-up tomatoes
- 1 can kidney beans, drained
- 1 teaspoon salt
- 2 teaspoons chili powder
- 1 bay leaf (optional)

Brown meat and onions in a pressure cooker. Add remaining ingredients, except bay leaf. Cover, set control and cook for 10 minutes after control jiggles.

Reduce pressure normally for 5 minutes, then place under faucet until the pressure is down. Add beans and bay leaf, then simmer for a few minutes. Remove bay leaf before serving.

Note: If you don't want to use a pressure cooker, after browning meat and adding the ingredients, cook over low heat for 40-45 minutes.

Disappearing Marshmallow Brownies

- ½ cup butterscotch chips
- ¼ cup butter
- ¾ cup all-purpose flour
- ⅓ cup brown sugar
- 1 teaspoon baking powder
- ¼ teaspoon salt
- 1 teaspoon vanilla extract
- 1 egg
- 1 cup mini-marshmallows
- 6 ounces chocolate chips
- ½ cup chopped nuts

Grease a 9-inch square pan. In a heavy pan, melt the butterscotch and butter, stirring constantly. Remove from heat and let cool to lukewarm.

Add everything except the chocolate chips, marshmallows and nuts and mix well. Then fold those three ingredients into the mixture until well combined.

Bake at 350 degrees for 20-25 minutes. Do not overbake. The center will remain soft.

Not-Too-Sweet Pecan Pie

- 1 cup white sugar
- ½ cup white corn syrup
- ¼ cup melted butter
- 3 eggs, well beaten
- 1 to 2 cups pecans
- 1 unbaked pie shell

Combine sugar, syrup and melted butter. Add beaten eggs and pecans to syrup mixture, mixing thoroughly.

Pour filling into pie shell. Bake at 375 degrees for 40 to 45 minutes. Do not overbake. Let cool before cutting.

Interest Leads to Career in Culinary Field

November 3, 2004

Kimberly Gibson

Kimberly Gibson grew up in Fayetteville.

Preparing food is a big part of her life.

For the past seven years, she has worked as a lab technician for the culinary department at Fayetteville Technical Community College, and she has a business baking and designing elaborate cakes. She is also married to a chef — her husband, Robert, works at Gates Four Golf and Country Club.

In her job at Fayetteville Tech, Gibson is responsible for making sure culinary students have everything they need. She not only supplies all the ingredients they need to cook with, but she makes sure the equipment and lights are working.

She says she has been interested in cooking since she was 15 or 16 years old.

"For the most part, my real joy is baking," she says.

She remembers trying to make doughnuts when she was 15.

"That was a real cooking experiment," she says. "I was always in the kitchen trying to do something."

About 10 years ago, she went to Fayetteville Tech to study food service management. She says she learned a lot from the college and also did research at the library and on the Internet, then practiced and experimented to hone her culinary skills.

Now, when she isn't working at the college, she can often be found creating elaborate cakes for weddings, baby showers or other events. She says she doesn't really advertise except to give out business cards, but people hear about her by word of mouth.

When she makes a wedding cake, she tries to come up with a unique design for the bride. After looking at pictures of cakes with the bride-to-be, she often combines elements from different cakes to create a design that hasn't been done before.

"We will make it whatever style, flavor, shape, within reason," she says.

A couple summers ago, a woman had a princess theme for her wedding, and she asked Gibson what was the most unusual cake she had ever made. Gibson showed the woman a picture of a cake she hadn't made but would like to try — a cake with a castle on top. The woman agreed; Gibson says it took her about 30 days to make the castle and about three days to make the cake.

Someday, when her oldest daughter, Paris, gets married, she plans to make her a cake shaped like the Eiffel Tower.

Until Paris, 18, left for college, she helped Gibson set up and deliver the cakes. Gibson also has a 16-year-old daughter, Felisha, and a 2-year-old son, Robert.

"I started doing this when my girls were small," she says of baking cakes. She would also save the children's shoe boxes, wrap the tops and bottoms, and fill them with cookies for their teachers.

"I guess I always shared my love of baking with my kids," she says. They can even be found in the kitchen baking cookies on Christmas Day.

Now, she says, she has more experience than when her girls were young, and she looks forward to teaching her son as he grows up.

– Chick Jacobs

Raspberry Marble Cheesecake

CRUST:

1¼ cups graham crackers

2 tablespoons sugar

⅓ cup butter, melted

FILLING:

1 10-ounce package of frozen raspberries

1 tablespoon cornstarch

3 8-ounce packages cream cheese

1 14-ounce can Eagle brand sweetened condensed milk

3 eggs

¼ cup lemon juice

Combine the graham crackers and sugar in a mixing bowl until well blended.

Stir in melted butter until moistened and press into the bottom of a 10-inch springform pan. Bake at 350 degrees for 10 minutes. Set aside to cool.

In a food processor, combine raspberries and cornstarch. Place this mixture in a heavy saucepan and cook over medium heat until thickened, then cool. Reserve ⅓ of the mixture.

In a mixer, blend cream cheese and sweetened condensed milk.

Add eggs and lemon juice. Pour half of the cheese mixture into the springform pan. Place several teaspoonfuls of the raspberry mixture on top and spoon the remainder of the cheese mixture over the top. Repeat with the raspberry mixture as before.

Using a knife, marble the two mixtures, being careful not to scrape the crust at the bottom, and bake in a 300-degree oven for 1 hour and 15 minutes. Allow to cool slowly. When completely cool, refrigerate or freeze until serving time.

Tuscany Grilled Chicken and Pasta with Sun-dried Tomatoes and Parmesan Cream Sauce

8 boneless, skinless chicken breasts

MARINADE:

1½ cups olive oil

⅔ cup lemon juice

1 tablespoon chopped garlic

1½ tablespoons Italian seasoning

CREAM SAUCE:

2 jars oil-packed sun-dried tomatoes, chopped

4 shallots, chopped

2 teaspoons garlic, chopped

2 tablespoons Italian seasoning

½ cup dry white wine

6 cups heavy cream

1¼ cups fresh grated Parmesan cheese

1 pound pasta

(penne or bowties)

Mix marinade ingredients. Marinate chicken for at least 1 hour or overnight. Grill on the charbroiler until done and grill marks are present. Slice on the bias and set in warmer until time to plate up.

Saute tomatoes, partially drained of oil, shallots and garlic in a saucepan until translucent. Add seasonings and cook 2 minutes, then add wine. Add cream and reduce until thickened. Just after the cream starts to thicken, add the Parmesan cheese. Serve over pasta and top with grilled chicken slices.

Sunday Calls for Different International Dishes

April 18, 2001

Gwen Whitmarsh

Gwen and Steve Whitmarsh are international junkies. They are both interested in cultures around the world and like to travel.

She is a former Army nurse and Steve was in Special Forces.

Four years ago while they were living in Toronto, Canada, where Steve was in a military school, they decided to entertain friends with East Indian food.

After researching they came up with some interesting recipes and learned about the country and people along the way.

That started a family tradition that has been going on ever since. Most Sunday nights the Whitmarshes invite friends to a dinner based on food from another country.

They have cooked German foods including sauerbraten, Irish corned beef and cabbage, Spanish paella, Welsh cucumber sandwiches, Italian fish, along with dishes from Alaska, England, Morocco, Austria, Mexican, China and Norway.

"Food really does seem to be the key to learning about other countries," she says.

To prepare for a dinner, the Whitmarshes research the country and diet on the Internet and find that it is a great learning experience for them and their children, Jeffrey, who is 5 years old, and Scott, 2.

The children like to dress in clothing from the country of the food they eat. Their favorite is the traditional dress of German boys.

Gwen says they have been blessed by having friends from a variety of countries who help them learn more about their dishes and customs.

One of Gwen's major food interests is the breads of different countries. She makes her own bread with and without her bread machine. Her favorite bread is East Indian naan bread made in a clay oven but she hasn't exactly figured out how to make that work in a home kitchen.

The Whitmarshes also do desserts from different countries. Gwen likes to make cakes and pastries that limit their intake of calories.

The couple's ancestors come from Germany, Wales, Norway and France.

Gwen grew up in Lake Forest, Ill., and moved to New England as a teenager. Steve lived all over the United States but mostly lays claim to Tennessee.

In 1991 they moved to Fayetteville and bought a home in Haymount. When Steve's career takes them to other places, they always come back to their Haymount home and consider themselves North Carolinians.

"I really do feel like this is our home," she says.

– Melissa Clement

Red Cabbage (Rotkohl)

- 6 thick slices bacon, diced
- 1 yellow onion, peeled and sliced
- 2 heads red cabbage (about 3 pounds), sliced
- 3 apples, cored and sliced
- 1 cup chicken stock
- 4 tablespoons red wine
- 4 tablespoons vinegar
- 4 tablespoons brown sugar
- 1 teaspoon salt
- ¼ teaspoon freshly ground black pepper

In an 8-quart pan cook bacon until translucent. Add onion, cabbage and apples to the pot.

Sauté, uncovered, until the cabbage begins to wilt some.

Add remaining ingredients and cover.

Cook over medium heat, stirring occasionally, until all is tender for about 1 hour.

Sauerbraten

- 1½ cups red wine vinegar
- ½ cup red table wine
- 4 medium onions, sliced
- 2 tablespoons sugar
- 4 bay leaves
- 3 teaspoons whole cloves
- 3½ teaspoons salt
- 1½ teaspoons mustard seed
- 1½ teaspoons peppercorns
- 1 4-pound beef bottom-round pot roast
- 3 tablespoons flour
- 2 tablespoons oil
- ½ cup ginger snaps, finely ground
- ½ cup sour cream

Two to four days prior to serving, combine 1 cup water, vinegar, wine, 3 of the onions, sugar, bay leaves, 2 teaspoons cloves, 2 teaspoons salt, 1 teaspoon mustard seeds and ½ teaspoon peppercorns. Put the roast in the marinade, cover and turn every day.

When ready to cook, remove roast from marinade. Reserve marinade. Pat the roast dry and coat meat with flour.

In a Dutch oven, brown roast on all sides. Add marinade, remaining onion, 1½ teaspoons salt, 1 teaspoon cloves, ½ teaspoon mustard seed and 1 teaspoon peppercorns. Heat to boiling. Reduce heat to low, cover and simmer 3 to 4 hours.

Remove roast from gravy, cover and set aside. Strain gravy and return it to the pot. Add ginger snaps and stir until thickened. Add sour cream and heat through.

Serve gravy over the meat.

Potato Pancakes

- 2 cups potato, grated
- 2 large eggs
- 1 large onion, grated
- 3 tablespoons pancake mix
- Salt, pepper and garlic powder to taste

Squeeze grated potatoes in cloth towel until very dry. Add the rest of the ingredients.

You may need to add extra pancake mix to make the batter have a sticky consistency.

Pour portions of the batter into a pan with vegetable oil and fry until brown.

Serve with sour cream.

Serve with whipped cream.

Cooking Is This Entrepreneur's Escape

May 2, 2001

Joe Riddle

Joe Riddle is a developer, builder and business owner who spends his days cooking up deals and running Riddle Commercial Properties, Riddle Building Inc. and other companies.

To help escape from the pressures of the business world, he can be found cooking up old fashioned comfort food at home for his family, employees and friends.

"It is almost like solitaire, just you and your creation," he says. "There is no one telling you what to do or arguing with you. In addition, a cook can receive instant gratification in the form of a job well done supported by appreciative eaters."

Riddle grew up in Fayetteville but has fond memories of going to visit his grandparents in Fairmont for Sunday dinners and holidays.

He says his maternal grandmother, the late Caroline Floyd, and his mother, March Riddle, always cooked full meals every day from scratch.

When he was in college at the University of North Carolina at Chapel Hill, Riddle says, his mother gave him a Betty Crocker cookbook.

He did the cooking for himself and two roommates.

That's when he started making lasagna. He says his mother put up tomatoes in Mason jars for him to use for his homemade sauce.

When he makes lasagna, he makes enough sauce to use for spaghetti later.

"I knew how to cook some things before I went to college," he says.

He was around cooking when he managed his family's Gates Four Golf and Country Club right out of college.

At home, he does a lot of the cooking for himself, his wife, Trina, and three sons.

In the past six months he has starting baking and making pies and other desserts.

"My approach to cooking is to buy a bunch of cookbooks, learn from your elders and use the best ingredients. I almost always select the difficult recipes that do not cut corners."

Banana Pudding

- ¾ cup sugar
- ⅓ cup flour
- 2 cups milk
- ½ teaspoon vanilla flavoring
- Dash of cream of tartar
- Dash of salt
- 4 eggs, separated
- 1 box of vanilla wafers
- 6 ripe bananas

Mix sugar, flour, milk, salt, eggs and vanilla flavoring in saucepan.

Cook over medium to medium-low heat. Mix will become thick like pudding.

Layer vanilla wafers and bananas in an 11¾-by-7½-inch baking dish, ending with bananas. Pour pudding mixture over bananas and wafers.

Beat egg whites with ¼ cup sugar and a dash of cream of tartar until stiff. Spoon over pudding mixture and bake in a 350-degree oven until meringue topping has browned slightly.

Riddle's favorite blueberry pie recipe comes from "Celebrations, Food Family and Food," a cookbook published by The Fayetteville Academy. He got his banana pudding recipe from Temple Baptist Church's cookbook "Cooking Together for God's Glory."

– Alice Thrasher

The Best Blueberry Pie

1 (9-inch) pie shell, unbaked

4½ cups blueberries (fresh or frozen)

4 tablespoons all-purpose flour

1½ tablespoons fresh lemon juice

¾ cup sugar

2 tablespoons butter

TOPPING:

1 cup all-purpose flour

¾ cup rolled oats

⅔ cup butter

½ cup packed brown sugar

Mix blueberries, flour, lemon juice and sugar. Pour into pie shell; dot with butter.

Crumble together all topping ingredients to form crumbs. Spread over pie.

Bake in a preheated 425-degree oven for 35 to 40 minutes.

Joe Riddle's Homemade Lasagna

10 lasagna noodles

2 pounds ground chuck

1 pound Italian sausage (hot or mild)

4 or 5 fresh mushrooms, sliced

1 medium yellow onion, diced

1 green pepper, diced

2 celery stalks, diced

3 cloves of garlic, minced and sautéed in margarine

2 teaspoons Texas Pete

2 or 3 drops Tabasco

1 teaspoon sugar

1 teaspoon dried oregano, crushed

1 teaspoon dried basil, crushed

1 teaspoon dried thyme, crushed

2 bay leaves

1 can (28-ounce) crushed tomatoes

1 can (28-ounce) tomato sauce

1 can (12-ounce) tomato paste

1 or 2 cans (28 ounce size) diced tomatoes (depending on how you like it)

18 ounces shredded mozzarella cheese

24 ounces ricotta cheese

8 ounces Parmesan cheese (you won't use the whole container)

Brown ground chuck and drain. You will need an oversized pot to prepare sauce.

Remove skin from Italian sausage. Tear into small chunks and roll into small balls.

Pan fry the sausage balls and roll over to brown complete surface. Drain.

Place meat into pot along with diced vegetables, mushrooms, sautéed garlic, tomatoes and tomato sauce.

Add spices and cook over medium heat for at least one hour.

Meanwhile cook lasagna noodles and drain.

Layer the bottom of a white ceramic oval dish (9 inches wide and 12 inches long by 3½ inches deep) with a good helping of sauce following with the noodles.

Continue with sauce, ricotta, mozzarella and Parmesan and repeat until full, ending with a good layer of Parmesan cheese.

Bake at 350 degrees for 50 minutes until top is lightly browned.

This dish will feed 10 to 12 people. You may have sauce left over that could be used for spaghetti.

Husband Is Taste-tester Before She Entertains Others

NOVEMBER 6, 2002

Fran Leeds

Like many other good cooks, Fran Leeds loves to collect and read cookbooks.

"I read them the way other people read novels, but I like to read novels, too," she says.

"I read every day."

She likes to try out new recipes on her husband, retired Army Lt. Col. Charles Leeds. She says he likes most things, except oysters.

That doesn't stop Fran from making her famous scalloped oysters — especially around the holidays.

"We always had them at Thanksgiving and Christmas," she says. "Today, I just don't think you can have a Thanksgiving or Christmas dinner without scalloped oysters."

She makes them sometimes when friends Charlie and Colleen Astrike come over for a monthly bridge night and dinner.

Fran grew up in Tignall, Ga., near the town of Washington. She and her mother lived with her aunt and uncle on a large farm where they grew vegetables and canned them for the winter.

Her uncle, Wade Griffin, served in the Georgia legislature for 25 years.

Fran says she learned to make chicken salad for all the entertaining that her aunt and uncle did — particularly during campaigns. "My uncle had 16 children when my aunt married him, and she cooked for them," she says.

Fran still likes the old family recipe. She says it is good as a salad or in little sandwiches, with the crusts trimmed. "You have to use just the white breast meat, not dark meat," she says.

Other favorite recipes include a banana pudding that she takes when there are dinners at her church, Cedar Falls Baptist.

"I am a member of the bereavement committee," she says. "I double it for a big gathering, and usually don't bring any home."

The basic recipe came from a church cookbook, but she adapted it a bit.

Her favorite potato salad recipe is based on one she found in Southern Living magazine years ago. She added the green onions and other touches.

She loves green onions, and adds them to many dishes, including deviled eggs and macaroni and cheese.

She also likes to cook out on a charcoal grill. "I barbecue a pork roast or do a turkey breast," she says. "I don't do much frying.

"I enjoy cooking. For some people, it's a job. I enjoy entertaining, what little we do now."

– Alice Thrasher

Chicken Salad

4 chicken breasts, boiled, boned, skinned and cooled

1 Red Delicious apple, peeled & chopped fine

2 eggs, boiled and chopped

⅓ cup sweet pickle cubes

1 to 2 ribs celery chopped

Salt and pepper, to taste

Hellmann's Real Mayonnaise

Juice of 1 lemon

Remove bone and skin from boiled chicken breasts. Chop into small pieces with kitchen shears.

Add chopped apples, chopped boiled eggs, pickles, celery, and mayonnaise; and mix well.

Needs to be moist, not dry.

After mixing, add lemon juice and stir again. Keep refrigerated.

Creamy Potato Salad

- 5 to 6 large red potatoes, peeled and cubed
- 2 boiled eggs
- ⅓ to ½ cup chopped celery
- ⅓ to ½ cup bell pepper
- ½ bunch green onions, chopped (tops also)
- ⅓ cup sweet pickle cubes
- ½ cup Hellmann's Real Mayonnaise
- ½ cup dairy sour cream

Boil cubed potatoes in salted water until fork tender, about 25 minutes. Drain well and cool in the refrigerator.

Remove yolks from boiled eggs and mash them in a small bowl. Chop whites and use in salad.

Add celery, bell pepper, green onions and pickles. Add salt and pepper to taste.

Mix mashed egg yolks. Add mayonnaise and sour cream to the egg mixture.

Mix with potatoes and other ingredients until all is well coated. Chill and serve.

Creamy Banana Pudding

- 1 (14-ounce) can Eagle Brand Condensed Milk (non-evaporated)
- 1½ cups cold whole milk
- 2 cups whipping cream, whipped or 1 large container Cool Whip
- Vanilla wafers
- 1 package (4-serving size) instant vanilla pudding mix
- 4 medium bananas, sliced and dipped in lemon juice

In a large bowl, combine Eagle Brand milk and the cold whole milk. Add pudding mix. Beat well. Chill 5 minutes. Fold in whipped cream or Cool Whip.

Spoon ½-cup pudding mixture into a 2½-quart-size glass serving bowl. Top with vanilla wafers, bananas and pudding mixture.

Repeat layering, ending with pudding mixture. Put Cool Whip or whipped cream on top. Chill thoroughly. Refrigerate leftovers.

Scalloped Oysters

- 2 to 3 cups crushed saltine crackers
- ½ cup melted butter
- 1 stick margarine or butter (Fran Leeds prefers Squeeze Parkay).
- 2 pints select oysters, reserving the liquid
- ½ cup half and half
- Salt
- Pepper
- 1 teaspoon Worcestershire sauce or soy sauce

Pour melted butter over cracker crumbs and toss together with a fork. Spread ⅓ of the cracker crumbs on the bottom of a greased casserole dish. Top with 1 pint of the drained oysters. Sprinkle with salt and pepper. Dot with margarine or butter; cut in small squares. Repeat layers, using ⅓ of the crumbs, a pint of oysters, salt, pepper and more pats of butter.

Mix the half and half, oyster liquid, and the soy sauce or Worcestershire sauce. Place over oysters, making sure some gets to the bottom and around the sides. Top with remaining buttered cracker crumbs. Bake in a 350-degree oven for 35 to 45 minutes. Serves at least six.

Southern Cooking Is a Family Tradition

November 30, 2005

Elaine Bryant

Elaine Bryant grew up in a household of good cooks. Her maternal grandmother, Golda Tanner Shaw, owned and operated a boarding house in Marion, S.C. After her husband was killed in an automobile accident in 1929, she had to do something to support her seven children, Bryant said.

"Mrs. Shaw's good home-cooking and hospitality was well known throughout South Carolina, North Carolina and Georgia. Everyone who passed through our beautiful town could find out where to get the best food–all they had to do was just ask," Bryant said.

"In fact, my mother, Vivian Shaw, met her future husband (my father), James Doares McCormick, because he was traveling through Marion and stopped to have dinner (the midday meal in the South). There he met Vivian (my mother). He always said she was the prettiest girl he had ever seen."

Through the years, Vivian McCormick helped her mother, and so did Bryant, so they all became good cooks.

Bryant shares her grandmother's recipe called Shaw's Boardinghouse coconut pie, which is a simple recipe using only coconut, milk, eggs, butter and vanilla. Mama's pecan pie, from Vivian Shaw, is the old-fashioned Southern kind with instructions to "whip eggs with a fork." Sugar and white Karo syrup are used for sweetening, and the pecans have to be coarsely chopped.

"I can still smell those wonderful desserts and breads that my grandmother cooked every day. I was always standing there, hoping that there would be a bowl for me to scrape, just a smidgen of icing to taste."

Bryant described Marion as a wonderful place to grow up.

"It was a beautiful small town where everyone knew everybody else," she said. "We felt so safe and free and were always encouraged by family and friends to take advantage of every good thing that came our way. What a blessing.

"I moved to Fayetteville, raised a family, and now my daughters are also very good cooks. I love to share my recipes and to share the things that I cook."

She is the arts education director at the Arts Council of Fayetteville/Cumberland County and does volunteer work in Fayetteville with the North Carolina Symphony and with the Cumberland Community Foundation.

– Melissa Clement

Shaw's Boardinghouse Coconut Pie

See photo in center of book

- 1 cup coconut, fresh or frozen
- 1 cup whole milk
- 3 eggs, beaten
- ¼ cup butter
- 1 teaspoon vanilla extract
- 1 unbaked pie shell, 9 to 10 inches

Beat eggs.

Add sugar, milk, coconut, butter and vanilla.

Pour mixture into unbaked pie shell.

Bake at 350 degrees for 40 to 45 minutes or until golden brown and firm.

Mama's Pecan Pie

See photo in center of book

3 eggs

4 tablespoons butter, melted

½ cup sugar

1 cup white Karo syrup

½ teaspoon salt

1 teaspoon vanilla

1½ cups pecans, coarsely chopped

1 unbaked pie shell

Whip eggs with fork.

Add melted butter and sugar and continue to stir with fork.

Add Karo syrup, salt, vanilla and pecans, mixing well. Pour mixture into unbaked pie shell.

Bake at 400 degrees for 10 minutes, then reduce heat to 325 degrees for 40 minutes.

May be served warm or cool.

Mile High Strawberry Pie

CRUMB CRUST:

1 cup plain or self-rising flour, sifted

¼ cup brown sugar

½ cup chopped pecans

½ cup butter, melted

FILLING:

2 egg whites

1 cup granulated sugar

2 cups fresh strawberries, sliced, or 20 ounces frozen strawberries, thawed and drained

2 tablespoons lemon juice

1 small container of Cool Whip

12 to 15 fresh, whole strawberries for garnish

Preheat oven to 350 degrees.

Stir together first 4 ingredients; spread evenly in shallow baking dish.

Bake 20 minutes, stirring occasionally.

Mixture should be light brown.

Sprinkle the crumbs in a 13-by-9-by-2-inch baking dish.

Combine egg whites and sugar.

Beat at high speed until stiff peaks form, about 15 minutes.

Gently fold in berries and lemon juice, then fold in Cool Whip.

Spoon this over cooled crumb mixture.

Top with remaining crumb mixture.

Cover and freeze 6 hours or overnight.

Cut in squares to serve, and top with fresh whole strawberries.

Yields 13 to 15 servings.

This dessert will keep indefinitely and will remain delicious.

Cook Carries on German Tradition

August 16, 2006

Elke Caesar

Elke Caesar grew up in Heidelberg, Germany, and came to this country as a bride in 1964. She has cooked for her husband, James Caesar, and her four children for 50 years and still cooks in her German tradition.

"Even though my husband is American, I stuck with my German cooking, taking only a few shortcuts here and there, to save time. My husband loves my cooking," she says.

Caesar remembers cooking her first dish, potato salad, for her family when she was 12.

"The majority of women are the cooks in the family, and I pass on the tradition," she says. "My daughter, Margarete, followed my steps. She is an excellent cook. Just the other day she prepared a fabulous meal for our weekly wine-tasting party with my neighbors.

"She cooks traditional food and likes to experiment with other dishes, eating it and testing it out. I don't like to experiment. I stick to the foods that I know are tried and true. I never measure anything. I just know how much needs to be in the food."

When the neighborhood got together for a recent wine-tasting party, she brought a pineapple cake that was the hit of the party. She took a shortcut and used a cake mix, she says.

One of the recipes she shares with readers is her rinder rouladen, or beef roll. Elke says her rouladen was served during holidays, since it is time-consuming to prepare.

"It is a traditional dish of hospitality," she says.

Rinder rouladen is often served with knodels, which are potato dumplings about the size of baseballs. They contain stuffing, such as onion and parsley, and are also time-consuming to make, so they are also a dish used for festive occasions.

These two dishes can be warmed over the next day and are just as good as they were the day before, she says.

The zwiebelkuchen (onion pie or cake) is something like a quiche with onions, bacon and sour cream and is sometimes eaten as a cold dinner served in the late afternoon with cold cuts and breads.

Her crazy cake is quick and easy and good, Caesar says. This one calls for a cake mix and is made like a sheet cake by laying the cake mix with cream cheese, eggs, vanilla and sugar.

– Melissa Clement

Crazy Cake

- 1 stick of butter
- 3 eggs
- 1 box white cake mix
- 1 teaspoon vanilla
- 1 (8-ounce) package cream cheese
- 1 box 10X powdered sugar
- 1 cup of pecans or walnuts

With a wooden spoon, mix butter, 1 egg and white cake mix together until moist. Spread mixture into a greased oblong pan.

Mix 2 eggs, vanilla, cream cheese, and sugar until combined and pour over batter in pan.

Spread pecans or walnuts on top. Bake at 350 degrees for 30 to 35 minutes.

Zwiebelkucken (Onion Pie or Cake)

See photo in center of book

- 1 (19-inch) pie shell, unbaked
- 6 thick slices bacon, cut in small cubes
- 2 onions, sliced
- ¼ teaspoon cumin
- ½ teaspoon salt
- ½ teaspoon pepper
- 2 eggs, well beaten
- 1 cup sour cream

Preheat oven to 400 degrees, saute bacon until crisp. Separate from grease (save grease) and set aside.

Add sliced onions to bacon grease and cook slowly until tender but not brown.

Sprinkle onions, bacon, cumin, salt and pepper over pie shell.

Bake at 400 degrees for 20 minutes. Remove from oven.

Blend eggs and sour cream together and pour over onions. Bake again for 15 minutes or until sour cream is set and pie is golden brown.

Serve at room temperature. Makes 6 to 8 servings.

Rinder Rouladen (Beef Rolls)

- 8 pieces of sirloin, cut ¼-inch thick, about 6 ounces each
- Pepper and salt to taste
- 2 teaspoons Dijon mustard
- 8 strips of bacon cut into long, thin strips
- 1 large onion, chopped
- 2 pickles cut into quarters, lengthwise
- ¼ cup vegetable oil
- 6 peppercorns
- 1 bay leaf
- 1 tablespoon corn starch
- 4 cups beef broth

Lay steaks on a flat surface. Spread each with salt, pepper and mustard. Add one slice of bacon and one sliced pickle. Roll up the steak and secure with toothpicks.

Heat oil in a large saucepan, add beef rolls and cook until they are brown on each side.

Add onion, broth, bay leaf and peppercorn. Cover and simmer for 1 hour and 20 minutes until tender. Remove beef rolls. Discard toothpicks and arrange on a serving plate.

Blend cornstarch with a small amount of water and add to the sauce until it forms a thick gravy. Pour gravy over beef rolls and serve with mashed potatoes or sauteed cabbage.

Cookie Recipe Takes First Place in Bake-off

October 6, 2004

Austin Lehmann

Austin Lehmann of Fayetteville is a first-time winner of the annual St. Patrick Catholic Church bake-off and bake sale.

"This was my first time entering the contest and my first time winning," the Lake Rim Elementary School physical education teacher said.

Lehmann had a lot of competition. There were 22 contestants in the bake-off, and three judges had to sample all the baked goods, from homemade pies to banana bread to cheesecakes and cookies.

"Two of the finishers were men, and the third winner was a boy in third grade," said Crystal Degroff, the bake-sale coordinator.

Contestant J.B. Erikson, 46, took third place with his Peanut Butter Fudge, and Connor Hohan, 8, took second place with a checker cake with chocolate icing.

Prizes were awarded for the bake-off: $25 for first place, $15 for second place and $10 for third place.

Something about Lehmann's entry stood out to the judges. His entry was named Big Chocolate Cookies.

"I wanted to go to breakfast at Haymont Grill. But my wife, Jolene, said I had to bake and drop off my entry before we could go eat," Lehmann said from his Clairway neighborhood home.

So the 54-year-old took the Nestle chocolate recipe, added "stuff to it" and then threw it in the oven.

"It took five minutes to prepare and 15 minutes to cook. I took it right out of the oven, wrapped it up and took it over to the church," Lehmann said.

"The judges said the cookies were so good and still warm when they tasted his entry," Degroff said.

Lehmann is the father of A.B., 19, and Rachel, 15, and has attended St. Patrick for 27 years. After winning the contest, he had to be called back to the church to get his prize and ribbon.

After his picture was taken, his cookies were cut up and placed in the bake sale. "My wife thinks my food is good but thought it was funny that I beat out the other contestants," Lehmann said.

The proceeds of the bake sale and bake-off will go to projects and programs at St. Patrick Catholic School.

"I didn't start cooking until high school. I was one of 10 children growing up in New Jersey," Lehmann said.

He has no plans to enter other competitions, although he was asked to enter the Cape Fear bake-off.

Lehmann finds comfort in taking requests from family members, teachers and friends for dishes such as his Big Chocolate Cookies and Stuffed Mushrooms. Now he will get ready for the upcoming holiday festivities.

Congratulations. You are a winner!

– Ealer S. Wadlington III

Stuffed Mushrooms

- 12 to 24 large mushroom caps (small mushrooms will work, too)
- 1 bag of herb stuffing mix
- 1 to 2 cans of crab meat
- 1 small onion, chopped
- Parmesan cheese
- Melted butter

Place the mushrooms in a cooking dish or pan. Cook stuffing according to directions.

Mix some of the stuffing and onion with the crab meat and press into the mushroom cap as much or as little as you like.

When finished, sprinkle Parmesan cheese all over the stuffed mushrooms and then pour melted butter over each one.

Bake at 350 degrees until the tops of the mushrooms look toasted.

Big Chocolate Cookies

- 2 sticks of butter
- ¾ cup brown sugar (packed)
- ¾ cup plain sugar
- 1 teaspoon vanilla
- 2 eggs
- 3 cups flour
- 1 teaspoon salt
- 1 teaspoon baking soda
- 24 ounces semi-sweet chocolate morsels
- 1 to 1½ cups chopped walnuts or pecans

Cream the butter, sugar, vanilla and eggs. Mix the flour, salt and baking soda. Add the flour mixture to the butter mixture in thirds and then fold in the chocolate and nuts. Use a big spoon to put the dough on two cookie sheets. Bake at 375 degrees for 15 to 18 minutes or until the cookies look done to your liking. Makes 18 large cookies.

Vegetarian Makes People Feel at Home

June 23, 2004

Penny McMillan-Hughes

Penny McMillan-Hughes says she tries to make eating fun at home. As a vegetarian, she says, eating out can be hard, so she tries to provide tasty and nutritious meals for her husband and 6-year-old daughter.

McMillan-Hughes and her family moved to Fayetteville two years ago when the military stationed her husband here.

Earlier they lived in Germany, where she was inspired to try gourmet cooking. She started baking bread and trying to replicate other foods she tasted in Europe.

"I love to do homemade pastas; I love to make all kinds of international foods," she says.

Her and her husband's roots also influenced her cooking style. She is from the mountains in North Carolina, and he is from northwest Indiana.

McMillan-Hughes worked until recently as a visual coordinator at Haverty's and would bring in food for her co-workers. In fact, Alice Quigley, who handles customer relations at Haverty's, likes McMillan-Hughes' cooking so much that she recommended her for "Cook's Corner."

McMillan-Hughes and her husband also invite people to their house who live far away from their families — especially at Thanksgiving.

For the Thanksgiving feast, her husband cooks a turkey, and she makes a tofu turkey. She also tries to make a pie or other dessert for everyone there.

"Some people live so far away from where they came from," she says. She tries to make them feel at home.

McMillan-Hughes says she learned a lot from her mother, who does a lot of "old-fashioned cooking" without recipes. "She gave me the basics," she says.

Now McMillan-Hughes' own daughter likes to help cook. When McMillan-Hughes is working in the kitchen, her daughter stands on a stool and helps add ingredients.

"I hope that she can keep that interest going in cooking," McMillan-Hughes says.

– Cathryne Meeks

"Veggie" Wiener Schnitzel

1 package Quorn 'Naked Cutlets,' slightly thawed

Salt

Pepper

Paprika

½ to ¾ cup refrigerated egg substitute

Fine bread crumbs (packaged)

Light oil for frying

Fresh lemon juice

Season cutlets with spices. Place egg substitute in a shallow dish, and place the bread crumbs in another. Heat 1 tablespoon oil in a skillet over medium-high heat, or until water droplets sizzle when added. Working one at a time, coat cutlets in egg substitute, then dredge through bread crumbs until coated. Cook cutlets on each side for approximately 4 minutes. Sprinkle cooked cutlets with lemon juice and serve with french fries and salad.

Kahlua-glazed Carrots

3 cups diagonally sliced carrots

1 tablespoon butter

1 tablespoon brown sugar

1 tablespoon honey

3 tablespoons Kahlua, divided

1 teaspoon cornstarch

¼ teaspoon salt

Steam carrots for 4 to 5 minutes, or just until tender. Remove from heat. Melt butter in a large skillet over medium heat. Stir in brown sugar, honey and 2 tablespoons Kahlua. Cook until bubbly. Combine remaining Kahlua and cornstarch; stir well and add to brown sugar mixture. Stir in salt. Continue cooking until thickened and bubbly. Add carrots, tossing gently to coat. Cook just until carrots are thoroughly heated. Serve immediately.

Fabulous Brownie Bottom Pie

4 squares semi-sweet baking chocolate, or 1 4-ounce package sweet baking chocolate

¼ cup (½ stick) butter

¾ cup sugar

½ cup refrigerated egg substitute

1 teaspoon vanilla

½ cup flour

½ cup chopped pecans

2½ cups cold plain or vanilla soymilk

2 packages (4-serving size) chocolate instant pudding

½ pint whipping cream

¼ cup confectioners' sugar

5 to 6 various candy bars, frozen

Preheat oven to 350 degrees (325 degrees for glass pie plate). Grease bottom and sides of a 9-inch pie plate. Combine sugar, egg substitute, and vanilla in a large, heat-resistant mixing bowl. Microwave chocolate and butter in a microwavable bowl on high for 2 minutes. Stir until chocolate is melted. Add chocolate to sugar mixture, stirring well to combine. Mix in flour, then nuts. Spread in pie plate and bake for 25 to 30 minutes. Cool on cooling rack. While cooking the pie, pour whipping cream into a chilled metal bowl. Begin beating with an electric mixer, slowly adding confectioners' sugar. Beat until stiff peaks form. Chill until needed. Pour soymilk into a large bowl. Add pudding mixes and beat with a wire whisk for 1 minute. Let stand for 2 minutes. While waiting, coarsely chop candy bars, leaving several large pieces intact. Spread pudding over cooled brownie pie. Top with whipped cream, then begin to decorate with candy bars, standing larger pieces up in whipped cream for a dramatic presentation. Sprinkle small bits lightly over the surface. Keep chilled until ready to serve.

Recipes Came From Travels Around the World

January 28, 2004

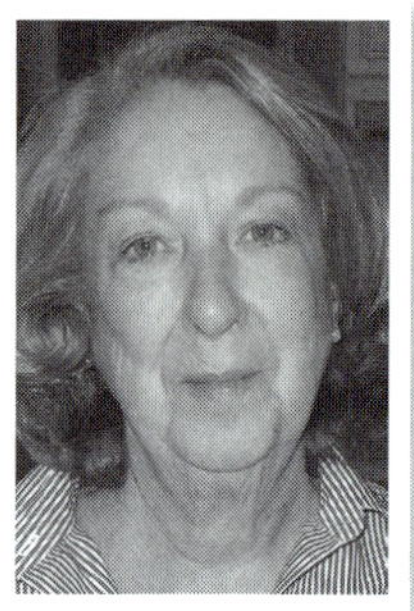

Mary Adams

Mary Adams loves a party — even when she has to do the cooking.

"Oh, I love to cook," she said, settling into the dining nook of her King's Grant home. "I've been doing it all my life, from the time I learned from my mother and granny.

"I had five children, and with my husband in the military, we cooked for lots of people. I've always said I've fixed meals from coast to coast and ETO (European Theater of Operations)."

Husband Harvey Adams is retired now, and the traveling family calls Fayetteville home. Like many military wives, Mary picked up recipes in stops around the world.

"We've been so many places," she said. "We were fortunate to be stationed in Hawaii. That was my favorite. Plus the children really enjoyed it."

Of course, Mary's cooking education began in a less exotic location: the down-home kitchens near Pacolet Mill in upstate South Carolina. She recalled family friends who'd drop by after their shift, only to find her mom whipping up something to eat.

"There was no one who could fix fried chicken like my mother," she said. "Of course, my children say mine was the best. I guess it depends what you grew up with."

Mary grew up learning home-style cooking — which helped her land Harvey, a young football player at Wofford College.

"Dad would always say, 'Have you fixed that boy something to eat, yet?'" she recalled with a laugh.

She did most of the cooking ("Harvey has so many wonderful qualities, but I do the cooking," she said), including meals for bachelor officers and friends. Her favorite company meal, a pasta dish called Zotoni, originally made servings for 24 people. She cut the recipe in half. "It's probably the most successful thing I make," she said. "More than 30 years later, people still want the recipe."

The Italian pie is a simple dish for single soldiers "or just about anyone who wants to make something easy that tastes good," she said. "Just serve it with a green salad, and it makes a great dinner."

Mary prefers cooking to baking, but she has a couple of good desserts to share. One, her Blizzard Blues Ice Cream Pie, is probably better for summer, but the Apple Pie Mess is perfect for winter.

"I really like it because it doesn't have to look pretty," she said. "I'm not one of those folks who spend hours making things look just right. When we're entertaining, I like to be with friends, not stuck in the kitchen.

"I think that it's important to be with people. The food will be gone soon, but these are your friends."

–Chick Jacobs

Zotoni

- ¼ cup cooking oil
- 1 large onion, chopped
- 1 small green pepper, chopped
- 1 clove of garlic, minced
- 2 cans tomato soup
- 1 can whole-kernel corn, drained
- ½ of small can of tomato paste
- 1 large can of mushrooms, drained but juice reserved
- Juice of 1 lime
- 2 pounds ground beef
- 1 pound spaghetti
- 3 cups grated cheddar cheese

In a medium saucepan, saute onion, pepper and garlic in oil until tender. Add tomato soup, tomato paste, corn, mushrooms and lime juice. Heat thoroughly.

Meanwhile, cook spaghetti according to package directions and drain. In a skillet, brown the ground beef in the reserved mushroom liquid. Do not drain.

Layer into a 9-by-13-inch casserole in the following order:

All the spaghetti.
1 cup grated cheddar cheese.
Meat mixture (undrained).
1 cup grated cheddar cheese.
Sauce.
1 cup grated cheddar cheese.

Cook at 350 degrees for 20 to 25 minutes, or until the cheese melts.

Italian Pie

- 1 can crescent rolls
- 1 10-ounce package Monterey Jack cheese, cut into ½-inch cubes
- 2 packages Little Smokie sausages, cut into ½-inch slices
- ⅛ teaspoon salt
- ⅛ teaspoon pepper
- 1 tablespoon Parmesan cheese
- 2 eggs, slightly beaten

Unroll crescent roll dough and separate into 8 triangles in an ungreased 9-inch pie pan. Press the pieces together to form a crust. Reserve 3 triangles for a top crust.

Combine remaining ingredients in a mixing bowl and pour into crust. Roll out each remaining triangle so the longest side is 9 inches and cut them into ½-inch strips. Crisscross strips over the top of the filling to create a lattice top. Flute the edge.

Bake at 250 degrees for 60 to 70 minutes, or until a toothpick inserted in the center comes out clean. Let pie stand for 10 minutes, then cut into wedges.

Blizzard Blues Ice Cream Pie

FOR THE CRUST:

1½ cup graham cracker crumbs

3 tablespoons sugar

⅓ cup melted butter

FOR THE FILLING:

1 8-ounce chocolate bar with almonds

½ cup strong brewed coffee

1½ quarts coffee ice cream

½ cup chopped toasted almonds

For the crust: Combine crumbs and sugar. Stir in butter and press mixture into a 10-inch pie plate. Bake at 350 degrees for 8 minutes and cool.

For the filling: Melt chocolate with coffee in the top of a double boiler. Pour into cooled pie shell and place in freezer until completely chilled. Turn ice cream in a mixer to soften slightly. Add almonds. Beat mixture until smooth, but not melted. Pour mixture over chocolate in pie shell. Garnish with chocolate curls or almonds if desired before freezing.

Freeze several hours. Remove from freezer 15 minutes before serving.

Apple Pie Mess

6 cups thinly sliced apples

½ cup sugar

1 cup all-purpose flour

1 stick butter

1 tablespoon cinnamon

½ cup grated cheddar cheese

Place apples in a 10-inch pie pan. Mix the remaining ingredients together and cover apples. Bake at 375 degrees for 30 to 40 minutes. Serve warm with vanilla ice cream.

Family Helps Create a Good Cook

FEBRUARY 21, 2001

Amber McNamara

Amber McNamara doesn't have an Italian heritage she knows of, but she says she may have because of her love for Italian foods.

"I like fresh tomatoes. I love garlic, and I love anything with cheese on it," she says.

She used to work in an Italian restaurant in Colorado Springs as a manager/waitress/bartender and helped cook sometimes in a pinch.

"It was a real pleasurable experience working there," she says. "They had a lot of great recipes and they used to make real Italian cannolis, stuffed pizzas, stromboli and spumoni. I would love to go to Italy."

One of McNamara's favorite recipes is Three-Pepper Lasagna. It is a recipe she got from her Aunt Sue Lynch in Colorado.

McNamara says her aunt adapted the recipe from the cookbook *"365 Ways to Cook Pasta."*

"My aunt invites people over for pasta parties and everyone makes a pasta dish," she says.

She's thinking of organizing one to try to get a gourmet cooking club started in her Bataan Hills neighborhood at Fort Bragg.

"The lasagna is a little spicy, and if you want to make it not so spicy you can use two packages of mild Italian sausage instead of using a hot one," she says.

McNamara likes to make the lasagna for special occasions such as birthdays for her husband, Staff Sgt. Mark McNamara, and their 3-year-old son, Cole.

"My son likes it too," she says.

McNamara likes to learn to make regional dishes whenever she moves to another Army post with her husband.

She found a recipe for Eastern North Carolina barbecue sauce and made it for a pig picking for her husband's unit.

She says it was a hit.

Another Italian dish that McNamara likes to make is a cream-filled dessert called Tiramisu.

"I make it just for company, not for my family because it is so rich," she says.

McNamara likes to try new recipes and looks for interesting ones on the Internet. She saves ones she likes on floppy disks.

"I like unusual things, and not just one style," she says. "I just got a couple of Indian cookbooks recently and I like the cookbooks published by community groups."

She says she got her love of cooking from her mother, her aunt, her grandmother, grandfather and great-grandmother.

Her great-grandmother cooked on a wood stove in West Virginia until her death.

"All the holidays with my family center around food," she says.

– Alice Thrasher

Three-pepper Lasagna

- 12 cooked lasagna noodles
- 1 package hot Italian sausage links (casings removed)
- 1 package mild Italian sausage links (casings removed)
- 1 large red bell pepper
- 1 large green bell pepper
- 1 large yellow bell pepper
- 1 bunch of fresh parsley
- 6 tablespoons flour
- 6 tablespoons unsalted butter
- 2 cans (14½ ounce size) chicken broth
- ¼ teaspoon nutmeg
- Salt and pepper to taste
- 1 pound grated Monterey Jack cheese
- 5 tablespoons grated Parmesan cheese

Wash and remove stems, seeds, and the white pithy part of the peppers.

Cut peppers in half and slice into ½ inch wide strips, set aside.

Chop a large handful of rinsed parsley, set aside.

In a large skillet, brown the sausage until crispy, but not burnt. Add peppers and parsley to sausage mixture and cook for 7 minutes.

Remove from heat and drain, set aside.

In a saucepan melt butter over medium heat. Whisk flour into the butter, cooking a couple of minutes.

Add chicken broth, heat over medium heat, whisking constantly until thickened. Stir in nutmeg, salt and pepper, set aside.

In a 9x13-inch pan, pour enough white sauce to coat bottom of pan.

Layer four noodles on top of sauce. Spread half of sausage mixture over noodles.

Sprinkle small amount of Monterey Jack cheese over sausage.

Layer four more noodles. Then layer the other half of sausage mixture.

Then pour half of sauce over the sausage and add another layer of 4 noodles.

Then top with rest of sauce leaving enough room to cook without bubbling over. Top with Monterey Jack and Parmesan.

Bake at 375 degrees for 45 minutes or until golden brown.

Eastern North Carolina Barbecue Sauce

- 1 pint apple cider vinegar
- 1 pint apple juice
- 3 tablespoons salt
- 2 teaspoons cayenne pepper flakes
- 2 teaspoons black pepper

Combine all ingredients into a plastic container with lid.

Pour over chopped, cooked pork, chicken or other meat before serving.

Tiramisu

2 packages (12-ounce size) ladyfingers

½ cup water

½ cup sugar

2 packages (8-ounce size) light cream cheese or 1 pound mascarpone cheese (room temperature)

5 eggs, separated

1½ cups strong brewed coffee

1 tablespoon orange liqueur

1 tablespoon brandy

1 tablespoon amaretto

Unsweetened cocoa powder

Combine water and sugar and heat it in a pan over medium heat for about 5 minutes until it is syrupy, but not caramelized, and reaches the "soft-ball" stage.

Don't stir. Let cool for a couple of minutes, and then slowly add unbeaten egg yolks one at a time, stirring briskly after adding each one.

Place the egg yolk mixture back on a medium-hot stove for 40-60 seconds stirring constantly, not allowing yolks to cook.

Take the yolks off the heat and set aside to cool.

Once cooled, mix the yolks until creamy. Add cream cheese, brandy and orange liqueur. Mix well.

In a separate bowl, beat egg whites until stiff. Fold egg whites into cream mixture.

In a separate bowl stir together coffee and amaretto. Dip ladyfingers in the coffee mixture and arrange a single layer in a 9x13-inch pan.

Pour half of cream mixture on top of ladyfingers and dust with cocoa powder.

Repeat layer again. Dust top generously with cocoa powder. Cover with plastic wrap and refrigerate overnight.

Garnish with chocolate curls.

Culinary Arts Teacher Passes on Her Skills

October 15, 2003

Elaine Pearce

Elaine Pearce cooks differently at home than she does at school.

But that doesn't mean students in her culinary arts classes at E.E. Smith High School are getting off easy.

The students' last cafe program for teachers featured flank steak with Parmesan rice pilaf, grilled zucchini, homemade rolls and ice cream cake.

Pearce came to teach culinary arts through her love of cooking. Her passion drove her to major in home economics education at East Carolina University. Over the years she has taught students in Greene County and at Douglas Byrd Middle School. For the past two years, she has taught at E.E. Smith.

"It's something where I can work with small groups of kids who are interested in the industry," she said. "They're not allowed to stand back. They have to participate."

At home, Pearce loves to cook Cajun food, her favorite style of cooking. The secret, she says, is using a good fish sauce and perfecting the roux.

Her favorite meals are shrimp and broccoli Alfredo and shrimp Creole. Her most difficult recipes are berry bisque and angel food cake made from scratch.

Her husband, David, loves more traditional fare such as pot roast.

When she takes a break to dine out, Pearce likes the Hilltop House in Haymount. One of her national favorites is Bubba Gump's in San Francisco and Charleston, S.C.

Pearce said about 30 percent of her students are interested in culinary arts as a profession. Half of them are already working in kitchens for part-time jobs.

The E.E. Smith culinary arts classes are known to cater for school functions. They most recently provided food for the junior varsity football meal and at the Student Government Association Inaugural Ball.

Pearce said cooks and people who love cooking are often the type of people who love to share.

She said she is no different.

"I like to take conventional recipes and then play," she said.

– Stacy Peterson

Pecan Pie Muffins

- 1 cup chopped pecans
- 1 cup firmly packed brown sugar
- ½ cup all-purpose flour
- 2 eggs
- ½ cup butter or margarine, melted

Combine nuts, sugar and flour in a large bowl; make a well in the center of the mixture.

Beat eggs until foamy. Stir together eggs and butter; add to dry ingredients, stirring just enough to moisten.

Spoon batter into greased muffin cups, ⅔ full.

Bake at 350 degrees for 20 to 25 minutes for regular size muffins, 10 to 12 minutes for miniature size.

Remove pans and cool on wire rack.

Yield: Nine regular size; 30 miniature size.

Bacon Cheesy Bread

- 1 pound bacon, fried and crumbled
- 1 jar Old English cheese
- 2 or 3 cans canned biscuits, torn into quarters
- 1 stick butter or margarine, melted

Place crumbled bacon in the bottom of a bundt or ring pan.

Spoon Old English cheese on top of bacon. Layer biscuit pieces on top of cheese. Pour melted butter over all.

Bake at 350 degrees for 20 to 25 minutes or until biscuits are golden brown. Invert on serving platter.

Yield: One bread ring.

Baileys Irish Creme Pound Cake

- 1 cup butter or margarine, softened
- 3 cups sugar
- 6 large eggs
- 3 cups all-purpose flour
- ¼ teaspoon baking soda
- ⅛ teaspoon salt
- 1 8-ounce carton of sour cream
- ½ cup Baileys Irish Creme
- 1 teaspoon vanilla extract
- ¼ teaspoon almond extract

Beat butter at medium speed with an electric mixer for two minutes or until creamy. Gradually add sugar, beating for five minutes. Add eggs, one at a time, beating just until yellow disappears.

Combine flour, soda and salt; add to butter mixture alternately with sour cream, beginning and ending with flour mixture. Beat at a low speed just until blended after each addition. Stir in Baileys and remaining ingredients. Spoon batter into a greased and floured 10-inch tube pan.

Bake at 325 degrees for 1½ hours or until a wooden toothpick inserted in the center comes out clean. Cool in a pan on a wire rack 10 to 15 minutes; remove from pan and cool completely on wire rack.

Yield: one 10-inch cake.

Science Teacher Loves to Cook

December 17, 2003

Gay Rose

Science teacher Gay Rose kicked her love of cooking up a notch three years ago when she decided to prepare meals before Wednesday night Bible study at Fayetteville Christian Church.

Her leadership caught on, and the church still has Wednesday night meals as a form of fellowship.

"I've always liked cooking," Rose said. "That's why I started the meal group at church."

At first the meals served about two dozen people. Today, 50 to 75 come out for the Wednesday meals.

"The menu has expanded since then," she said.

Rose teaches sixth- and seventh-grade science at Fayetteville Christian School. She took a break from the classroom recently to share some of her favorite recipes.

Rose's favorite foods are spicy Mexican dishes. But she is also fond of Italian dishes she learned from friends while her family was stationed in Italy.

Rose is married to Martin Rose, an Army civil affairs officer.

The Roses have been in Fayetteville for the past three years after being stationed in Italy, Kansas, Virginia, Maryland and once before in Fayetteville.

Of all the places they have lived, Rose said, Italy was the best.

One of the recipes that reminds her of Italy is Ragu, a pork dish she learned from the Rocchetto family they befriended during their stay.

The dish is unique for its use of thick spaghetti, smaller amounts of tomato sauce and the use of finely chopped carrots and celery stalk along with the usual garlic clove and onion.

Rose said the family hopes to retire in Fayetteville so her children can finish school with their friends.

– Stacy Peterson

Sesame Chicken

3 tablespoons sesame seeds

2 tablespoons soy sauce

2 tablespoons honey

1 teaspoon sesame seed oil (or vegetable oil)

1 teaspoon ground ginger

1 minced garlic clove

4 boneless, skinless chicken breasts

Sliced fresh vegetables

Rice

Combine sesame seeds, soy sauce, honey, sesame seed oil, ginger and garlic. Marinate chicken in sauce for at least 30 minutes. Broil on a grill with sliced fresh veggies, and serve on rice.

Beef Tips

1 to 2 pounds stew meat

1 packet Lipton onion soup mix

1 cup water

1 can cream of mushroom soup

Noodles or rice

Cut stew meat into cubes and trim off fat.

Braise in a pan before placing in a baking dish.

Add onion soup mix and water. Bake at 350 degrees in a foil-sealed baking dish for 1 hour. Add cream of mushroom soup and spread on the top. Bake an additional 30 minutes until a nice gravy is formed.

Serve beef tips on a bed of hot noodles or hot rice.

Ragu Italiano Meat Sauce

1 pound ground pork

Salt

1 garlic clove, minced

½ onion, chopped

1 stalk celery, finely chopped

1 carrot, finely chopped

2 tablespoons olive oil

4 tablespoons tomato sauce

Bigoli (or very fat spaghetti)

Simmer ground pork in a sauce pan; season with salt. Add garlic, onion, carrot and celery to the pork.

Then add olive oil and continue simmering for up to one hour, covered.

In the last 10 minutes, add tomato sauce to simmering sauce. Serve on top of pasta.

Chalupas

1- to 2-pound pork roast

2 packets taco seasoning

2 tablespoons chili powder

2 cloves minced garlic

1 teaspoon cumin

Corn tortilla chips

Place pork roast into a large slow cooker and cover with water. Add taco seasoning, chili powder, garlic and cumin and cook on high for most of a day.

When tender, remove the pork roast and shred with a fork, removing fat and bone.

Return it to the juices and spices in the slow cooker before serving on a bed of corn tortilla chips.

Add taco toppings as desired.

Stay-at-home Mom Creates Her Own Recipes

August 18, 2004

Heather Santon

Heather Santon didn't really cook much until she got married. Now she not only cooks, she creates her own recipes while experimenting in the kitchen.

Santon said she always watched her mother cook when she was younger. When she started cooking on her own as an adult, she learned a lot from cookbooks.

"As I got more comfortable with things, I started creating my own dishes here and there," she said.

One original recipe is her method of making stuffed mushrooms. She also experiments with ways to season different types of meat, figuring out through trial and error what flavors complement each other.

Santon and her husband are from Kentucky, and she said her family likes home-style country cooking, such as a breakfast of eggs and biscuits with gravy — a favorite of her husband.

Santon is a stay-at-home mother with a 1-year-old son, Jacob. Even at his age, he is learning about cooking.

"He helps me make cakes," Santon said. When she makes biscuits, she gives him a piece of dough to play with.

"I'm usually holding him on my hip while I'm making dinner, so he's learning as he goes."

When she has questions, she calls her own mother.

"Moms are a good source of 'How do you do this?' " she said.

After Santon's son was born, her mother passed on a family baking tradition in the form of a cookie cutter. Santon said that when she was a child, she and her mother would make cookies and cut them out with a Santa Claus cookie cutter that left a three-dimensional impression of Santa's face. They would add raisins for the eyes and decorate the cookies with frosting. Her mother gave her the cookie cutter on her son's first Christmas. Now Santon hopes to create similar memories with her son.

– Cathryne Meeks

Potato Casserole

- 2 pounds frozen hash browns (shredded)
- 2 cups sour cream
- 1 cup cheddar cheese
- 1 cup Velveeta
- 1 can cream of mushroom soup
- 1 small onion, chopped
- 1 teaspoon salt
- ½ teaspoon black pepper
- ½ teaspoon garlic salt
- Parmesan cheese, grated
- Hormel Real Bacon Bits

Thaw hash browns.

Mix sour cream, cheddar cheese, Velveeta, cream of mushroom soup, onion, salt, pepper and garlic salt. Add to hash browns. Spoon into a large baking dish.

Sprinkle the top generously with Parmesan cheese and Hormel Real Bacon Bits.

Bake at 350 degrees for 45 to 50 minutes or until lightly browned.

Stuffed Mushrooms

- 1 package whole mushrooms (about a pint)
- 1 cup stuffing mix (herb or chicken)
- ¼ cup water
- 1½ tablespoons butter, divided use
- 1 small can clams
- 2 tablespoons pimentos
- 1 teaspoon garlic salt
- ¼ teaspoon black pepper
- Basil (optional)
- Oregano (optional)
- ¼ cup Parmesan cheese (freshly grated)

Remove stems from mushrooms. Using a spoon, gently scrape out caps.

Add ½ tablespoon butter to water and bring to a boil. Stir in stuffing mix. Remove from heat; let stand 5 minutes.

Drain clams (reserving juice). Mix stuffing, clams, 1 tablespoon clam juice, pimentos, garlic salt, pepper, a pinch of basil and oregano, and Parmesan cheese.

Arrange mushrooms in baking dish. Stuff mushrooms with filling.

Mix remaining clam juice and 1 tablespoon of butter (melted). Spoon over mushrooms. Sprinkle tops with Parmesan cheese.

Bake at 350 degrees for 5 to 10 minutes or until cheese is melted and bubbly.

Chicken Enchiladas

- 8 6-inch flour tortillas
- ½ cup chopped onion
- 4 cloves of garlic, minced
- 1 teaspoon ground coriander (cilantro)
- ¼ teaspoon black pepper
- 2 tablespoons margarine
- 3 tablespoons all-purpose flour
- 8 ounces sour cream
- 2 cups chicken broth
- 1 can (4 ounces) chopped green chilies (drained)
- 1 cup shredded Monterey Jack cheese
- 2 cups chopped chicken
- Garnish (optional):
- Sliced pitted ripe olives
- Chopped tomatoes
- Chopped green onions

Wrap tortillas in foil. Heat in a 350-degree oven for 10 to 15 minutes.

For sauce, in a saucepan cook the onion, garlic, coriander and pepper in margarine until onion is tender. Stir flour into sour cream; add to onion mixture. Stir in broth and chili peppers all at once. Cook and stir till thickened and bubbly. Remove from heat; stir in ½ cup of the cheese.

For filling, stir ¼ cup of the sauce into chicken. Place about ¼ cup of filling atop each tortilla; roll up. Arrange rolls, seam side down, in a baking dish. Top with remaining sauce. Bake, covered, in a 350-degree oven for 35 minutes or until heated through.

Sprinkle remaining cheese on top. Bake uncovered for 5 minutes longer or until cheese melts. If desired, sprinkle the top with olives, onion and tomato.

Let stand 10 minutes.

Stewart Finds Opportunities to Share Recipes

MARCH 9, 2005

Marie Stewart

"I just always loved to cook," says Marie Stewart.

It's a good thing, because as the mother of six children, she needed to be skilled in the kitchen.

Although those children have grown up and now have families of their own, Stewart still loves to cook and often cooks for church groups or for company.

"I try to eat healthy and light," she says. She often reduces the sugar in recipes and finds other ways to make them more healthy. "I hardly ever follow the recipe exactly."

Stewart's mother gave her her first cookbook when she was 8 or 10 years old. She still has the book, although the pages have come unbound. Over the years, she has added many other cookbooks to her collection.

She also collects recipes from other sources, such as the newspaper. A bran-muffin recipe she saved from the newspaper in 1989 has become a favorite choice for breakfast. She adds dried fruit to the muffins and eats them in the morning along with toasted almonds.

Stewart bakes her own bread, including sourdough. Baking bread can be time-consuming, but while she's kneading the dough, she uses the time to pray for friends and family members, she says.

When her children were young, she was a stay-at-home mother and cooked a lot. One of the family's favorite meals was meatloaf with steamed cabbage and baked potatoes. The family always ate supper together.

Now only two of her sons live in town, and her husband died a few years ago, so she doesn't have a big group to cook for at home. But she often cooks for events at Saint Patrick Catholic Church, where she is a member. That includes cooking vegetarian soups to serve on Fridays during Lent; Stewart's soup recipes can be made in large batches. In fact, she made up her vegetable soup recipe herself; she says it can easily be doubled to feed a large group.

She also has many friends in town and likes to invite them over. She says scallops au vin is a good company recipe, and "It's really not as complicated as it might sound."

A simple dessert, she says, can be made by mixing together a pint of vanilla ice cream, a pint of Cool Whip and a small can of limeade or lemonade; putting the mixture in a graham-cracker pie crust; and freezing it.

With a large collection of recipes to choose from, Stewart makes a wide range of meals and desserts, and she finds many opportunities to share her skills. As she says, she just loves to cook.

–Cathryne Meeks

Potato Soup

2 tablespoons butter

1 medium onion, diced

1 can chicken broth (vegetable broth for vegetarian version)

3 large potatoes, peeled and diced

2 teaspoons white vinegar

2½ cups milk

1 teaspoon pepper

Salt to taste

Saute onion in butter until tender. Add broth, potatoes and vinegar. Cover and bring to a boil. Reduce heat and simmer until potatoes are very tender. Stewart likes to lightly mash the potatoes, leaving lumps. Add milk, salt and pepper. Cook at low heat for a while, stirring occasionally to prevent sticking.

Serves 6 to 8. This soup can also be made as a vegetarian soup and can be doubled and tripled as needed for large crowds. It is a good Lenten dish.

14 Day Slaw

1 medium head cabbage (2 pounds), shredded

1 medium onion, thinly sliced

1 medium green pepper, thinly chopped

¾ cup salad oil

1 cup garlic-flavored wine vinegar

¾ cup sugar

1 teaspoon dry mustard

1 teaspoon celery seed

1 tablespoon salt

Mix all vegetables in a container with a tight lid. Put all dry ingredients in a saucepan, then gradually add oil and vinegar to blend. Bring ingredients to a boil. (Watch closely; it will boil over quickly.) Remove from heat. Cool and pour over vegetables. Cover tightly and shake well to mix. Refrigerate. This lasts refrigerated for well over 2 weeks. Makes 12 to 14 servings.

Easy Vegetable Soup

1 pound ground beef

1 can tomato juice (46 ounces)

2 onions, sliced, or onion flakes

1 cup shredded cabbage

1 large potato, diced

1 package frozen mixed vegetables

1 package frozen, sliced okra

3 beef bouillon cubes

½ cup diced celery

1 tablespoon parsley

½ teaspoon oregano (optional)

1 teaspoon salt, or to taste

Cook and crumble ground beef, but do not brown. Skim off fat. Add tomato juice, onions, cabbage, celery, potato, bouillon cubes, oregano, salt and parsley. Bring to a boil. Add frozen vegetables and return to the boiling point. Immediately reduce heat to a simmer and cook 2 hours or longer. It can't be overcooked. If the soup is too thick, add water or tomato juice. This soup freezes well.

Moms Club Member Makes Healthy Meals

July 21, 2004

Jade Wu

In a way, food brought Jade Wu and her husband together. Not much of a cook herself at the time, she was visiting her aunt and uncle in Fayetteville five years ago. While here, she met one of the customers at her relatives' Chinese restaurant, and someone set them up on a date. She returned to Taiwan, where she lived, but the two kept in touch and were eventually married.

Once she was married and living in Fayetteville, Wu decided she needed to learn how to cook. She says she learned a lot from her aunt and uncle.

She combines the styles of Chinese and American cooking. "I like to try new stuff," she says.

One of her goals is to create healthy meals for her husband and son. She doesn't want her 2-year-old son, Jett, to grow up eating fast food.

Jett doesn't like vegetables much, so she tries to sneak them into his diet. One of her methods is to make chicken noodle soup with lots of vegetables cooked in.

"When he was little, he had no problem," she says, "but now he's bigger, he's picky."

Wu is a member of the local Moms Club, and she likes to invite the other mothers and their kids over and show them how to cook things like dumplings and spring rolls. It's fun for the moms to try different recipes, she says, "and the kids love it, too."

She says the Chinese restaurants here serve food that is a lot different from what she ate in Taiwan. "In Taiwan, we use more light stuff, like steamed vegetables," she says, and they don't cover everything with soy sauce.

Sesame Shrimp Toasts

8 ounces cooked and peeled shrimp

1 scallion

¼ teaspoon salt

1 teaspoon light soy sauce

1 tablespoon cornstarch

1 egg white, beaten

3 thin slices white bread, crusts removed

4 tablespoon sesame seeds

Vegetable oil for deep frying

Put shrimp and scallion in a food processor and grind to a fine consistency (or they can be chopped finely). Put in a bowl and stir in salt, soy sauce, cornstarch and egg white.

Using a butter knife, spread the mixture evenly over bread slices. Spread sesame seeds on top of the spread and press down to keep the seeds from falling off.

Cut each slice of bread into four equal triangles or strips.

Heat the oil until it is almost smoking for deep frying in a wok. Carefully place the triangles in the oil with the coated side down and cook for 2 to 3 minutes or until golden brown. Remove with a draining slotted spoon and drain on paper towels. Serve hot.

"They have good food, too, here," she adds — it's just different.

Wu says sometimes it's hard to find the ingredients for the foods she likes to make. She shops in the Raleigh-Durham area about once a month, visiting an Asian market.

"One of my favorite desserts is sweet almond bean curd," she says. It's kind of like a sweet soup and is great during the summer. She can't find it here, so she has to make it herself.

Wu also likes to bake. She says her birthday cakes are Chinese-style: not too sweet, and with whipped cream instead of icing.

Wu says she hopes to teach her son to cook when he is old enough. For now, he is growing up with nutritious, homemade meals rather than fast-food hamburgers and french fries.

–Cathryne Meeks

Sweet Almond Bean Curd

- 3 cups water
- 2 envelopes unflavored gelatin
- ½ cup sugar
- 1 cup milk
- 2 tablespoons almond extract
- 1 29-ounce fruit cocktail
- ¼ cup sugar
- ½ cup hot water
- 2 cups cold water

To make almond bean curd, add 3 cups water to a small saucepan. Sprinkle with gelatin and let stand one minute. Stir; bring to boil over medium-high heat, stirring occasionally. Remove from heat and stir in sugar until dissolved. Add milk and almond extract; stir and cool. Cover with plastic wrap and chill in refrigerator until set.

To make syrup, dissolve sugar in hot water. Add cold water and chill in refrigerator.

Cut almond bean curd into small cubes. Add fruit cocktail and cold syrup. Stir and serve.

Dumplings

- 4 10-ounce packages frozen chopped spinach, thawed
- 2 to 3 (12- or 14-ounce) packages of dumpling wrappers (May be purchased at local grocery stores. If unable to find, can use wonton wrappers.)
- 2 pounds ground pork
- ¼ cup water
- 4 tablespoons soy sauce
- 1 teaspoon salt
- ¼ teaspoon white pepper
- 2 tablespoons cornstarch
- 2 tablespoons cooking wine
- 6 scallions, chopped
- 2 tablespoons sesame oil
- ½ cup water

Combine pork and ¼ cup water, stir one minute.

Add soy sauce, salt, white pepper, cornstarch, cooking wine and scallions to pork. Mix well.

Squeeze out excess water from chopped spinach and mix well into pork.

Place 1 tablespoon filling onto each dumpling wrapper, moisten edges and fold in half over filling. Pinch edges to seal.

To fry, heat 2 tablespoons oil in a frying pan over medium heat. Arrange dumplings in a single layer in pan.

Drizzle ½ cup water over dumplings. Cook until water has evaporated and dumpling sides in contact with pan are golden brown (6 to 10 minutes).

This recipe makes about 100 dumplings.

Cooking Since 8 Years Old and Still Going

March 5, 2003

Sam Bass

Sam Bass is a good cook. Just ask anyone who has ever eaten his breakfast at Village Baptist Church.

For years he cooked Sunday morning breakfast and sometimes Saturday breakfast for about 40 men of the church.

It included bacon and country ham, redeye gravy, grits, eggs, buttermilk biscuits and coffee.

He learned to cook as a youngster of 8 years while growing up in Charlotte.

His mother worked as a candymaker and left home early in the morning, so Sam took over the job of cooking breakfast for his three brothers and two sisters. He remembers rising early to mix buttermilk biscuits for the family before he headed off to grammar school.

He later worked in the same candy store and learned how to make coconut candy with three different colors of coconut as well as peanut brittle and suckers. He said when he first went to work they told him to eat as much candy as he wanted.

"You eat as much as you want and then after a while you just don't want to eat much candy," he says.

But he never tires of eating his own pound cake called "Colonial Never Fail Friendship Cake."

"You get the starter from a friend and then it takes about 30 days to brandy the fruit you use."

He uses sugar, pineapple, and maraschino cherries and ferments the mixture until it becomes alcohol.

"Then you drain the liquid off and use a cup and a half of the fruit in the cake. The alcohol burns off and you still have the flavor. You pass the liquid starter on to a friend. That's why it is called friendship."

Bass likes to barbecue pork or chicken for his daughter, Deborah Foster.

"I fix a pretty good sauce when I'm grilling out-of-doors on the gas grill. I just start putting it together until I get a taste of what I like," he says.

Beef Stew is another of his well-liked recipes. For this he uses a slow cooker or a cast-iron Dutch oven, adding potatoes, onions, mushrooms, carrots and garden peas to taste.

He and his wife, Ercel, split the cooking duties, he says. When he cooks, she washes dishes and cleans up. When she cooks, he cleans up.

– Melissa Clement

Colonial Never Fail Cake

2 cups sugar

4 eggs

3 cups flour

1 teaspoon lemon flavoring

1 cup butter (2 sticks)

1 cup sweet milk

2 teaspoons baking powder

1 teaspoon vanilla

Cream butter. Add sugar. Add eggs one at a time, beating well after each egg is added.

Add flavoring, then milk and flour that has been sifted with baking powder three times.

Bake at 350 degrees in a greased and floured loaf pan one hour or layer pans for 30 minutes.

Country Grits and Sausage

2 cups water

½ teaspoon salt

½ cup uncooked grits

4 cups (16 ounces) shredded extra sharp cheddar cheese

4 eggs beaten

1 cup milk

½ teaspoon dried whole thyme

⅛ teaspoon garlic salt

2 pounds mild bulk pork sausage, cooked crumbled and drained.

Tomato roses

Fresh parsley sprigs

Bring water and salt to a boil; stir in grits. Return to boil and reduce heat. Cook four minutes, stirring mixture occasionally.

Combine grits and cheese in a large mixing bowl; stir until cheese is melted. Combine eggs, milk, thyme and garlic salt.

Mix well. Add a small amount of hot grits to egg mixture, stirring well. Stir egg mixture into grits mixture. Add sausage, stirring well. Pour into a 12-by-8-by-2 inch baking dish. Cover and refrigerate overnight.

Remove from refrigerator. Let stand 15 minutes. Bake at 350 degrees for 50 to 55 minutes. Garnish with tomato roses and parsley sprigs. Yield: 8 servings

Note: Recipe may be halved and baked at 350 degrees in a 10-by-6-by-2 dish for 45 minutes.

May be cooked and frozen, remove from freezer and let thaw. Heat in a 350-degree oven for approximately 20 minutes.

Thirty Day Friendship Cake

- 1¼ cup starter juice
- 7½ cups sugar
- 2½ cups sliced peaches and juice
- 2½ cups pineapple chunks
- 2 jars (9-ounce size) maraschino cherries, drained
- 1 box Duncan Hines yellow cake mix
- 1 box (3-ounces) instant vanilla pudding
- 4 eggs
- 1½ cup fermented fruit
- ⅔ cup Wesson oil
- 1 cup chopped pecans

In a large bowl or jar place starter juice, 2½ cups of the sugar and peaches. Ferment for 10 days in a warm area with lid loose.

On the 10th day add another 2½ cups sugar and pineapple. Let ferment for another 10 days.

On the 20th day add cherries and remaining 2½ cups of sugar.

On the 30th day drain juice off the fruit. You will have enough juice for four starters and enough fruit for three cakes.

For your cake, mix the yellow cake mix, pudding, eggs, fermented fruit, oil and pecans together. Pour into a greased and floured tube pan.

Bake at 350 degrees for 1 hour. Cake freezes well.

Don't forget to pass a starter on to a friend.

Buttermilk Biscuits

- 2 cups self-rising flour
- 1 cup buttermilk
- ½ cup Crisco, butter flavored shortening

Put flour in bowl, cut in the shortening until it looks like coarse meal. Add milk and mix until the flour is moist.

Turn out on board and knead (be sure the board is floured), until you can handle it without it sticking to your hands.

Pat out and cut the biscuits. Bake at 450 degrees for approximately 10 to 12 minutes or until lightly brown.

It's Law Books at Work, Cookbooks at Home

February 20, 2002

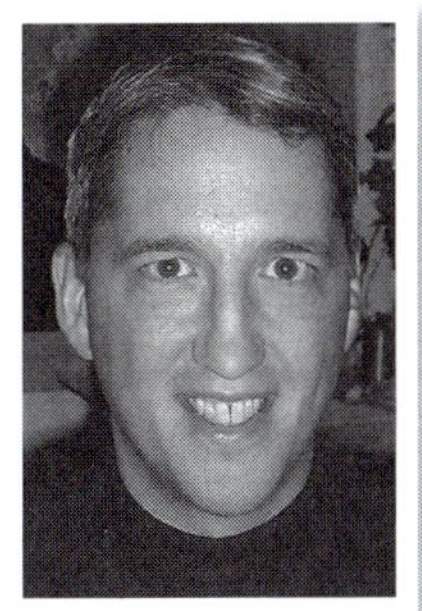

Brad Sutera

Army Capt. Brad Sutera says friends tell his wife, Arlene, how lucky she is all the time.

Sutera likes to cook and loves to prepare dinner for his wife, who gets home from work at night later than he does.

Arlene sells cars at a local dealership and doesn't get home until 8:30 or 9 most nights and works on Saturdays.

Brad is a lawyer and is assigned to a judge advocate's office at Fort Bragg. In his off-hours when he's not cooking or watching TV chefs prepare exotic dishes, he can be found on the golf course at Bayonet at Puppy Creek.

He's earned fame for his cooking outside the home as well. He was invited to cook as a celebrity chef at Trio Cafe last year and has been asked to make a repeat visit.

Brad got his start cooking breakfast when he was only 6 or 7 years old.

"Some were good, and some were not," he says of his early creations. "The scrambled eggs with pineapple was a disaster."

His father worked for IBM and the family moved frequently. He says he considers Texas his home state. It's where he went to law school at Southern Methodist University and where he returns each January to go deer hunting.

He likes to prepare game dishes as well as Southwestern, traditional French and northern Italian cuisine. Because of the unusual work schedules, he says it is difficult for him and his wife to entertain in their home.

For his guest chef appearance at Trio he helped prepare the menu, made some of the dishes and worked with the restaurant chefs and assistants to prepare the others.

One of Arlene's favorites is scones. "But I have been forbidden to make them except on request, because she likes them so much," Brad says.

One of the dishes he makes often is a Southwestern-style roasted red bell pepper soup. "I serve it as a first course or a main meal with homemade ravioli," he said. He fills the pasta with herbed goat cheese or smoked duck mousse.

He brings home venison in a cooler from his hunting trips and butchers it when he gets home. He says the secret to cooking it right is in the handling and not cooking it too long.

"Once venison gets past the point of medium rare it starts to taste like shoe leather," he says.

One of his favorite ways to cook vension is with his Parmesan-herb crusted medallions of venison with dried cherry sauce.

Brad says he and Arlene like to travel and try out new dishes. They sampled northern Italian cuisine last year and are planning a trip to France this year.

"It is hard to get away from classic French cooking because it is so technique driven," he says.

– Alice Thrasher

Classic Haricots Vert

- 8 ounces haricots vert (baby green beans, about 3 inches long and no more than ¼ inch in diameter)
- 1 tablespoon butter
- 2 cloves minced garlic
- 1 tablespoon chopped parsley (optional)
- Salt and pepper to taste

De-stem beans. Bring a large pot of salted water to a boil. Make an ice-water bath in a large bowl.

Add beans to boiling water and cook until beans are still crisp, perhaps 1-3 minutes depending on the beans.

Remove from boiling water and immediately plunge them into the ice-water bath until the beans are fully cooled. This sets the doneness and color.

Drain and dry. The beans can be held up to a day like this.

To serve, heat a large skillet over medium heat. Add butter and melt. Add beans, garlic, parsley, salt and pepper. Toss until the beans are heated through, about 1 minute. Serve immediately.

Serves 4

Parmesan-herbed Crusted Medallions of Venison with Dried Cherry Sauce

- Whole venison backstrap, fat and silverskin removed
- 6 ounces Parmesan reggiano cheese, grated
- ½ cup plain bread crumbs
- ½ cup chopped fresh rosemary
- 3 eggs beaten
- 1 teaspoon salt
- Olive oil

DRIED CHERRY SAUCE:

- 1 minced shallot
- 3 tablespoons butter
- 4 ounces dried cherries
- 4 tablespoons fresh chopped basil
- 1 cup red wine plus small amount for deglazing
- ½ cup demiglace (or ½ cup canned beef consomme.)

Cut venison into ¾-inch medallions.

Combine bread crumbs and rosemary.

Lightly beat 3 eggs with salt. Heat a large non-stick skillet and coat with olive oil.

Dredge each medallion lightly in egg wash, then bread-herb mixture. Shake off excess.

Dredge in egg wash again and then in cheese. Press mixture into medallions, ensuring each is well coated. Saute until brown and crisp, about 2 minutes. Turn to brown other side. Medallions will be medium rare. Serve with dried cherry sauce.

Serves six.

CHERRY SAUCE: Saute minced shallot in 1 tablespoon butter for 30 seconds. Deglaze with small amount of wine. Add cherries, basil, wine and demiglace (or beef consomme). Cook about 3 minutes. Pour in blender and puree. Return to heat. Taste and adjust seasoning. Keep warm until ready to serve. When ready to serve, remove from heat and whisk in 2 tablespoons softened butter. Serve immediately.

White Divinity Candy

- 2 cups granulated sugar
- 1 cup white corn syrup
- ½ cup water
- ¼ teaspoon salt
- 2 egg whites
- 1 cup finely chopped pecans
- 1 teaspoon of vanilla

In a large saucepan, combine sugar, corn syrup, water and salt. Stir that mixture over low heat.

Make sure all sugar is dissolved. If you have difficulty with it dissolving, you may cover the mixture for 1 to 2 minutes.

Pour cold water into a saucer and set aside. You can test to see if it is dissolved by dropping a small amount of the hot mixture into the cold water. A small, firm ball should form if it is ready.

Remove mixture from the heat when ready.

Next whip egg whites in a large bowl. Beat the egg whites until stiff. They should have little peaks.

Slowly pour the syrup mixture into the egg whites, mixing until the mixture no longer has a gloss. (You should be able to drop a small amount from a spoon and it should hold its shape).

Add the pecans and vanilla.

Using a teaspoon, place drops onto a lightly buttered cookie sheet or wax paper.

At Christmas you can also crush peppermint in a Ziploc bag and sprinkle over the top. Shaved chocolate is also a good topping.

Peanut Brittle

- 2 cups sugar
- ½ cup light corn syrup
- ¼ cup boiling water
- 2½ cups dry roasted peanuts
- 1 tablespoon butter
- ½ teaspoon vanilla (optional)
- 1 teaspoon baking soda

Combine the first three ingredients in a heavy sauce pan. Turn heat to low and stir constantly.

Stir until all of the sugar is dissolved.

Cover and cook on low heat for about 3 minutes, adding peanuts occasionally until the mixture becomes hard or looks cracked.

Stir in butter and baking soda. Pour into a lightly buttered 9-by-13-inch metal pan and spread mixture quickly and let the candy cool.

Use the handle of a butter knife to break the candy into pieces.

Travels Add Variety to Family's Menu

March 27, 2002

Laura Efird

Laura Efird grew up in Hephzibah, Ga., a small town near Augusta. Her family got together frequently for meals and her aunt, Pattie May, cooked a favorite dish, poppy seed chicken.

Today it is still a family favorite, especially for her husband, David. It was the first meal she cooked for him in their first home after they were married and the first meal he ate after coming home from Saudi Arabia.

She says it is not only easy to cook and delicious, but it can be used as leftovers on baked potatoes, sandwiches or subs. It is one of the few "real meals" her two children, Cory, 7, and Rebecca, 8, will eat without hesitation.

Efird says military wives are exposed to different cultures, different foods and ways of preparing meals. She has picked up a variety of recipes in her travels. In Panama she learned to cook Sausage Stars made with crumbled sausage, peppers and cheese, and baked in won ton wrappers.

In Panama she was the leader of a family-support group and helped produce newsletters for about 30 military families. She collected recipes from each wife. The recipes, especially the Poppy Seed Chicken and the sausage stars, were great successes.

When the family moved to Fort Lewis, Wash., they picked wild blackberries and blueberries by the bucketful. She learned to make berry jelly and jam. A neighbor taught her how to make a fried bread to dip in a berry sauce called berry gravy.

When she moved to Fayetteville she discovered a recipe made by her sister-in-law, Eva. It is a breakfast casserole that can be made, or just assembled, the day before. Efird says the casserole is filling and easy to make. It is made with sausage, eggs, cheeses, mushrooms and onions.

Efird and her Aunt Pattie are busy collecting recipes they remembered were used by Efird's grandmother, the late Elizabeth Park. The recipes include broccoli casseroles, sweet potato casserole, spaghetti and lasagna and goulash.

She says they intend to compile the recipes, along with photos of Park and stories about her, into a cookbook. After it is complete they will share it with friends and relatives who remember Park's great cooking.

– Melissa Clement

Poppy Seed Chicken

1 package boneless, skinless chicken

1 can cream of mushroom soup

1 8-oz. container sour cream

2 tablespoons poppy seeds

1 sleeve Ritz crackers

Butter

Boil chicken until done. Drain, then cut into bite-sized pieces.

Mix sour cream, mushroom soup and poppy seeds together. Add chicken and mix well.

Place in casserole dish and top with crumbled Ritz crackers and 5 pats of butter.

Bake at 350 degrees for 25 minutes.

Sausage Stars

2 cups (1 lb) cooked crumbled sausage

1½ cups grated sharp cheddar cheese

1½ cups grated Monterey Jack cheese

1 cup prepared Hidden Valley Ranch dressing

1 can (2.25 oz) sliced, ripe black olives

½ cup chopped red pepper

1 package fresh or frozen won ton wrappers

Vegetable oil

Preheat oven to 350 degrees.

Blot sausage dry with paper towels and combine with cheeses, salad dressing, olives and red pepper. Set aside.

Lightly grease a muffin tin and press one wrapper into each cup. Brush with oil.

Bake for 5 minutes or until golden brown. Remove from tin. Place on baking sheet. Fill with sausage mixture.

Bake 5 minutes until bubbly.

Makes 4 to 5 dozen.

Eva's Breakfast Omelet Casserole

1 package au gratin potatoes

3 cups very hot water

1 package hot sausage (12 to 16 oz.)

1 onion, diced

1 green pepper, diced

1 can sliced mushrooms, drained

½ cup very hot tap water

½ cup milk

6 eggs

1½ cups shredded cheddar cheese

In a large bowl, cover the potato slices with 3 cups hot water. Let stand. Sauté in oil, mushrooms, onions and bell pepper until done. Set aside.

Brown sausage until done, drain.

Drain potato slices. Combine the contents of the seasoning mix envelope, found in the au gratin potato box, and ½ cup hot water. Beat in the milk and eggs. Grease 13-by-9-inch baking pan. Place sausage, potatoes and vegetables in the bottom of the pan. Pour egg and milk mixture over the top layer of casserole. Top with cheddar cheese.

Bake at 350 degrees for 35 to 40 minutes.

CEO Changes Her Lifestyle Thanks to Health Classes

August 1, 2001

Jean Hodges

Several years ago Jean Hodges, CEO of Hodges Associates, an advertising, marketing and public relations agency, volunteered to be in the Women's Health Initiative Dietary Change Group.

It is a 10-year national study funded by the National Institutes of Health. The mission is to see if a diet low in fat and high in fruits, vegetables and grain can improve the health of women.

Hodges says she joined because she hoped the study, which includes other women's health issues, such as hormone studies, would help others in the future, particularly her three daughters and three granddaughters.

In trying to help others, she helped herself.

In the first year she lost 20 pounds by changing her diet using information she learned from the weekly classes given by dietitian Karen Gantt.

She started eating more fruits, vegetables and grains. Although she never cared much for bread she began to eat cereal in the morning and pasta and bagels during the day.

"One of the main things I learned is that it's not what you eat so much as what you put on what you eat. It's not the bread, it's what you put on it — pasta, what you put on it. I have learned to substitute low-fat products in sauces and gravies, switching from creams to things like marinara sauces. I don't fry foods. I learned to bake, broil and grill."

She uses olive oil, and instead of pouring in a spoonful for cooking, she uses sprays.

"I changed from eating rib-eyes to sirloin steak. I use seven percent ground meat instead of hamburger meat. I eat more fish."

Hodges didn't give up eating what she likes; she only modified her diet gradually until she reached her goal.

She switched from whole milk by bumping down the percentage of fat until she reached her goal of skim milk.

Now she says drinking whole milk "tastes like you've got a mouth full of butter."

Occasionally she will eat a fat, juicy steak to satisfy a craving because she does not believe in denying herself.

She learned ways to modify her favorite recipes to meet her requirements, such as using applesauce as a substitute for oil in baking. Because she loves fruit ice cream, she has changed her recipe to use fat-free Eagle brand milk and low-fat milk with pureed fresh fruits.

She learned to read labels to find out what foods have the most fat and cholesterol.

"I never read a label before in my life. Now I believe in eating right, exercising and keeping your mind sharp."

– By Melissa Clement

Crab Dip

2 cans lump crab. Rinse and squeeze very dry.

1 cup green onions, chopped fine

1 cup celery, chopped fine

1 envelope unflavored gelatin

1 can 98 percent fat-free cream of mushroom soup

8 ounces light or fat-free cream cheese

2 tablespoons cold water

Combine cream cheese and mushroom soup in a saucepan. Heat until melted together.

Remove from heat.

Add 1 cup low-fat or fat-free mayonnaise to crab, onion and celery.

Dissolve 1 envelope unflavored gelatin with 2 tablespoons cold water.

Add at once to soup and cheese mixture.

Mix and add to the rest of ingredients.

Pour into mold and refrigerate until set.

Catfish Parmesan

⅔ cup freshly grated Parmesan cheese

¼ cup all-purpose flour

½ teaspoon salt

¼ teaspoon pepper

1 teaspoon paprika

1 egg (I use the Egg Beater equivalent)

¼ cup skimmed milk

5 to 6 small catfish fillets (about 2 pounds)

¼ cup low-fat margarine, melted

⅓ cup sliced almonds

Combine cheese, flour, salt, pepper, and paprika; stir well.

Combine egg and milk; stir well.

Dip fillets in egg mixture; dredge in flour mixture. Arrange in a lightly greased (I use non-fat olive oil spray) 13 x 9 x 2 inch baking dish; drizzle with margarine.

Sprinkle almonds evenly over tops of fillets; bake at 350 degrees for 35 to 40 minutes or until fish flakes easily when tested with a fork.

Yields 6 servings.

Spaghetti alla Carbonara

5 ounces smoked turkey bacon

1 medium onion, chopped

1 to 2 garlic cloves, crushed

⅔ cup chicken stock

⅔ cup dry, white wine

7 ounces low-fat cream cheese

1 pound chili and garlic flavored spaghetti

2 tablespoons chopped fresh parsley

Salt and pepper

Shavings of Parmesan cheese.

Cut the turkey bacon into ½ inch strips. Fry quickly in a non-stick pan for 2 to 3 minutes. Add the onion, garlic and stock to the pan. Bring to a boil, cover and simmer for 5 minutes until tender.

Add the wine and boil rapidly until reduced by half. Whisk in the cream cheese until smooth.

Meanwhile, cook the spaghetti in a large pan of boiling, salted water for 10 to 12 minutes.

Drain thoroughly.

Return to the pan with the sauce and parsley, toss well and serve immediately with shavings of Parmesan cheese.

Serves 4

Presentation Is Key to This Cook's Desserts

August 8, 2001

Jane Horrocks

When Jane Horrocks goes to a restaurant, she checks out the desserts on the menu before the main dishes.

"Every cook has a specialty," Horrocks says. "I like to do desserts more than anything, and I like pretty desserts."

She doesn't cook desserts every day for her husband, Harry, or daughter, Hallie, who is 15, and son, Hampton, who is 12.

"Sometimes on the weekend I will make one and I cook them for company, special dinners or to give to someone," she says.

"When we get together with my family I usually cook the desserts. My daddy loves lemon pie and I'll fix it for him."

Horrocks likes to make birthday cakes from scratch and apple cakes in the fall.

Hallie got a special chocolate cake this year made from a recipe from *Bon Appetit* magazine.

Horrocks has some favorite recipes collected over the years and likes to look for new ones on the Internet.

"She makes the best chocolate chip cookies," Hampton says.

Horrocks always make the Foothill House Sweet Dream cookies to take on trips to eat on the road. She makes them for teachers and neighbors at Christmas, too.

She clipped the recipe from a magazine years ago.

"The powdered sugar makes them so good," she says. "They come out crinkly."

The Fudgy Brownie Pie is an easy dessert for children to learn to make, she says.

"Hallie makes that pie all the time. She probably started making them when she was 10 or 12."

Another favorite is Lemon Luscious Pie with Raspberry Sauce. The pie recipe came from a Fayetteville Junior League cookbook, and Horrocks came up with the raspberry sauce.

She garnishes the plate with blueberries and fresh mint.

"I always use real butter and real sour cream," she says. "I feel like if you are going to make a dessert, you might as well make the real thing."

The desserts are not low-calorie, Horrocks say. She walks and plays tennis to keep trim.

Horrocks say she learned to cook from her mother, the late Ellen Hollinshed.

"When she went back to school to become a librarian, my sister and I would try to cook dinner," she says. "Mary's specialty is hors d'oeuvres."

Horrocks likes to watch the television cooking shows.

"I've learned from watching 'Emeril Live' that it's all in the presentation and to use color."

– Alice Thrasher

Fudgy Brownie Pie

2 ounces unsweetened chocolate

1 stick butter

2 eggs

1 cup sugar

½ cup flour

1 teaspoon vanilla

1 frozen pie shell, unbaked (not deep dish)

Preheat oven to 325 degrees.

In a double boiler melt chocolate and butter.

Whisk in eggs, one at a time. Whisk in sugar, flour and vanilla.

Pour into pie shell and bake for 30 to 35 minutes.

Foothill House Sweet Dreams

- 1 cup (2 sticks) unsalted butter
- 1½ cups firmly packed light brown sugar
- 1 egg, room temperature
- 1 teaspoon vanilla
- 2 cups unbleached, all-purpose flour
- 1 teaspoon baking soda
- 1 teaspoon cinnamon
- 1 teaspoon ground ginger
- ½ teaspoon salt
- 1 package (12 ounces) semi-sweet chocolate chips
- 1 cup chopped walnuts
- 1 cup powdered sugar

Cream butter using electric mixer.

Beat in brown sugar, egg and vanilla.

Combine flour, baking soda, cinnamon, ginger and salt. Blend into butter mixture.

Fold in chocolate chips and walnuts.

Refrigerate until firm. (Dough can be prepared 1 day ahead.)

Preheat oven to 375 degrees. Lightly grease baking sheets.

Break off small pieces of dough; roll between palms into 1-inch rounds. Dredge rounds in powdered sugar. Arrange rounds on prepared sheets, spacing at least 2 inches apart. Bake 10 minutes.

Let cool 5 minutes on sheets. Transfer to racks and cool.

Store in airtight container. Makes about 6 dozen.

Luscious Lemon Pie with Raspberry Sauce

See photo in center of book

- 1 cup sugar
- 3 tablespoons cornstarch
- 1 tablespoon lemon rind, grated
- 4 tablespoons butter
- 3 egg yolks, slightly beaten
- 1 cup sour cream
- 9-inch pie shell, baked (not deep dish)
- 1 cup milk
- ¼ cup fresh lemon juice

RASPBERRY SAUCE:

- 1 bag (12-ounce) frozen raspberries
- ½ cup water
- 1 regular-size tea bag
- ¾ cup sugar
- 2 tablespoons butter
- 1 teaspoon vanilla
- 2 tablespoons cornstarch

Combine sugar, cornstarch (stir with whisk to break up any lumps and mix together well), lemon rind, butter, lemon juice, milk and egg yolks in heavy saucepan.

Cook over medium heat until smooth and very thick, stirring constantly; cover and cool.

Fold sour cream into filling; pour into baked pie shell. Chill at least 2 hours before serving.

Top with whipped cream and raspberry sauce.

RASPBERRY SAUCE:

Combine raspberries and water in saucepan and bring to a boil. Reduce heat and simmer 5 minutes. Take off heat.

Add tea bag; cover and steep 5 minutes; remove tea bag. Pour mixture through a strainer, pressing mixture with back of spoon to squeeze out the juice.

Combine sugar and cornstarch in small saucepan; gradually add raspberry juice, stirring until smooth. Bring to a boil over medium heat, stirring constantly; boil 1 minute.

Remove from heat; stir in butter and vanilla. Cover and chill.

He's Spent a Lifetime Around Seafood

May 5, 2004

John Cook

When John Cook was growing up, cooking was just part of everyday life.

"I was born in the South ... my mom and dad both did a lot of cooking," he said. "I just sort of took a liking to cooking different meals."

In fact, he said, he moved to Fayetteville to manage a restaurant, although he has since switched jobs and now works as a martial arts instructor.

Cook and his wife celebrated their 19th anniversary last week. They have three children, ages 14, 13 and 11.

Cook said one of the kids' favorite dishes is Hobo Stew, in which meat and vegetables are wrapped in foil and cooked outside in the coals of a fire. "We do it a lot when we go camping with the Scouts," he said.

Another dish Cook likes to make is Shrimp Perlow.

"My dad was a fisherman, so we always had seafood," he said.

He said the shrimp dish is a one-pot meal kind of like a jambalaya; it uses shrimp, sausage, bacon, tomato sauce and rice, simmered together.

But the cook can be flexible and add whatever sounds good, such as bell peppers or different kinds of rice. "Just use your imagination with it."

He said he makes most of his dishes by feel, knowing from experience how much of the ingredients to add and how long to cook them. "I don't really cook by recipes," he said.

He also likes to cook on the grill. He sometimes soaks small tree limbs in water and then adds them to a charcoal grill to smoke chicken. The smoke from the wood penetrates the chicken.

He said his extended family lives in Florida, but they sometimes come up to visit. Then the family will have an oyster roast. "It's great."

Cook said he doesn't have as much time to cook now because the martial arts school is taking so much of his time, but he still loves to cook. "I've always enjoyed cooking."

– Cathryne Meeks

Shrimp Perlow

Rice
Shrimp
Sausage
Bacon
Onions
Tomato sauce
1 can whole tomatoes (optional)

Note: The amount of the ingredients depends on preference. If you like a lot of rice, use a lot; if you don't like bacon, use just a little or leave it out. The recipe is flexible and can be made with many variations.

Put a couple of cups of rice in a large pot and add water. Boil.

After a few minutes, take out some of the water and add the tomato sauce and the tomatoes, if using.

Simmer the onions in a frying pan. Add the bacon and sausage and continue cooking. Add the shrimp and cook for just a few minutes longer.

Add the meat mixture to the pot with the rice. Continue to cook until the rice is done.

Hobo Stew

Cube steak or hamburger meat
Vegetable oil
Potatoes
Carrots
Onions
Corn (canned)
Salt
Pepper

Divide the meat into single-serving portions and pat them flat, like hamburger patties.

Cut up the vegetables: Cut the carrots lengthwise. Cut the potatoes into rounds. Dice the onions.

For each serving, layer three or four pieces of aluminum foil, about 1 foot square, on a plate. Place 1 or 2 drops of oil on the foil. Then put a piece of meat on the foil.

Let each person pick what vegetables he or she wants and put those vegetables on top of the meat. Add salt and pepper.

Fold the foil over the top. Place the foil packets in the coals of a fire. (You can use the coals of a campfire or bonfire, or take the grate off a grill and place the packets directly in the coals.)

Let them cook 3 or 4 minutes, then flip them over and cook until done.

Smoked Chicken with Potatoes and Corn

Chicken breasts

Corn on the cob (fresh or frozen)

Potatoes

Teriyaki sauce

Butter (if desired)

Salt or season salt (if desired)

Skin the chicken. Soak in teriyaki sauce for several hours.

Gather some small tree limbs and break them up, so they're about the size of pencils. Soak in water.

Shuck the corn (if fresh) and add butter and salt or season salt if desired. Wrap in foil. Wash the potatoes and, while still damp, wrap in foil. Prepare charcoal grill.

Just before adding the chicken and vegetables, put soaked wood on coals. Put the chicken, potatoes and corn on the grill. Close the lid but leave the vent cracked so air circulates to keep the coals from going out.

At some point, the wood will dry out and flame up. Be prepared to take everything off the grill when the wood dries out, then put out the flames and put the food back on the grill to finish cooking. Or you can use a spray bottle to put out the flames, but this may get ashes on the chicken.

The chicken breasts usually cook the fastest. The corn will probably take 10 or 15 minutes, and the potatoes will take a little longer. When you can stick a fork in the vegetables and it slides right back out, they are done. (To make the potatoes finish about the same time as the chicken and corn, you can cook them in the microwave for a few minutes before wrapping them in foil and grilling them.)

Cajun Cuisine Eaten After Curtain Call

May 28, 2003

Clare Davis

Clare Davis is known to wear many hats at the Cape Fear Regional Theatre.

Her official job is stage manager, but when the curtains close Davis is known to whip up some of the best authentic Cajun food around for cast members and co-workers.

A native of Houma, La., Davis is Cajun through and through. Her father was a chef, her uncle a shrimp distributor and her grandfather was an oyster farmer.

Growing up 60 miles southwest of New Orleans, Davis learned her skills as a cook nearly by instinct.

She helped the family cook as soon as she could stand on a stool beside her four older brothers and sisters.

"Where I come from that's what people do to bond and hang out," Davis said. "It was something we all did together."

At 28, Davis has missed only two Mardi Gras festivals in her lifetime. And as many southern Louisiana natives know, the party is not limited to New Orleans. In fact, some of the best food and good times can be found in the smaller towns.

Davis lived in Louisiana until she was 18 years old. She then moved to California and next to Tennessee. She moved to Fayetteville eight years ago.

Her secrets for great Cajun food?

The secret is the roux. It simply has to be prepared correctly for any Cajun dish to thrill food lovers.

"Really good Cajun food — you have to have really good ingredients," Davis said.

Another secret for good roux is a flat, wooden spoon and a heavy-bottomed pot.

Her friends and co-workers swear by Davis' cooking. Why not become a chef?

"It's one of the many things in my life I'd want to do," she said.

One of Davis' favorite Cajun meals is the old favorite Red Beans and Rice. It's just one of her signature dishes along with huge portions of chicken and sausage gumbo.

Still, North Carolina has had some influence on Davis' taste buds.

She's a big fan of pig pickings and boiled peanuts.

– Stacy Peterson

Chicken and Sausage Gumbo

- 1 cup vegetable oil
- 1 cup plus one tablespoon all-purpose flour
- 8 pieces of chicken (legs and thighs, bone in, skin removed)
- 1 lb. smoked sausage or andouille, sliced
- 1 large onion, diced
- 1½ large bell pepper, diced
- 3 large stalks celery, with leaves, diced
- 2 large bay leaves
- Cajun seasoning to taste
- Salt and pepper to taste
- 3 quarts boiling water

Make sure all ingredients are prepared before you start. Make the roux by heating oil in a heavy-bottom pot over medium heat until a sprinkling of flour sizzles.

Next slowly add the rest of the flour, stirring constantly using a flat wooden spoon. Reduce the heat to medium-low until the roux, which thickens as it cooks, becomes a dark caramel color almost like maple syrup. (If the roux is not thick enough, the gumbo will taste like flour).

When the roux is completely browned, add onion and continue to stir. Add chicken pieces that have been coated with Cajun seasoning and sausage. Stir in the roux until chicken is slightly browned. Add celery, bell pepper and onion. Cook until slightly softened. Add spices and boiling water and cook, stirring occasionally for two hours. Serve over rice with a side of potato salad.

Red Beans and Rice

- 3 large cans light red kidney beans
- 2 lbs. smoked sausage
- 1 large ham hock
- 2 cloves garlic, minced
- 1 large onion, chopped
- 1 large bell pepper, chopped
- 2 stalks celery (with leaves)
- 1 bay leaf (remove when done)
- 1 handful chopped parsley (reserve a couple of tablespoons for garnish)
- 1 large can diced tomatoes (if desired)
- 1 teaspoon black pepper
- 1 teaspoon Cajun seasoning (Ex. Tony Chaserie's)
- 1 cup water

Note: The ham hock and sausage usually add enough salt.

Brown sausage in one tablespoon of olive oil.

Add onions and garlic, stirring often until slightly browned. Add bell pepper and celery and cook a few minutes until softened.

Add remaining ingredients, stir and cover.

Cook on low fire for approximately two hours, stirring often. The beans will stick and possibly scorch if not stirred often. Stirring often will also help the beans to break up and thicken. The ham hock can be removed when the beans are done so the meat can be taken off and put back in.

Serve over rice with a pinch of fresh parsley and cornbread.

Cajun Potato Salad

- 8 large white or red potatoes, approximately four lbs. (peeled and diced)
- 4 large eggs
- Approximately 1 cup mayonnaise
- 3-4 tablespoons mustard
- 1 handful sliced pickles (diced)
- ½ large bell pepper (diced)
- 2 stalks celery, with leaves (diced)
- 3 tablespoons chopped parsley
- 2 tablespoons pickle juice
- 1 small onion (diced)
- Cajun seasoning to taste
- Black pepper to taste

Boil potatoes until they are very tender. They should easily mash with a fork. The eggs can be washed and put in the same pot as the potatoes and will be done at the same time.

Drain potatoes and peel eggs.

Dice eggs or smash with a fork and add to the potatoes. Add all other ingredients and stir well.

The potato salad will have a kind of chunky mashed potato consistency.

FTCC Food Class to be Taught by Aspiring Author

MARCH 26, 2003

Marilyn Fender

Marilyn Fender has definite ideas about food — how to cook it and how to eat it.

"Cooking should not be drudgery. It should be fun to cook and to eat. People should sit down to dinner and commune at least once a week in these troubled times, enjoying each other's company and just being quiet."

She is set to teach a cooking class at Fayetteville Technical Community College called "Dinner from Scratch in the Nick of Time."

It begins April 12 and runs through May 17. The 20-hour class costs $45.

She retired and moved here last September to be near her son, who is in the military.

When she worked at a senior homeless center in New York, folks there were so glad to have her cooking rather than the frozen foods they were used to eating that they persuaded her to write a cookbook. She named it "Bones! Beans! & Greens! ... Funny Food ... and Some of the Foods I Cook So Swell." She hasn't found a publisher yet. In the book she makes personal comments about the food, the family she grew up in and how they cooked. She tells how her mother had a punishment chair that Marilyn says she sat in quite often. With nothing else to do, she watched her mother cook bread and special sauces on a coal-burning stove.

When she grew up she became a caterer in New York City with her own style of cooking. As a diabetic she had to learn to cook without using much fat.

"You don't have to cook everything with fatback, bacon and ham hocks, although the Southern fried chicken is the best in the world. You also don't have to soak beans overnight."

Here's why she named the book "Bones."

"There is absolutely no bones about it. You find the tastiest, most tender meat next to the bone. Some of these bones get passed over entirely and most of you

Bok Choy

1½ to 2 pounds fresh bok choy

½ cup extra virgin olive oil

1 clove fresh garlic, crushed

Kosher salt and fresh grated black pepper to taste

1 8- or 10-inch skillet with a top

Wash the bok choy by separating the leaves and washing off any sand on the stalks. Cut off the very root end (the white stem is part of the good part so leave it intact).

Slice the bok choy across in about ¼ inch slices, drain in colander.

Heat skillet until hot, not smoking. Add bok choy. It will sizzle. Stir and add salt and pepper. Cover and turn heat low. Let cook until the thickest white stalk is tender, about 20 minutes. Leave the cover on, no reason to peek.

When done, serve as an easy, quick side dish.

Makes 6 servings.

have not even thought of preparing such as oxtails, beef, lamb shank and veal shanks, country-style spare ribs, lamb riblets and veal breasts. You don't have to cook everything with fatback, ham hocks and bacon.

"Bones! is a concept I began in the early 1990s. Bones, beans and greens are amazing tastes you have probably been overlooking but will grow to love."

She says bean cuisine in soups, salads and as main courses is all the rage right now.

"Kale, Chinese and savoy cabbage, bok choy, broccoli rabe, and dandelions will be a welcoming change from spinach. These are all amazing tastes. In my recipes I use kosher salt, freshly ground black pepper and fresh herbs."

– Melissa Clement

Braised Lamb Shanks in Mint Sauce

- 6 lamb shanks
- ½ cup tightly packed fresh mint leaves, coarsely chopped
- 1 large, coarsely chopped Spanish onion
- 3 large cloves garlic, crushed
- ½ cup dry white wine
- ¼ cup flat leaf parsley, coarsely chopped
- 1 tablespoon dried oregano
- 3 crushed bay leaves
- 1 teaspoon kosher salt
- ½ teaspoon freshly ground black pepper
- 2 cups whole cranberry sauce
- 1 cup mint jelly

Buy six meaty, lean lamb shanks. Cut away as much fat as possible. Wash in cool running water or wipe clean with a wet paper towel, wipe dry. Salt and pepper and put them end to end in a shallow glass baking dish with mint, crushed garlic, coarsely chopped onion, parsley, oregano, and bay leaves. Pour the wine over all, cover with plastic wrap and refrigerate overnight.

Remove shanks from the marinade, shake off the onions and herbs.

Heat a skillet then add ½ cup canola oil, when hot, not smoking.

Brown the shanks in the oil, place in one layer in a shallow baking dish, set aside. In a saucepan bring the marinade to a boil and cook until the garlic and onions are wilted and liquid reduced, strain, pour strained marinade over shanks. Cover with aluminum foil and place in a preheated 300-degree oven. Cook for one hour.

In the meantime simmer the cranberry sauce, mint jelly and a few fresh mint leaves until syrupy.

Remove the shanks from the oven. Close oven and turn the temperature up to 350 degrees.

Pour the syrup over the lamb shanks, put back into the oven uncovered for another 30 minutes. In that last 30 minutes baste the shanks with the syrup often, coating nicely. Watch carefully. Do not burn.

This would go very nicely with a Boston lettuce, red onion and sliced tomato salad; a rice pilaf; sauteed fresh green beans; homemade dinner rolls and apple pie.

Makes 6 servings.

Pigeon Peas and Rice

- ½ pound smoked ham hock
- ½ pound beef chuck cut into ½ inch cubes
- 1 teaspoon kosher salt
- 1 teaspoon ground cloves
- 2 tablespoons extra virgin olive oil
- 1 cup peeled, seeded and chopped fresh tomatoes
- ½ cup chopped green pepper
- 2 fresh seeded, chopped hot peppers
- 1 cup coarsely chopped onion
- 1 cup fresh pigeon peas that you soak and set aside (if canned use 2 cups drained)
- 2 cups long-grain rice
- 3 cups beef or chicken stock

Note: This may be served as a side dish or a main course, or you may want to take it with you to "that covered dish social," Marilyn Fender said.

Soak ham hock overnight in water, drain, cut meat off the bone in ½ inch pieces.

Mix with the beef and season with salt, garlic and cloves.

Heat the olive oil in a Dutch oven, saute the meats until brown. Add a cup of chicken stock and simmer 1½ hours (meat needs to be tender). Add water from time to time, and stir if it seems dry.

When done, measure the liquid. It needs to measure 4 cups with the stock and liquid from the meat. If needed add water to bring the measurement to 4 cups. Add the tomatoes, peppers, onions, pigeon peas and rice.

Bring to a boil, cover and cook over very low heat until the rice is tender and all the liquid is absorbed.

Makes 6 servings.

Broccoli Rabe or Raab

- 2 bunches broccoli rabe
- 1 cup of chicken broth
- 1 tablespoon crushed red pepper
- 1 whole bulb of chopped garlic
- ½ cup extra virgin olive oil
- 1 8- or 10-inch covered skillet

Wash the sand off the leaves and stems under cold running water. Cut off the very thick part of the stems. You want the buds and the thin stems. Drain well (water will spatter in the oil).

Heat skillet and add the olive oil. Let it get hot and add coarsely chopped garlic. Saute quickly but do not brown. Remove cooked garlic, set aside.

Add the washed, drained broccoli rabe to the hot pan in a single layer. Saute a few minutes. Turn once keeping a fairly uniform layer.

Add the chicken broth and sprinkle the crushed red pepper on top. Cover and cook without opening for 15 to 20 minutes. Turn off the heat.

Remove the top, add a generous splash of olive oil. Serve as a side dish. It is best served over penne pasta with grated Parmesan cheese. Pass the fresh Italian bread and enjoy. Monja!

Hunt Wins 2004 Chicken Bog Cookoff

May 19, 2004

Billy Hunt

Some winning recipes are crafted by years of trial and error, worried and fretted over by their creators, and blended into a delicate mixture of time, ingredients and seasoning.

Then there are recipes such as the one that earned Billy Hunt top honors at this year's Chicken Bog Cookoff in St. Pauls.

Hunt's taste for bog and sense of adventure led him to a bog recipe that included everything from garlic to Lawry's seasoning salt, with most all of the chicken thrown in for effect.

"I know it should be some big secret, and should be real tough," Hunt said while accepting congratulations from hungry spectators eager to sample his bog. "But really, it's not hard at all."

And the genesis for his award-winning recipe?

"I had a big bunch of friends over at a get-together, and I had to feed them," he said. "A bog's a great way to feed a lot of people for little money."

Chicken bog, for the uninitiated, is a traditional dish in the Eastern Carolinas. The fine points vary from place to place, but essentially, you need a chicken, some rice and a big pot to cook them in. From there, cooks often add sausage, spices, whatever is handy to give the bubbling blob a kick.

"I don't know how you could make it very complicated," Hunt noted. He added Jimmy Dean sausage to his for a little extra flavor. "I started a few years ago, and folks seemed to like it. Then a friend of mine, Patrick Edge, suggested I come over here and make some."

Some people wonder about something called "bog." Hunt says he explains that it's "kind of like Brunswick stew," only different.

And while his recipe allows for variations in cooking temperature and spices, he has one warning for would-be boggers.

"Whatever you do, don't overcook it," Hunt warned. "Once it gets overdone, there's nothing you can do about it. It needs to stay moist, so a lower heat is better."

And what about folks who don't like picking bones out of their bog? They can use precut chicken, he says.

"But it won't be a genuine bog."

– *Chick Jacobs*

Billy Hunt's Chicken Bog

- 1 box Uncle Ben's converted rice, original recipe
- 1 good-sized chicken, whole or cut up; 4 to 5 pounds works best
- 1 diced large onion
- 1 clove of garlic
- 1 diced red pepper
- Crushed red pepper to taste
- Salt to taste
- Black pepper to taste
- Lawry's seasoning salt, to taste
- 1 pound Jimmy Dean Sausage; spiciness is up to the cook

Use a large pot or kettle for cooking. Put chicken in the pot and with enough water to cover the bird. Turn on heat and boil the chicken until tender.

While chicken is cooking, slice up onion, garlic and red pepper. Cook the sausage until done.

When chicken is tender, add sausage, chopped vegetable and spice and reduce heat to a simmer, stirring occasionally.

Thirty to 45 minutes before serving, add the rice and stir occasionally. If additional moisture is needed, add water or chicken broth. Do not let the mixture get dry. When rice is tender, remove and serve.

Pilot Likes to Experiment in Kitchen

FEBRUARY 4, 2004

Kent Hellman

Chief Warrant Officer Kent Hellman recently returned from Afghanistan. He is a Chinook helicopter pilot and works at Simmons Army Airfield on Fort Bragg.

When he isn't working, he can sometimes be found in his kitchen or at his backyard grill, fixing food for his family or guests. He said that when he and his wife, Dawn, and their daughter are home together, he makes a lot of the meals, especially on weekends.

Hellman said he likes to cook a little of everything.

He likes to make up recipes or alter existing recipes — "just whatever comes to my mind."

His favorite dish that he has made up is a pasta creation with cheese, onion vinaigrette salad dressing and shrimp. He has also been known to make homemade pizza or grill bratwursts for friends.

"I always like to grill," he said.

Hellman said he used to experiment in the kitchen as a child. He mostly learned by watching his mom.

"By the time I was a teenager, I had to make most of my own meals because I was on a different time schedule than my parents," he said.

As an enlisted soldier, he cooked in the barracks with a hot plate, a coffee pot and a microwave. The most common themes were macaroni and cheese and ramen noodles, but he added his own variations. But he didn't do a lot of cooking until he had his own kitchen in flight school.

Hellman said his favorite utensil is the George Foreman lean mean green grilling machine.

His words of advice to adventurous cooks: "If you ever decide to cook snake, make sure you boil it first and then grill it."

– Cathryne Meeks

Quesadilla Casserole

- 1 can green enchilada sauce
- 2 to 4 cans diced green chilies
- 1 large package flour tortillas
- 1 pound of chicken
- 1 8-ounce package low-fat cream cheese
- 8 ounces or more cheddar cheese
- Jalapenos (optional)
- Red chili peppers (optional)

Dice chicken. Cook in a pan.

Put green chili sauce in another pan and melt cream cheese with it. Add chilies. Let it all heat together. Add chicken. Add hot peppers to taste.

Tear up tortillas into little pieces. Put a layer of tortillas in a casserole dish. Pour half of sauce over. Add a layer of cheese. Repeat layers, ending with cheese. Cover with foil.

Cook at 400 degrees for 25 minutes. Remove foil. Broil until cheese browns.

Mint Iced Tea

- 1 gallon water
- 6 to 8 tea bags – half camomile, half green tea
- Mint extract
- ¼ cup sugar (optional)

Put the tea bags in a clear container of water and let it sit in the sun until the water becomes tea. (If you don't want to make sun tea, you can make tea by boiling the water. Use the same amount of tea bags.) Add about ¾ capful of mint extract. Add sugar if desired. Chill.

Big Family Enjoys Mother's Culinary Skills

NOVEMBER 9, 2005

Joy Van Hout

When Joy Van Hout moved to Haymount, a neighbor called to ask her whether she was into voodoo.

She did not know what gave him that idea until he said he was referring to a dead bird pinned inside her window.

It seems she was preparing Peking duck, which had been saturated with soy and honey, and she was trying to dry it out. It has to dry in order for the skin to puff up when it is roasted, she said.

"Peking duck is really marvelous," she said. "It takes a lot of imagination and dedication to get it just right. I took the duck out of the window and hung it in the attic to dry. It takes a good day or two to dry out."

Now her duck doings are a family joke, and when she told her daughter she was going to share her recipes in this column, her daughter asked whether she was going to include Peking duck. She declined.

There was also the incident of the cobra that slithered into her kitchen when the family lived in the Philippines. Her husband, the late Col. Harold Van Hout, was stationed there with the Army.

The snake was killed with a trash can lid, and the house had to be searched for others. But that didn't give Joy a fear of the kitchen. She has cooked for many since the snake incident.

Her offspring range in age from 59 years to 16 months and include nine children, 29 grandchildren and two great-grandchildren. When the whole family gets together, there are 46. Once when the whole clan was at the beach, someone asked whether the gathering was a church picnic. She said, "No, but the Pope started it all."

She decided to share her daughters' favorite recipes. One is hot chicken salad, which includes unusual ingredients such as crushed potato chips, grated cheese and toasted almonds. Another is sweet-and-sour green beans with bacon bits. The most unusual is cranberry spinach salad; it can be made with a variety of greens, nuts and poppy seeds. You may even add feta cheese.

Someone usually brings these dishes to family gatherings, along with a huge turkey, a big roast, a large ham, eight pounds of shrimp, mashed potatoes, salads, homemade bread, scalloped corn and cookies.

When they all gather at Joy's house, she uses her mother's best china and crystal.

When they all come for Thanksgiving, she said, "This house looks small from the outside, but it stretches. You'd think they would have worn the walls out with all that rubbing of elbows against the walls. The children eat in the kitchen. It's like an Army mess hall, and it's really a mess when we're all through. They're a good bunch with a funny sense of humor. If I didn't have a funny sense of humor, I don't think I would have survived."

– Melissa Clement

Sweet and Sour Green Beans

3 (16-ounce) cans green beans, drained, or Italian flat beans

1 large onion, thinly sliced

½ cup vinegar

½ cup sugar

½ cup bacon bits

Mix beans and onion slices together. Bring to a boil vinegar, sugar and bacon bits. Pour over beans and onions. Marinate in the refrigerator at least 24 hours. Stir about 4 times while marinating.

Heat in oven at 350 degrees for 40 minutes or so just before serving.

Serves 8 to 10.

Sometimes mix the whole green beans and Italian beans together.

Hot Chicken Salad

4 cups cooked chicken chunks

2 cups celery, chopped

4 hard-boiled eggs, diced

2 tablespoons onion, finely minced

1 teaspoon salt

2 tablespoons lemon juice

¾ cup mayonnaise

¾ cup cream of chicken soup

1 cup cheese, grated

½ cup potato chips, crushed

⅔ cup toasted almonds, finely chopped

Combine chicken, celery, eggs, onion, salt, lemon juice, mayonnaise and soup, mixing well.

Spread in 9-by-13-inch casserole dish. Combine cheese, potato chips and almonds and spread over top.

Cover and refrigerate overnight.

When ready to bake, preheat oven to 400 degrees and bake 20 to 25 minutes. Makes 8 servings.

Spinach Cranberry Salad

See photo in center of book

SALAD:

¾ cup slivered almonds

1 tablespoon butter

1 pound salad spinach or romaine lettuce torn into bite-size pieces

1 cup dried cranberries

DRESSING:

1 tablespoon poppy seeds

½ cup sugar

2 teaspoons minced onion

¼ teaspoon paprika

¼ cup white-wine vinegar

¼ cup apple-cider vinegar

½ cup salad oil

Feta cheese (optional)

Saute the almonds in butter until lightly toasted.

Remove from heat and let cool.

Toss greens with toasted almonds and cranberries.

Whisk together the poppy seeds, sugar, onion, paprika, both vinegars and salad oil in a bowl.

Toss with salad just before serving. May add crumbled feta cheese.

Heirloom Recipes Become Family Traditions

May 25, 2005

Becky Lee

Becky Lee enjoys cooking, entertaining with food and taking food to others.

She says she comes from a long line of good cooks and married into a line of more good cooks when she and Tom Lee wed.

Even her son, Jack Lee, a 28-year-old sound engineer in Chicago, likes to cook and calls her frequently for some of the family's heirloom recipes.

Once he asked what to substitute for fatback, because he couldn't find it up north. She advised him to use bacon instead.

At Christmas and Thanksgiving she cooks with heirloom recipes, which she keeps on the same time-worn manila cards on which they were written years ago.

Some of those are from her mother, Shirley Kenton of Sanford, who frequently entertained her literary club and other organizations and friends. She was well-known for her peach chutney and apricot preserves, and she gave programs on cooking. Some of her dishes often grace the Lees' holiday dinners.

Tom's grandmother, Gram Rebecca Lee, loved to cook and eat, and the richer the food the better, Becky says. She cooked with a lot of rich cream at her home in Fremont, Neb. Her son is Jackson Lee, who was the mayor of Fayetteville from 1971 to 1976 and owned WFAI Radio Station.

Gram Lee made steamed chocolate pudding for young Tom Lee's birthday every year until her death at age 97. Now Becky follows that tradition. She admits it's quite a lengthy process and the pudding is extremely rich, but she offers the recipe to readers.

"Just go ahead and cut your calories some other way," she says.

Becky offers one of her favorite recipes from her grandmother Rebekah Ingram, called "Mema." Her grandmother called the recipe "six-week bran muffins" because she could keep the batter in the refrigerator for up to six weeks at a time without it going bad. But Becky says it never lasted that long because the muffins were so good.

Mema Ingram lived in South Boston, Va., and Becky says her fondest memories are of family members gathering at her home, where she would do all the cooking for both sides of her family. "The aroma of dill or boxwoods brings back fond memories of those reunions," she says.

Becky's own special recipe was given to her by a college roommate when she attended Stratford College in Danville, Va. She smiles when she describes the fresh tomatoes baked in a pie with onions, oregano and cheese.

– Melissa Clement

Becky Lee's Tomato Pie

- 2 cups Bisquick
- ½ cup milk
- 6 to 8 fresh tomatoes, peeled, sliced and drained
- Oregano to taste
- Minced dried onions to taste
- Salt and pepper to taste
- 1½ cups grated cheese
- 1½ cup mayonnaise

Make crust with Bisquick and milk. Roll out and put in pie pan. Prepare filling with a layer of tomatoes, a layer of oregano, a layer of dried onions, salt and pepper. Repeat layers three times. Mix the cheese and mayonnaise and use the mixture to top the pie. Bake at 400 degrees for 25 to 30 minutes.

Mema's Bran Muffins

3 cups dry bran cereal
1 cup boiling water
2 eggs, beaten
½ cup oil
1½ cups sugar
2 cups buttermilk
2½ cups flour
1 teaspoon salt
2½ teaspoons soda
1 teaspoon cinnamon
½ box seedless raisins, if desired

Mix the bran cereal with the boiling water and let it sit while you assemble the other ingredients.

Mix together eggs, oil, sugar and buttermilk.

Stir together flour, salt, soda and cinnamon.

Combine all ingredients. Fold in raisins if desired. Put in greased muffin tins, and bake at 375 degrees for 25 to 30 minutes. If mini-pans are used, cook for 10 to 12 minutes.

Becky Lee says her Mema kept batter in the refrigerator for up to 6 weeks. It never lasts that long, she says, because it is so good.

Steamed Chocolate Pudding

½ cup sugar
1 cup milk
2 squares unsweetened chocolate
1 egg at room temperature
2 cups sifted flour
2 teaspoons baking powder
Salt to taste

You will need a metal steamer with a cover. Melt the chocolate. (Do not microwave.) Cool.

Combine with other ingredients.

Put into a greased and floured metal steamer.

Cover and set inside a pan of water.

Steam at 325 degrees for an hour and a half.

Remove from oven and flip onto plate. Slice and serve hot with cold sauce.

Cold Sauce

4 tablespoons butter
2 cups powdered sugar
2 eggs, room temperature
1 cup whipping cream
1 teaspoon vanilla

Separate egg yolks from whites.

Cream butter and sugar.

Add egg yolks and set aside.

Whip egg whites until stiff. Whip cream. Carefully fold egg whites into cream. Fold egg-and-cream mixture into sugar mixture.

Cover and refrigerate. This sauce is also good with plum pudding.

German Native Is Known for Her Baking

June 18, 2003

Ilse Hutcheson

Ilse Hutcheson, a native of Germany, came to the United States as a war bride in 1960.

Each time she went home, she said her mother would say, "'Don't they feed you in America? You need to put on weight. Don't you know that your nerves have to be buried in fat so you can face the everyday tribulations?'

"Then she would proceed to feed me for the next three weeks. It was easy to put on weight with all that good German food."

German food, she says, is better seasoned because German cooks use a variety of spices and seasonings to make things taste good, while in this country seasonings are often just salt and sugar.

Hutcheson is well known for her baking, especially the cookies she bakes and shares with friends and family at Christmas.

"My cookies are never as sweet as those made with American recipes."

She tries two new cookie recipes each Christmas and gets the cookies tested by her friends.

She also makes stollen, a German yeast bread that is also not overly sweet.

One of the secrets of her excellent baking is the ingredients she uses.

"I always use the best I can find like pure vanilla,

Little Rascals

2 sticks and 2 tablespoons butter (must be butter — unsalted)

1 cup sugar

1 egg

1 teaspoon pure vanilla extract

1 cup almonds measured, then finely ground

3 cups flour

Raspberry jam

Powdered sugar

Cream butter until fluffy. Add sugar, add egg, add vanilla extract. Mix well after each addition. Add almonds and then knead in flour.

Chill in refrigerator a minimum of 1 hour or longer.

On floured surface roll out small portions of dough to inch thickness. Cut out with round 2-inch cookie cutter. Cut out centers of half of the unbaked cookies with a mini cookie cutter (inch).

Remove the centers and reroll dough to reuse. Bake in preheated 350 degree oven until edges are firm and bottoms are lightly browned, approximately 8 to 9 minutes. Remove cookies carefully from cookie sheet and cool completely.

Assembly of cookies:

Spread raspberry jam onto the bottom of cookies without cutouts. Top with cookies with cutouts (sandwich fashion). Dust tops with powdered sugar.

Makes approximately 50 cookies.

because I feel that if I'm going to put that much effort into baking, I might as well start with the best ingredients. After all you don't eat it all in one sitting."

Hutcheson learned to bake when she was 10 or 11 because her mother did not like to bake.

One thing she did learn from her mother was to wear an apron. Hutcheson was born during World War II when clothing was at a premium. Women wore aprons in order to save wear and tear on their garments. Now she finds it difficult to cook unless she wears an apron and it is hard to find a full apron now, she says. So when she goes back to Germany for a visit she always brings several back.

Her cookie recipes here were translated from German and all are cut out and decorated, and when she serves them, they are stacked on a plate covered with a white doily.

"I put emphasis on pretty. That is important. When I put different kinds of cookies on a plate it really is a feast for the eyes. Your eyes eat also. First your eyes feast, then you feast."

– Melissa Clement

German Butter Cookies

- 3 sticks butter (must be butter — unsalted)
- 1 cup sugar
- 5 egg yolks
- 3 cups flour

Cream butter with mixer until fluffy. Add sugar and mix well. Add egg yolks and mix well. Add flour, a little at a time and knead into a smooth dough.

Form ball, put on plate dusted with flour and chill in refrigerator a minimum of one hour or longer.

Roll out small portions of dough to inch thickness on floured surface. Cut out with small cookie cutters.

Bake in preheated 350-degree oven for approximately 10 minutes until lightly golden. Remove carefully from cookie sheet and cool completely.

Makes about 10 dozen cookies.

Crisp Almond Cookies

- 1 stick and 2 tablespoons butter
- 1 cup and 3 tablespoons sugar
- 1 egg
- 1 teaspoon almond or rum extract
- 1 cup whole unblanched almonds measured, then finely ground
- 1 cup flour

Cream butter, add sugar, add egg, add almond extract. Mix well after each addition. Stir in almonds and flour. Knead into a smooth dough and chill in refrigerator (minimum 1 hour).

Shape dough into 1 inch balls and place 1 inch apart on cookie sheet. Press whole almond on top of each cookie.

Bake in a preheated 350 degree oven about 12 to 13 minutes. Cookies are done when edges are slightly brown.

Remove carefully from cookie sheet and cool completely.

Makes about 4 dozen cookies.

Almonds can be replaced with hazelnuts.

Businessman Likes to Experiment with Recipes

May 15, 2002

Patti Pollitt

Patti Pollitt says she's the most spoiled person in Fayetteville.

That's because her husband, Bill, loves to cook and has been doing most of the shopping and cooking for more than 20 years.

"She's a great prep cook and good at clean-up," Bill says.

"We were married for about 10 years when we were having a frank talk one day and Patti said she hated having to plan meals and get dinner ready," he says. "She never enjoyed cooking. I told her I liked to cook, so I would just start doing the cooking."

"We were both working full time and the children were little," Patti says. The three daughters and son all are grown now, married and living in other cities. The Pollitts have five grandchildren and another on the way. They will celebrate their 33rd wedding anniversary in June. They work together at their framing and gift shop in Westwood Shopping Center.

Bill Pollitt

"I like to cook," Bill says. "It's evolving all the time. We do things a little different now and eat more fish and seafood."

He likes to fish in a sound near Emerald Isle, but says most of the fish he cooks he has to buy.

"And I buy frozen salmon steaks from Sam's and like them cooked on the grill with a little chili powder and lime," he says.

Bill says he has had to adapt his cooking radically in the past year.

"Patti just this year found out she has severe food allergies to eggs, dairy products and wheat," he says.

He has been searching for recipes that he can use without eggs, cheese, butter, or wheat. He uses soy milk to make gravies and soy sour cream for some sauces.

"We use a lot of olive oil," he says. "And I have found some sources on the Internet to order 20 pounds of corn spaghetti.

Shrimp and Scallops with Pasta

- 1 pound cleaned shrimp (can use frozen, cooked shrimp)
- 1 pound fresh, large scallops
- 5 cloves minced garlic
- 1 chopped medium onion
- 1 can black beans, rinsed
- 1 can (2½-ounce) sliced ripe olives
- ¾ cup olive oil
- ¼ cup fresh lemon juice
- 1 cup white wine
- 1 bunch fresh basil leaves
- 4 Roma tomatoes, quartered
- Salt and pepper, to taste
- Cooked pasta (for 6 to 8 servings)

In a large stock pot or skillet, saute garlic and onion in a little olive oil until tender.

Add wine to reduce slightly, then olive oil, lemon juice, beans, olives and chopped basil.

Add salt and pepper to taste. Add shrimp and scallops. Heat to cook through (but don't overcook), about 5 minutes.

May want to thicken with a tablespoon of cornstarch mixed with water.

Stir in tomatoes before serving on cooked pasta. Makes 6 to 8 servings.

"We have gotten really good at reading ingredients, but that's not a bad thing to do anyway," he says.

Patti says for years she was taking medicine for allergy-induced asthma. "I wanted to get off the drugs and inhalers and asked to get more extensive testing and blood work done," she says.

After finding out the foods Patti was allergic to, Bill began searching for ways to prepare foods she could eat.

"We have a lot of stir-fried type things," he said. "And we eat a lot of grits." He looks at recipes in *Southern Living*, *Cooking Light* and other magazines to get ideas for what ingredients go well together.

He likes to cook with black beans and likes to use fresh herbs. He is a master gardener and grows herbs that he can snip to enhance his home-cooked dishes. He grows tomatoes, peppers and eggplants in pots at home, too.

"He is really good with the presentation, too," Patti says.

"He has really been great to find ways to cook things that I can eat."

– Alice Thrasher

Fish with Chipotle Butter and Baked Beans

FOR CHIPOTLE BUTTER:

3 tablespoons unsalted butter, softened

1 canned chipotle chili in adobo, chopped fine (about 1 tablespoon)

½ teaspoon fresh lime juice

FOR BLACK BEANS:

3 cans (15-ounce size) black beans, rinsed and drained (about 4½ cups)

1½ teaspoons chopped fresh oregano leaves or ½ teaspoon dried, crumbled

1 tablespoon vegetable oil

3 tablespoons fresh lime juice

6 squares (15-inch) parchment paper

3 plum tomatoes, cut lengthwise into 6 slices

6 pieces (6- to 7-ounces each) grouper or cod fillet, skinned

24 pitted green olives, halved lengthwise

1 small red onion, cut into ¼-inch-thick slices

¾ cup dry white wine

4 tablespoons fresh lime juice

6 sprigs oregano, if desired

6 pieces (7-inch each) kitchen string

Make chipotle butter:

On a small plate with a fork blend together well the chipotle butter ingredients and chill. Chipotle butter may be made 5 days ahead and chilled, wrapped tightly.

Make black beans:

In a bowl mix together black bean ingredients with salt and pepper to taste. Black beans may be made 1 day ahead and chilled, covered. Season beans with salt and pepper before using.

Preheat oven to 400 degrees.

On a work surface arrange 1 parchment square and put ¾ cup black beans and 3 tomato slices in center. Top tomato and beans with 1 piece of grouper or cod.

Top the fish with 8 olive halves, about one sixth of onion slices, 2 tablespoons wine, 2 teaspoons lime juice, 1 oregano sprig and about ⅙ of chipotle butter and season well with salt and black pepper. Gather sides of parchment paper up over fish to form a large sack and gently squeeze middle of sack together to form a waist. Tie 1 piece of string tightly but gently around waist of sack and transfer sack to a large shallow baking pan. Make 5 more sacks in same manner with remaining parchment squares and ingredients.

Bake sacks in lower third of oven (being careful that tops of sacks do not touch heating element) 15 to 20 minutes, or until fish is cooked through.

Divide sacks among 6 plates and at table snip strings with scissors. Serves 6.

Meatballs and Vegetables with Horseradish Dressing

6 ounces ground chuck (or use frozen meatballs and simply steam them with vegetables)

1½ tablespoons seasoned, dry bread crumbs

⅛ teaspoon salt and pepper

¼ teaspoon browning and seasoning sauce

Vegetable cooking spray

½ cup cauliflower flowerets

⅓ cup julienne cut carrots

¼ cup chopped onion

1 cup sliced zucchini

¾ cup snow pea pods, fresh or frozen

4 cherry tomatoes

¼ cup plain low-fat yogurt

1½ tablespoons mayonnaise

1 teaspoon prepared horseradish

½ teaspoon lemon juice

Combine first 5 ingredients; shape into 6 meatballs. Coat a vegetable steamer with cooking spray; place over boiling water. Add meatballs, cover and steam 5 to 7 minutes. Add cauliflower, carrots and onion and steam 10 minutes. Add zucchini, snow peas and tomatoes; cover and steam 2 to 3 minutes.

To make the horseradish dressing, combine room-temperature yogurt, mayonnaise, horseradish and lemon juice in sauce pan. Place over low heat, stir constantly until heated (do not boil).

Serve horseradish dressing over vegetables and meatballs and brown rice. Makes two servings for a simple but pretty company supper.

Flank Steak Pot Roast

1½ pounds flank steak

2 cups prepared bread dressing

¼ cup chopped onion

1 tablespoon minced fresh parsley

½ teaspoon celery salt

½ teaspoon salt and pepper

½ teaspoon dried sage

1 tablespoon butter or margarine

1 tablespoon cooking oil

1 cup hot water

½ teaspoon peppercorns

1 tablespoon garlic wine vinegar

1 cup hot water

1 beef bouillon cube

¼ cup flour, mixed with 6 tablespoons cold water

Score flank steak on one side in a diamond pattern.

Combine bread dressing with next six ingredients; arrange on unscored side of steak, patting it nearly to edge. Dot with butter.

Roll steak like jelly roll and secure with skewers or string.

Heat oil in Dutch oven or large skillet and brown steak on all sides.

Add cup of water with peppercorns; sprinkle with vinegar.

Cover and simmer for 1 to 1½ hours or until tender.

Remove peppercorns, arrange steak on platter and remove skewers.

Stir in remaining water and bouillon cube into liquid. Thicken with mixed flour and water.

Meals Adjusted for Grandchildren

January 8, 2003

Norma Maness

Norma Maness has a special challenge when cooking meals. She and her husband, Len Maness, have the care of three grandchildren, ages 5, 11 and 13. She tries to keep them eating healthy and liking it.

She experiments with a lot of different recipes. If the children do not like a dish they have to eat a portion, but then she tries another healthy dish.

"They keep us young," she says. "We have to be flexible. We try to keep them busy and happy. They have soccer, band practice, plays, piano lessons, school projects and Scout meetings, so I try to take a lot of shortcuts in preparing meals because we move pretty fast."

She uses packaged frozen Potatoes O'Brien with onions and peppers in her lasagna casserole and fat-free wieners in her hot dog casseroles. Her fruit salad is made with canned fruits.

"On a cold day they like lasagna soup. It is made with a packaged mix and is real nutritious. I get a good hearty bread to go with it."

She says her husband, a former coach and assistant principal at Terry Sanford High School, is easy to please, likes about everything she cooks, and will eat broccoli steamed. There is always fruit on the table for snacks.

Norma Maness also constantly watches her own diet as she is one of the participants in the national Women's Health Initiative (WHI) study in which women volunteer to eat a low-fat diet including lots of grains, vegetables and fruit. After the 10-year study is completed, the data will be calculated to see if the diet did improve the health of women.

She says she did not think much about eating healthy until she was in her 50s. Then she began eating a balanced diet, counting grams of fat and calories and eating more fruits and vegetables. She lost 30 pounds.

"You are what you eat," she says. "I feel much better now."

– Melissa Clement

Lasagna Soup

1 pound lean ground beef

1/2 cup chopped onion

1 package lasagna dinner mix

5 cups water

1 (14-ounce) can diced tomatoes, undrained

1 can whole corn, undrained

2 tablespoons grated Parmesan cheese

1 small zucchini, chopped (You may use green beans instead of zucchini.) Brown the beef and onion. Add everything but the noodles and cheese. Bring to a boil. Put on simmer. Add noodles and cook until they are tender. Add cheese as served so it won't stick to pot.

Serves 6.

Hot Dog Casserole

1 pound red potatoes, cubed (may substitute 1 pound 12-ounce package frozen Potatoes O'Brien with onions and peppers

10 hot dogs (1 pound), sliced across (can use fat free.)

2 tablespoons diced onions (when not using O'Brien potatoes)

1 cup frozen peas, thawed

1 can (10 ounces) condensed cream of mushroom soup, undiluted

3 tablespoons butter or margarine, melted

1 tablespoon prepared mustard

1/8 teaspoon pepper

In a saucepan, cook the potatoes in boiling salted water until tender, drain. If using Potatoes O'Brien, don't cook ahead of time. In a greased 2-quart baking dish combine the potatoes, hot dogs, onions and peas.

Combine soup, butter, mustard and pepper; gently stir into potato mixture.

Bake, uncovered, at 350 degrees for 25 minutes or until heated through.

Serves 6.

Fruit Salad

See photo in center of book

1 can peach pie filling

2 cans (15 ounces) fruit cocktail

1 small can Mandarin oranges, drained

1 can (15 ounces) pineapple tidbits, drained

2 bananas, sliced

Mix all ingredients together and cool in refrigerator 1 hour before serving.

Linden Resident Celebrates Family Events With Feasts

April 28, 2004

Winifred McKethan

When there's a birthday, graduation, anniversary or holiday, it means a gathering with family and close friends to Winifred McKethan, who lives in Linden.

"I started cooking around 12 or 13 years old when I was in the sixth grade," she said. "I was the baby of 12 siblings from Dunn."

"The first meal I made was pork chops, pinto beans and rice," she said as she smiled. "Mother had to help me with the potato pie."

McKethan's mother, Julian M. Dixon, taught her children to cook. The three sisters who are still living are known for their desserts. McKethan has a brother who is a caterer in New York and one who cooks for his church members in Detroit. He recently cooked for a Men's Day event at his church and served more than 500 people.

"My brothers usually pack up lots of my Southern food and carry it back with them so they can share the food with others," McKethan said.

The housewife's brother-in-laws are cooks, and many of her ideas have come from them. Her husband, Kenneth, cooks as well. The couple married on June 6, 1976, and they have three grown boys.

"The first meal she cooked for me was chicken or a pot roast, pinto beans and a sweet potato pie," Kenneth McKethan said. "It was on a Sunday."

While gospel music is being played in the McKethan house, she is preparing a list of all the foods that will be served at a Mother's Day and birthday celebration.

"We are expecting more than 100 people to come for my mother's 90th birthday party," she said.

"People will even come off the street and try to blend in to get something to eat," Kenneth McKethan added with a chuckle.

The couple stressed that if strangers do come over, they do not turn anybody away. McKethan is an evangelist at Westwood Church of God of Prophecy in Erwin, and she sees her cooking as a way of ministering to others.

"I will even invite Mattie McInnis, my pastor, and sometimes we invite the congregation over after church for dinner."

So what is on her food list? "I plan to make potato salad, macaroni and cheese meaty casserole, Winifred's chicken and pork chops, Winifred's Beefy Seasoned Barbecue Pinto Beans, Winifred's Meaty Rice Casserole, Winifred's Fried Seasoned Pork Loin With Cayenne Pepper and all kinds of cakes," she said. "Don't forget the specialty — Kenny's fish and maybe my chitterlings," Kenneth McKethan said.

The chitterlings take a lot of time to prepare, but it is worth the wait, Kenneth explained.

No matter what will be served, people are expected to leave with full stomachs and with plates of food in their hands.

Celebration and food really go together for this family. "Cooking is something I really love to do," McKethan said.

– Ealer S. Wadlington III

Beefy Seasoned Barbecue Pinto Beans

- 1 pound cooked and drained seasoned pinto beans
- 2 pounds barbecue sauce
- 1 pound ground chuck or sirloin
- 1 pound ground beef
- 1 pound ground hot sausages
- 1 medium bell pepper, diced
- 2 medium onions, diced
- 1 pound pork sausage
- 1 teaspoon seasoned salt
- 1 teaspoon garlic powder
- 2 tablespoons sugar
- ½ teaspoon crushed cayenne pepper
- 1 teaspoon Italian seasoning
- ½ teaspoon allspice
- ½ teaspoon black pepper
- 1 can Italian tomatoes
- Onion powder, to taste

Combine the beef and sausage in a large saucepan. Add onion and pepper, then add seasoned salt, garlic powder, onion powder, sugar, crushed cayenne pepper, Italian seasoning, allspice and black pepper.

Cook over medium heat until meat is well done, then drain and return to heat for about 15 minutes, stirring constantly.

Add barbecue sauce, and let it simmer on low for about 20 minutes. Add the seasoned pinto beans. For added flavor, add one can of Italian chopped tomatoes.

Meaty Rice Casserole

- 1 pound ground chuck
- 1 teaspoon cayenne pepper
- 1 pound ground beef
- 2 teaspoons Lawry's Seasoned Salt
- 1 pound sausage
- 2 teaspoons garlic powder
- 4 Brightleaf Red Hot Sausages
- 2 teaspoons onion powder
- ½ teaspoon black pepper
- 5 Brightleaf Franks
- 1 bag of four cheeses
- 5 dashes Texas Pete hot sauce
- 1 pack of Italian sausage
- 1 large green and red pepper
- 2 teaspoons sugar
- 1 large onion
- 4 celery stalks
- Small jar of diced pimentos
- 1-pound box of Uncle Ben's Original Rice, cooked

In a large skillet, cook ground beef, chuck, sausage and Italian sausage (diced), peppers, onion, celery, pimentos and seasonings until meat is medium done. Add red hots and franks, cook until done; drain the meats. Add Uncle Ben's Original Rice. (Cook rice before adding it to the meats.)

Mix rice and the meats well; add one bag of four cheeses on top of the casserole, and let it set for about 20 minutes. Serve.

For added flavor, you can add 1 can of tomato sauce and 1 can of tomatoes with chives and herbs (Italian tomatoes with garlic and herbs).

If you use the tomatoes with this recipe, don't add the rice to the meats until you let the tomatoes and sauce cook in the meat for 20 minutes on medium heat. Then add the rice and let set for an additional 10 minutes.

Fried Seasoned Pork Loin with Cayenne Pepper

Vegetable oil

8 large pork loin chops

1½ teaspoons cayenne pepper

2 teaspoons garlic powder

2 teaspoons onion powder

½ teaspoon black pepper

1 teaspoon Lawry's Seasoned Salt

5 dashes Texas Pete hot sauce

½ cup self-rising flour (Golden Eagle)

1 cup of Moss Chicken Breader mix

Wash the chops thoroughly. Lay each chop on a cooking board. Sprinkle cayenne pepper on each chop, and chop them with a food chopper. After chopping the chops, place them in a large bowl; then add the seasoned salt, garlic and onion powders, Texas Pete hot sauce and black pepper. Mix well. Put self-rising flour and Moss Chicken Breader in a large bag.

Mix and shake the flours until they are well blended and add 3 pork loins. Shake them up in the bag until they are evenly covered. Shake off excess flour and drop the chops in a Fry Daddy.

While you are mixing the chops, you should have your fryer heating at 375 degrees.

Cook the chops for about 15 minutes or less. When the chops rise to the top of the oil, turn 1 time.

Let the chops cook for a few minutes and remove from the hot oil. Crisco or Wesson vegetable oil can be used. If using a skillet, also use oil, and do not put too many chops in the skillet, maybe 3. For added flavor, after chops are cooked, you may add more hot sauce or ketchup or ranch dressing on top of them.

Teacher Shares Japanese Traditions

OCTOBER 5, 2005

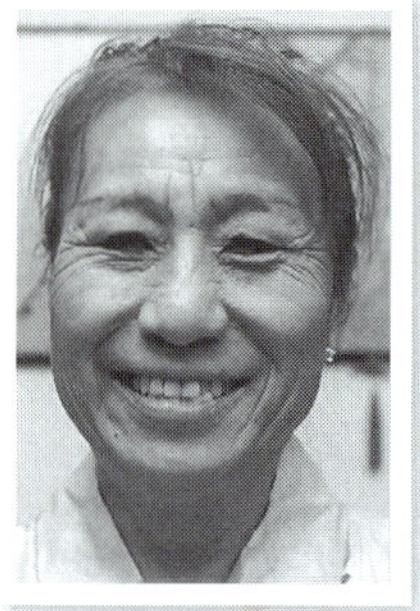

Etsuko Martin

Etsuko Martin's Japanese father is very traditional. He believes that women's happiness is in the home, cooking for a husband and changing diapers, she says.

He believes that a girl who would marry well into a traditional household must go to Bride's School to learn the five different duties of a wife. They are the cooking, the tea ceremony, flower arranging, sewing and kimono making.

Although Martin didn't want to go there, she took all of the classes for brides to be, but she yearned to go to college. Her father was still against her getting an education, but he paid her tuition. She worked to pay other expenses and graduated from the well-known Mushasino Art University in Tokyo.

She didn't realize it at the time, but all those traditional Japanese skills would later help her make a living. For many years, she has taught classes in traditional Japanese cooking at Fayetteville Technical Community College in continuing-education classes. She makes most of her money from sewing and making alterations. She also teaches other skills such as flower arranging and origami and is often called on to do the traditional tea ceremony.

After college, Martin toured this country and came to Fayetteville to visit a friend. Here she met her husband to be. Later she attended Methodist College to get a better understanding of our culture so she could have a better relationship with her husband. There she majored in fine art and sculpture, which has helped her earn money from commissions and art-show prizes. So both her father's influence and her own motivation for education have been useful in her life.

When she teaches cooking, she cooks in the traditional Japanese style.

"Anything goes in Japanese cooking today. Some cooks even use hot dogs in their tempura," she said.

Tempura is made with vegetables and seafood that have been battered and deep fried. She insists that her students learn the traditional cuisine before inventing their own dishes.

One of the first things Martin stresses in her classes is that sushi is not raw fish, as so many people believe. Sushi is boiled rice flavored with rice vinegar. The rice is then mixed with chopped vegetables, tofu and other ingredients and made into a roll, which is then cut into slices. Raw fish can be one of the ingredients in

Noodle Salad

- Dried clear noodles (long kou bean threads)
- Water
- Salt
- Pepper
- Mayonnaise
- Dashinomoto
- Cucumber, sliced paper thin
- Red bell pepper, chopped fine
- Green onion, sliced thin
- Parsley, chopped

Break noodles and drop into boiling water. Boil until noodles can be cut easily. Drain and cool noodles (not ice cold, just enough so they don't cook the vegetables). Add salt, pepper, mayonnaise and dashinomoto to taste. Add vegetables.

sushi and then it is called nigiri sushi.

"Japanese diet is the best diet for a long life," she said. "My grandmother lived to be 104. I believe the average life is close to 92. We drink green tea, don't eat much fatty food, eat lots of vegetables and seafood and not much meat or grease. I don't use sugar and not much salt. When my father was here, he couldn't understand why the food here is so salty."

– Melissa Clement

Sushi

- ½ cup sugar
- Pinch salt
- Pinch of dashinomoto (dried bonito-flavored soup stock)
- 1 cup rice vinegar
- 4 cups rice, cooked (directions follow)
- Nori (seaweed sheet)
- Fillings of choice (see instructions)
- Ginger and parsley for garnish

Mix sugar, salt and dashinomoto with rice vinegar until dissolved. Spread rice on a flat dish. (Wet rice paddle to prevent sticking.) Pour vinegar mixture over rice. Fan rice and use a cutting motion with the rice paddle to mix rice and vinegar. Lay nori on rolling mat and pat rice into layer on top, leaving an inch at edge for sealing. Place filling in a line across center of rice. Wet sealing edge of nori and roll up. Wet knife before slicing. Arrange sushi on plate and decorate with ginger and parsley.

FILLINGS FOR SUSHI

Use multiple fillings for Hutomaki (big roll), but only one or two for Hosomaki (small roll).

Eggs: Lightly beat eggs with a pinch each of sugar, salt and dashinomoto. Oil skillet (used oil works best), and pour egg into pan. Rotate pan to distribute egg into thin layer. When set, flip over gently. Remove from pan, cool and cut into long, thin strips.

Fish cake: Slice into long slices about ¼-inch square.

Spinach: Fresh is best, but if using frozen spinach, heat to separate leaves and squeeze out water.

Cucumber: Slice into long slices about 1 inch square.

Tuna salad.

Shiitake mushrooms: Boil in cup water, 2 tablespoons soy sauce, 1 tablespoon sugar and teaspoon dashinomoto until liquid is gone.

Kanpiyo (dried gourd): Wash in salt water until pliable. Boil as with the mushrooms.

Credit Summers at Beach for Recipes

October 17, 2001

Susan McMillan

When Susan McMillan cooks for a crowd, one of her favorite recipes is for paella — a Spanish dish of saffron-flavored rice combined with a variety of meats and shellfish (such as shrimp, clams, chicken and spicy Spanish chorizo sausage) garlic, onions, peas and red peppers.

"Some people make it with lobster and no chicken," Susan says. "And if you have high cholesterol, they will leave the pork out."

Her recipe calls for half a young chicken, cut into pieces. She says she cooks it with chicken breasts now.

Her late husband, Allen McMillan, liked dark meat, so she used a whole chicken when she cooked it for him.

Susan says she grew fond of paella (pronounced py-AY-yuh) while spending summers on the family's boat in Wrightsville Beach with her now-grown daughters, Dorsey and Page. She is a former teacher and heads a family business now.

An older Bahamian man who was a captain on a boat owned by the Flagler family of Florida used to make paella on the dock. He was at the marina while his boat was under repair and would share in the communal Sunday dinners with the boating families, Susan says.

"He did this on an open flame on the dock and he would put conch in it," she says. "He put newspaper over the entire thing and said that was imperative.

"His was the best in the whole world. It was wonderful."

Susan says she's afraid of using newspaper to cover the dish and can't find conch to put in her paella here.

"I do like to leave the heads on shrimp because it makes it flavorable," she says. She finds the clams and mussels at Harris-Teeter and orders the saffron strands from Williams-Sonoma.

"We eat it in a rustic manner and I always have a plate for everybody for their shells and shrimp heads."

Susan says Grand Vegetables is another favorite dish she used to prepare in the boat's small galley.

"It is a pretty accompaniment to any entree," she says. The vegetables are all raw and the dish can be prepared ahead of time.

Another family favorite is Chicken with prosciutto. Prosciutto (proh-SHOO-toh) is a thinly sliced, spicy, air-dried Italian ham.

"My mother takes shortcuts, and when she can't find prosciutto she will use the dried beef. But the prosciutto makes all the difference in the world."

Susan says she likes to experiment with recipes when she cooks.

"It feeds the creative side," she says.

– Alice Thrasher

Grand Vegetables

1½ cups cauliflower, broken into pieces

1½ cup broccoli

1 can artichoke hearts, drained and sliced in half

1 large red onion cut in chunks and separated

1 can heart of palm, cut in bite-size pieces

½ jicama, peeled and julienned

1½ cups cherry tomatoes

1 yellow bell pepper, chopped

3 tablespoons capers

Cardini's Original Caesar Salad Dressing

Salt and pepper, to taste

Carefully wash all fresh vegetables and dry thoroughly.

Split tomatoes in half. Toss everything in large bowl.

Add Cardini's Original Caesar Salad Dressing to coat.

Season with salt and pepper to taste. Best when prepared about 30 minutes before serving.

Toss just prior to serving.

Chicken with Prosciutto

Canola oil (enough to cover bottom of pan)

4 large chicken breasts (bone-in provides more flavor.)

Flour for dusting

½ pound thinly sliced mozzarella

½ pound prosciutto (sliced paper thin)

2 cans cream of mushroom soup

1 cup good dry, red wine

Salt and pepper, to taste

Preheat oven to 325 degrees.

In a large, heavy frying pan, add just enough canola oil to cover bottom of pan.

Dust chicken in flour and salt and pepper it.

Brown thoroughly in pan. Remove from pan. Pour off any excess oil, being careful to save all browned bits.

Deglaze pan with wine. Immediately lower heat.

Add 2 cans of soup to pan, stirring constantly until quite smooth. Remove pan from heat.

Spray a large baking dish with Pam. Place prosciutto in bottom to completely cover.

Add chicken. Cover with mozzarella, then pour sauce over all, evenly covering.

Bake at 325 degrees for 30 to 35 minutes.

Serve over rice.

Paella

2 tablespoons olive oil

1 large yellow onion, chopped

3 small green onions with tops, sliced on the diagonal

1 to 2 cloves garlic, minced ¼ teaspoon salt

2 cups Calasparra rice or Arborio (short-grained)

½ cup dry white wine

½ young chicken, cut into pieces (or chicken breasts)

½ pound chorizo (or other spicy, air-dried sausage)

3 strands saffron, soaked in chicken broth.

4 cups good chicken stock (or low-sodium canned chicken broth)

12 mussels, carefully cleaned

12 clams (small neck), carefully washed

½ pound 16-20 count shrimp, deveined (heads on)

½ cup red bell pepper, chopped

⅓ cup fresh flat-leaf Italian parsley, chopped

1 teaspoon kosher salt (or to taste)

1 teaspoon freshly ground black pepper

1 cup fresh English peas (parboiled)

Lemon wedges, for garnish

In a paella pan or other large bistro pan warm oil over medium-high heat.

Add onions, red peppers, garlic and chorizo (cut in small pieces) and saute until vegetables are translucent (3 to 4 minutes); being careful not to burn garlic.

Parboil chicken or microwave it for a few minutes ahead of time to cut down on cooking time of paella.

Dust chicken in light flour and brown in saucepan, adjusting heat to avoid burning (7 to 10 minutes).

On low heat, add saffron, wine, 2 cups chicken broth and rice.

Stir occasionally to prevent sticking. Add salt and pepper. Cook approximately 15 minutes.

Add broth as needed. Finally, add mussels, clams, shrimp and remainder of chicken broth and peas. Cook 5 to 7 minutes longer. Add parsley. Stir.

(Rice should be tender, chicken cooked completely, mussels and clams opened and shrimp pink and tender. One may head shrimp, but the flavor is far more intense when heads are left on while cooking.)

Serves 8 to 12. Provide extra dish for guests to discard shells and shrimp heads.

Trip to Africa Adds to His 'More Eclectic Flair'

April 14, 2004

Ricardo Morgan

People do different things with their spare time. Ricardo Morgan's passion is cooking.

"If I'm not reading a book or listening to some jazz, I'm cooking," Morgan said. "It's a hobby, and it's really relaxing."

And what he cooks ranges from simple items such as an original pasta dish to mushrooms stuffed with such items as shrimp, scallops and Italian sausage. And while his mother, Louise, is the queen of greens and his sister Marcia makes a mean beef stroganoff, Morgan said he specializes in a variety of foods.

"I have a more eclectic flair," he said.

It's a flair he acquired from his grandmother and great-grandmother.

Morgan remembers when he was younger how his grandparents would cook huge meals virtually every day of the week.

"I always remember something smelling good, something sweet, and something tasty at my grandmother's house," he said. "She always cooked my grandfather full breakfasts. She would cook Sunday dinner on Saturday. The greens were chopped like confetti, and everything was just so good."

As a child, Morgan liked things most adolescents would probably turn down. To this day, he cooks with many of those same items and often turns to television cooking shows for ideas to incorporate them into his dishes.

"I liked things like olives, anchovies and bell peppers. I like cooking with those things. I'm addicted to the cooking channel."

One thing Morgan likes to do is keep folks who frequently eat his food off guard. He may use the same recipe but add a different ingredient to give it a different taste.

"I do something different each time, and that frustrates people," he said. "I might add something the next time to make it better.

"I'm always saying to someone, 'Here, try this.' I'm adventurous. I'm willing to try new flavors, new things, new tastes."

Part of Morgan's quest to try new and different things occurred when he was a teaching fellow in Gabon, a country on the west coast of Africa. Resources in the African country were limited, so Morgan had to come up with a little ingenuity when it came time to eat.

"We made use of the things we had," he said. "It was a French-inspired country, so I tried to take everything I knew about cooking and incorporate it into the items that were available.

"When you are in another country, you should try to immerse yourself and try things indicative of that culture. I try to experience things to the far right or left."

Morgan came up with a pasta dish while in Gabon that he frequently makes today. Eggplant is common, and Morgan made a tomato-based sauce utilizing the vegetable. He sauteed the eggplant in butter along with some garlic and onion.

"The eggplant was my meat source," he said. "It was quick and easy."

–Jeffery Womble

Lime Pork Chops

- 1 package lean pork chops, wash and pat dry
- Garlic powder
- Lowry's Seasoned Salt
- Black pepper
- Lemon pepper
- 2 medium-size fresh limes or bottled lime juice
- ½ cup Italian salad dressing
- Butter

Soak the chops for at least 1 hour or overnight in about ⅓ cup fresh lime juice and ½ cup Italian salad dressing. Dust with the dry ingredients and put a small pat of butter on each chop to give them color when cooking.

Put 2 cups water, ½ cup lime juice (may use bottled) and a generous amount of the listed seasonings in the broiler pan.

Place the pork chops on the rack in the broiler pan.

Broil for 15 to 20 minutes until done.

Suggestions: Serve with mashed potatoes and your favorite sides. Reduce the pan drippings for gravy. Excellent with Texas toast.

Leftovers make great sandwiches. Try roasting a few Granny Smith apples and a few pears with a little brown sugar and butter as a side dish.

Eggplant Pasta

- 2 large eggplants
- 1 (28-ounce) can tomato puree
- 1 pound linguini
- 2 tablespoons olive oil
- 1 pinch dried, crushed red-pepper flakes
- 1 onion, chopped
- 1 green pepper, chopped
- 2 garlic cloves, minced
- ½ stick lightly salted butter
- 1 tablespoon sugar (optional)

Peel and dice eggplant into bite-sized pieces.

In a large skillet, saute the onion and pepper in olive oil until translucent.

Set aside. In the same skillet, add a little more olive oil and the butter. Over medium heat, cook the diced eggplant until almost done.

Combine the onion, pepper, garlic and red-pepper flakes and saute until fragrant, folding in the eggplant as the last step.

Simmer until the flavors blend and the eggplant fully cooks. At this point, you may want to add a tablespoon of sugar to blend all the ingredients. Meanwhile, boil the pasta in a large pot of salted water until tender but still firm to the bite, stirring occasionally. Add the tomato puree and serve over linguini. Garlic bread and tossed salad complement the meal.

Note: Once I returned to the states, I've modified this dish by adding 1 pound cooked shrimp or scallops or both to the dish. If using both, add 1/2 pound each. Saute separately, and place the cooked seafood on top of the sauce.

Ric's Hearty Stuffed Mushrooms

1-pound shrimp peeled and deveined

1 pound sea scallops

4 links mild Italian sausage

2 pounds large mushrooms (reserve the stems)

1 8-ounce block Philly brand cream cheese (softened)

1 stick lightly salted butter

2 diced jalapeno peppers

½ tablespoon minced garlic

Lime juice

2 tablespoons olive oil

Cajun seasoning

Old Bay seasoning

Seasoned bread crumbs

In a medium skillet cook the shrimp and scallops in butter, lime juice, olive oil and garlic.

Dust with Old Bay and Cajun seasonings for flavor. In a separate skillet, brown and crumble the Italian sausage. After the seafood and sausage have been fully cooked, drain. Chop the meat mixture to a coarse consistency.

Wash and de-stem the mushrooms, saving 1 cup of stems. Brown the stems in the drippings from the sausage. Pat the mushroom caps dry and dust with Cajun seasoning and bread crumbs. Align them evenly on a baking sheet or shallow casserole dish. Mushrooms will reduce some in cooking.

STUFFING:

In a large bowl, mix cream cheese with ½ cup bread crumbs. Add the meat mixture and 1 or both of the jalapeno peppers (finely diced and seeded) for bite. Fold in the remaining stems as well. With a tablespoon, stuff the caps; top with more bread crumbs. Bake at 350 degrees 7 to 10 minutes or until golden and brown.

Suggestions: This may be used as an appetizer or an entree. For those who are allergic to shellfish, you may omit the seafood. Pork may be omitted and substituted with ground beef.

Marinated Shrimp

1 pound medium-size shrimp, cleaned and deveined

2 tablespoons Old Bay seasoning

1 sprig of fresh dill

1 garlic clove (minced)

24-ounce bottle Kraft Zest Italian salad dressing

1 medium-size onion, sliced into rings

1 large green pepper, sliced into rings

½ can Budweiser Beer (optional)

2 to 3 cups water

In a medium-size pot, bring to a boil the water and beer. Add shrimp. Make sure there is enough water to cover the shrimp.

Once the water begins to boil, add the Old Bay seasoning. Cook until shrimp are pink. Immediately after cooking, immerse the shrimp in an ice bath to stop the cooking.

Drain. Combine shrimp, fresh garlic, dill, pepper and onion and cover with the entire bottle of Italian dressing. Chill for at least one hour before serving.

Serving suggestion: Great with orzo, couscous, garlic bread and a fresh salad of choice.

Woman Considers Herself a 'Mad Scientist'

February 5, 2003

Alison Minard

Alison Minard has seen the best of both worlds in foods. She grew up in Batavia, N.Y., near Buffalo and loved her mother's old-fashioned recipes and her father's "Galloping Gourmet" type cooking.

In high school she took home economics and learned a different cooking style. When she and her husband, Gordon, who is from Philadelphia, moved south to restore a 150-year-old house in Harnett County, she learned to love Southern cooking. She says the cooking she grew up with uses a lot of nuts and fruits such as orange peels and dates. Here the food is apt to be fried.

In Batavia they had fried food only on Friday, usually fish, she said. She has learned that recipes that call for spinach can be made with collards or turnip greens.

She calls her own style of cooking "mad scientist" because she mixes recipes to create her own, each time a little different.

After she married and moved away from home she got a craving for Velveeta cheese and developed a party recipe called "I Can't Stop Eating It Cheese Fondue." It calls for jalapeno peppers, olives and pimientos, tomatoes and chilli peppers.

She still loves muffins for breakfast and uses her family's favorite recipe, Oat-Apple Breakfast Muffins. She remembers when her sister bought muffin recipe books and the whole family tried different kinds of muffins until they came up with a recipe made with quick or old-fashioned uncooked oats, spices, honey and apple slices.

Another of her family favorites is Tuna Florentine made with frozen spinach, onions and a can of tuna, adding hard boiled eggs, mushroom soup, sour cream, butter and bread crumbs.

This year she and her husband grew a garden full of different kinds of tomatoes, peppers, cucumbers and eggplants. The garden was so abundant that she gave away what the couple didn't make into eggplant parmigiana, salsa and sauces.

They grew oregano, rosemary, anise, garlic and thyme to add a little spice to their fresh salads.

– Melissa Clement

Oat-Apple Breakfast Muffins

- 1 cup quick or old-fashioned oats, uncooked
- 1 cup flour
- 1 teaspoon baking soda
- 1 teaspoon cinnamon
- ½ teaspoon allspice
- 1 cup honey
- ¼ cup milk
- ¼ cup vegetable oil
- 1 egg
- 2 medium cooking apples, cored, peeled and sliced

Preheat oven to 400 degrees. Mix dry ingredients in large bowl.

Mix the remaining ingredients in a smaller bowl and then add to the dry ingredients until they are a little moist. It's okay for the batter to be lumpy.

Spoon into muffin cups. Bake 25 minutes or until firm.

I Can't Stop Eating It Cheese Fondue

- 1 pound Velveeta cheese
- ½ pound cheddar or Colby cheese
- Pimientos to taste
- 1 12-ounce can of tomatoes with chilies
- 2 jalapeno peppers or 1 or 2 small 7-ounce cans of jalapenos according to taste
- Olives with pimientos to taste

Cut cheese into cubes, dice olives and pimientos, remove seeds from peppers and shred or dice.

Cook in double boiler or crock pot until cheese is melted and blended.

Serve with favorite crackers, vegetables or chips for dipping.

Date Squares

- 1 cup chopped nuts (your favorite)
- 1 cup plus 2 tablespoons unsifted flour
- 1 tablespoon baking powder
- ½ teaspoon salt
- 1 cup sugar
- 2 well-beaten eggs
- ¼ cup melted butter
- 1 tablespoon hot water
- 2 teaspoons grated orange rind
- 2 cups finely chopped dates

Mix flour, baking powder and salt. Gradually beat sugar into eggs. Add butter, water and rind.

Stir in dates and nuts. Gradually add flour mixture, beating well. Spread batter into 13-by-9-inch cooking pan.

Bake at 325 degrees for 25 to 30 minutes and cool.

Tuna Florentine

- 2 packages (10-ounce size) frozen, chopped spinach, thawed
- 2 tablespoons minced onion
- 1 can (12-ounces) tuna, drained
- 6 hard-boiled eggs, sliced
- 2 cans (10-ounces) cream of mushroom soup
- 1 cup sour cream
- ¼ cup melted butter
- 2 cups soft bread crumbs, about 4 slices of bread
- Salt and pepper to taste

Remove excess liquid from spinach and spread into 2-quart casserole dish. Sprinkle with onion and tuna over the spinach. Layer sliced eggs over top.

Mix mushroom soup and sour cream together and pour mixture over the eggs. Mix melted butter and bread crumbs and sprinkle over all.

Bake in preheated oven at 350 degrees for 30 to 35 minutes or until bubbly and golden brown.

Daughter's France Trip Helps Cook Go 'Bon Apetit'

April 25, 2001

Nina Godwin

Unlike many other good cooks, Nina Godwin says she didn't learn to cook while growing up in her native state of Massachusetts.

"My mother didn't like to cook," she says.

Godwin and her husband, Dr. Harold Godwin, moved to Fayetteville in 1951.

When she was rearing her own four children, Nina Godwin says, she did not experiment with new dishes.

"I was cooking ordinary food," she says. "With four children it was just a question of getting something on the table."

When daughter Lisa was in college and went to France, she came home raving about the food.

"About the same time I got hooked on *Bon Apetit*," Godwin says.

She began experimenting with recipes she found in the magazine. "I like *Bon Apetit* better than *Gourmet* because it cuts corners and you can make substitutions," she says. "And I like *Cooking Light* magazine too."

She subscribed at one time to Craig Claiborne's 60-minute Gourmet series and still refers to that recipe box for dishes. Godwin loves to cook and likes to entertain family and friends.

"I do a right much entertaining in the summertime at the beach where it can be informal," she says.

She has a vegetable and herb garden at the family's home on Figure Eight Island and one in Fayetteville, and likes to use herbs in cooking.

Godwin has some favorite standby recipes, like Nancy Reagan's Crabmeat Casserole recipe that was printed in a Wilmington Junior League cookbook years ago.

Mandarin Salad

SAUCE:

1 green onion, minced

3 garlic cloves, minced

2 tablespoons soy sauce

¼ cup white vinegar

Dash of Accent

¼ to ½ cup sugar

1½ tablespoons sesame oil

SALAD:

1 to 2 cucumbers, peeled and cut into julienne strips

1 stalk celery, slivered

1 carrot, slivered

½ teaspoon salt

Water

½ package bean threads

1 medium green pepper, slivered

2 or 3 fried eggs, slivered

2 chicken breasts, cooked and slivered

Mix together sauce ingredients; set aside.

Combine cucumbers, celery and carrots; sprinkle with salt. Let stand 30 minutes. Drain liquid.

In small saucepan, bring water to a boil. Boil bean threads for 10 seconds; separate while boiling. Drain and cut into 2-inch lengths.

Layer all ingredients. Pour sauce over the mixture and mix well.

Serves four.

Note: Bean threads can be found in the Oriental food section of some grocery stores or Oriental markets.

Another favorite is Mandarin Salad, which she clipped from the *Fayetteville Observer* in 1981.

"It's a winner," she says.

She looks for new recipes all the time.

Most recently, she has been trying out soups, including a cream of cauliflower soup recipe printed in *Southern Living* magazine.

"Our guests asked what was in it because the flavor was so subtle.

"I probably cook a new thing every week," she says. "My husband is good to try new things. He says, 'I don't say I didn't like it until several days later.' "

– Alice Thrasher

Cream of Cauliflower Soup

- 1 large onion
- 2 shallots
- 1 garlic clove
- 1 tablespoon olive oil
- 2 (14½-ounce) cans chicken broth
- 1 large cauliflower, cut into flowerets
- 1½ cups whipping cream
- 1 teaspoon salt
- ⅛ teaspoon ground white pepper
- Garnishes: asparagus tips, cracked black pepper

Slice first 3 ingredients; sauté in oil in a Dutch oven until tender.

Stir in broth; bring to a boil. Add cauliflower; cook, stirring occasionally, 15 minutes or until tender.

Process soup in batches in a blender until smooth; return to pan.

Stir in cream, salt and white pepper. Cook over low heat, stirring often, until thoroughly heated.

Ladle into bowls and garnish, if desired.

Yields 2 quarts.

Crabmeat Casserole

- 1 (20-ounce) can artichoke hearts
- 1 pound crabmeat
- ½ pound fresh mushrooms, sautéed
- 4 tablespoons butter
- 2¼ tablespoons flour
- 1 cup cream
- ½ teaspoon salt
- 1 teaspoon Worcestershire sauce
- ¼ cup medium-dry sherry
- Paprika, to taste
- Cayenne, to taste
- Pepper, to taste
- ¼ cup Parmesan cheese, grated

Preheat oven to 375 degrees.

Place artichokes in bottom of 2½-quart baking dish; spread a layer of crabmeat.

Add a layer of sautéed mushrooms.

Melt butter in a saucepan; add flour, cream, salt, Worcestershire sauce, sherry, paprika, cayenne and pepper.

Stir well after each addition to form a smooth sauce.

Pour sauce over artichoke-crab layer and sprinkle with cheese on top. Bake 20 minutes.

Serves 8.

Veteran Loves 'Feeding the Multitude'

April 11, 2001

Clifton Montgomery Yarn

When Clifton Montgomery Yarn was in high school he used to play hooky from school and to have something to do he would bake pies and cakes.

"I just acquired a desire to make pastry," he says. "Cooking is a science. You have to have the right amount of ingredient at the right time. But it's an art too. You have to be creative."

As a young man he joined the Army as an infantryman. When he found that cooks had one day on and two days off he took the job.

"It was awfully hard work. I cooked the supper meal, then breakfast and lunch, but I enjoyed the two days off."

Then he was asked if he could bake and that's when he began to shine and have the kind of flexible hours he needed to pursue his many interests. He worked as a baker until 1955 when he was sent to Korea and took over an officers' mess.

"I devoted a lot of time to making pastries and making up my own recipes."

When he returned from Korea he became a baker for the 82nd Airborne Division. He served the commanding general's open mess and then worked for a general in his home for a year and a half.

He served in Vietnam cooking for the commanding general's open mess. After that he became a mess steward, food service supervisor, dining service supervisor and dining service manager.

The officers he has cooked for include Brig. Gen. James M. Shephard.

"His favorite was soup and peanut butter sandwiches with honey. When I worked for Gen. Melvin Zais in Vietnam he was not particular. He ate anything that was on the menu. He had a war to run.

"I went to all the food service schools the Army had and I cooked so much, that's why I've got the belly I have today," he says with a grin.

At one time he catered wedding receptions and school functions and worked as the area manager for three of Mrs. Winter's Chicken and Biscuits.

The quality of food is important to him and his family. He grinds his own grain for bread to create just the right consistency for the hearty bread they prefer.

He picks his own wild plums, blueberries and strawberries and makes 35 to 40 pints of jam each summer.

When his family gets together, he cooks a pig outdoors on two grills.

He has six children and 24 grandchildren.

"It's a lot of fun," he says, "feeding the multitude."

– Melissa Clement

Potatoes

- 6 medium-sized baking potatoes, peeled, cubed and parboiled (tender but still firm)
- 2 medium-sized onions, chopped
- ¾ cup butter
- 2 cloves chopped garlic
- ½ cup bacon bits

Sauté onions and garlic in butter until opaque and tender.

Stir in bacon bits. Coat well-drained potatoes with butter mixture.

Place in baking dish. Heat in 325 oven until browned.

Nitwit's Nightmare

1 quart each vanilla, strawberry and butter pecan ice cream

1 can crushed pineapple

1 can peach slices

16 oz. frozen strawberries

1 cup pecan chips

Let butter pecan ice cream thaw enough to spread over the bottom of a 9 x 9 baking pan or dish and refreeze.

Drain crushed pineapple and spread over butter pecan ice cream and freeze.

Spread softened strawberry ice cream over frozen pineapple and freeze.

Drain and crush peach slices and spread over frozen strawberry ice cream and freeze.

Spread softened vanilla ice cream over peaches and freeze.

Spread thawed strawberries over vanilla ice cream and top with pecan pieces and freeze.

Cut into 3-inch squares.

Makes 9 servings.

Baked Chicken Breast with Pecans

6 boneless chicken breast

1 egg

½ cup milk

¾ cup plain flour

½ cup pecans

2 tablespoons butter (melted)

¼ cup sugar

salt and pepper to taste

Marinate chicken overnight in buttermilk.

Preheat oven to 325 degrees. Whip egg and milk together.

Combine butter and sugar. Coat pecan chips with butter, sugar mixture and place on plate.

Heat in microwave 3 to 4 minutes. Drain away excess butter and mix pecans with the flour.

Coat chicken breast with egg, milk mixture and then dredge in flour, pecan mixture.

Place in baking dish and bake for 35 - 40 minutes.

Asparagus, Bacon and Cheese

2 cans asparagus spears (well drained)

6 pre-cooked bacon slices (not crisp)

6 strips of cheese as long as the asparagus spears

salt and pepper to taste

Chill asparagus spears about 2 hours (makes them easier to work with).

Place strip of cheese in the middle of 4 or 5 asparagus spears and wrap a slice of pre-cooked bacon around the asparagus.

Place on butter flavored sprayed baking dish.

Cover dish with foil and bake at 325 for about 10 minutes or until bacon is done and cheese is melted. Season to taste with salt and pepper.

Diabetic Helps to Promote Good Eating Habits

May 23, 2001

Betty Parker

Betty Parker is a diabetic. She found that out two years ago. It not only inspired her to do research and change her own diet, but she volunteered to help others change their style of eating and living.

She got involved with a research program through the University of North Carolina at Chapel Hill and the National Institute of Cancer. The program was designed to improve the health of black Americans through healthy eating in a one-year program.

It is called the "Praise" (Partnership to Reach African-Americans to Increase Smart Eating) Project. Ten churches in this area were involved, including St. Luke AME Church where Parker is a member. She volunteered to be the church liaison for the Praise Team and did research and wrote monthly columns in a news publication called "Voices of Praise." Her column was called "Food Taster's Corner, In the Kitchen with Betty." It gave tips and recipes.

A retired registered psychiatric nurse and writer, Parker coordinated the programs that met to discuss healthy eating and taste food prepared in a healthy manner.

In one column she wrote about introducing members to "foods which are delicious but low in fat content and low in sugar. We tried to show how foods contribute to different diseases and heart problems and how an increase in fruits, vegetables and grains are essential to good health and lower cholesterol."

Parker talked about eating regular meals, and a different way of cooking, especially for children who do not

Peanut Butter and Jelly Muffins

- Vegetable cooking spray
- 1 cup all-purpose flour
- 1 teaspoon baking powder
- ½ teaspoon baking soda
- ¼ teaspoon salt
- ⅓ cup firmly packed brown sugar
- ½ cup drained vanilla low-fat yogurt
- 3 tablespoons reduced-fat creamy peanut butter
- 2 tablespoons vegetable oil
- 2 egg whites
- 3 tablespoons strawberry or grape jelly

Preheat oven to 400 degrees. Lightly spray 24 mini muffin tins with cooking spray. Set aside.

Combine flour, baking powder, baking soda and salt in a medium mixing bowl.

Combine sugar, yogurt, peanut butter, vegetable oil and egg whites in a bowl.

Beat at low speed with an electric mixer until blended. Add to dry ingredients, stirring just until moistened.

Spoon batter into muffin cups, filling half full. Top each with ¼ teaspoon jelly and top with remaining batter.

Bake for 12 minutes or until muffins test done.

Remove from pans immediately and cool on a wire rack.

Makes 24 muffins.

like to eat vegetables. "Instead of collard greens cooked with ham hocks I suggested using smoked turkey."

During holidays she planned healthy menus and cooked dinners and handed out recipes. She took old recipes and adapted them toward better health by using healthier ingredients. She also introduced new recipes.

At Christmas she wrote about using all low-fat deserts and dessert with no sugar.

"We had plenty of different activities to get them interested in coming to the meetings for food testing. I wrote a funny dieting monologue and passed out recipes."

The 25 church members who participated weighed in at the end of the year and had their blood pressure and cholesterol tested.

Most saw a noticeable improvement, she said.

"It was a lot of work and research but was worth it."

– Melissa Clement

Pistachio Chocolate Chip Cream Pie

See photo in center of book

- 1 (4-serving) package Jell-O sugar-free instant pistachio pudding mix
- ⅓ cup Carnation Nonfat Dry Milk Powder
- ¾ cup Yoplait plain fat-free yogurt
- ¾ cup water
- 3 tablespoons (¾ ounce) mini milk chocolate chips
- 1 cup Cool Whip Free
- 1 6-ounce Keebler chocolate pie crust
- 2 teaspoons Hershey's Lite Chocolate Syrup

In a medium bowl, combine dry pudding mix and dry milk powder. Add yogurt and water.

Mix well using a wire whisk. Blend in chocolate chips and ¼ cup Cool Whip Free.

Evenly spread mixture into pie crust. Refrigerate for at least 15 minutes.

Just before serving, spread remaining ¾ cup Cool Whip Free over set filling and drizzle chocolate syrup over top.

Cut into 8 servings.

Cookies and Cream Pie

- 1 (6.5 ounce) package sugar-free chocolate sandwich cookies (Murray)
- 1 cup fat-free milk
- 1 (1.5 ounce) package vanilla sugar-free, fat-free instant pudding mix
- 4 cups fat-free frozen whipped topping, thawed and divided
- 1 (6 ounce) graham cracker crust

Crush cookies in plastic bag with rolling pin.

Reserve ¼ cup for topping. Combine milk and pudding mix in a bowl; stir with a wire whisk until blended.

Fold in 3 cups whipped topping and crushed cookies. Spoon mixture into cracker crust.

Cover and freeze 4 to 6 hours until firm. Top with the reserved whipped topping.

Sprinkle evenly with reserved ¼ cup crushed cookies.

Cooking Is all About the Flavor

August 3, 2005

Richard Kugelmann

Richard Kugelmann loves to cook. He says his motivation for cooking is the "wow" factor.

"That's when you set a plate in front of someone, and they go, 'Wow.' Ninety percent of that is making it look beautiful. Then they taste it, and wow."

He didn't start out to be a chef, but that's what he is today, along with being a businessman.

At Methodist College, he earned a degree in business administration. For a few years, he worked in banking in Florida, but he still wasn't sure what he wanted to do in life.

Then on a visit home to Fayetteville, he was in the kitchen with his mother, Helene Kugelmann, when it came to him.

"Being the son of a German mother who is known as a good cook, I just loved being in the kitchen with her, watching what she was doing."

That's when he realized that his real passion was cooking. Soon after, he enrolled at Central Piedmont College in Charlotte. In 1993, he got an associate's degree in culinary arts, and he has been cooking ever since.

A few years ago, Richard and a partner started their own restaurant, called South City Grill, on Raeford Road. The food was good, but the restaurant went out of business, perhaps because of its location, he says.

But one thing did stick: his nickname, "Da Cook." When anyone in the restaurant asked a question, the answer was always, "Ask Da Cook." He even signs his e-mail Da Cook.

Today he teaches culinary arts at Fayetteville Technical Community College and is a loan officer with Carolina Mortgage Company.

Richard likes to throw big, elaborate theme parties at times such as Halloween. At Thanksgiving, he is known for his Turducken, which is a turkey, a duck and a chicken bundled up together with the turkey on the outside.

Kugelmann says experimentation is how he has learned to make some of his original dishes and the many sauces he creates.

He says his wife, Rachel, loves virtually everything he cooks, but her favorites are his lemon basil chicken, and pignolia-encrusted shrimp with sun-dried tomato pesto aioli.

His children, Jamisson, 12, and Brooklyn, 7, are typical kids.

"They like pizza, hot dogs and chicken fingers, but my son, at 12, is actually starting to eat some of my cooking."

When Richard cooks for people who are on diets, he simply tells them, "This is your splurge meal."

– Melissa Clement

Tiramisu Fondue

See photo in center of book

- 2 teaspoons instant espresso powder
- 2 tablespoons boiling water
- 17 ounces mascarpone cheese
- ½ cup powdered sugar (10X)
- 2 tablespoons amaretto liqueur
- 2 teaspoons cornstarch
- 3 egg yolks
- 2 tablespoons bittersweet-chocolate shavings
- 12 ladyfingers
- 12 strawberries

In a small bowl, dissolve the espresso powder in the boiling water.

In a double boiler, combine the espresso coffee, mascarpone cheese, sugar, amaretto and cornstarch.

Stir occasionally until the mixture is melted and thoroughly combined.

In a medium bowl, lightly beat the egg yolks. Add a small amount of the cheese mixture, stirring constantly to prevent cooking the egg yolks. Add a small amount more, and then add the egg mixture to the mascarpone batter and bring to 180 degrees. Do not overheat, or the eggs will curdle.

Place in a small butter warmer or fondue pot and top with chocolate shavings.

Serve with ladyfingers and fresh strawberries. Makes 2 cups.

White Pizza

See photo in center of book

- 9-inch pizza crust
- ½ cup Alfredo sauce (recipe follows)
- 4 Roma tomatoes, sliced
- ¼ cup baby spinach, fresh
- 2 tablespoons red onions, diced
- ¼ cup mushrooms, sliced
- 2 tablespoons bacon bits
- 6 chicken strips, grilled
- ½ cup mozzarella cheese, shredded
- ½ cup cheddar cheese, shredded

You can use a store-bought pizza crust and Alfredo sauce or make your own.

Place pizza crust on a sheet pan. Evenly coat with the Alfredo sauce and layer the remaining ingredients evenly on top of the sauce, ending with the cheeses.

Bake in a 425-degree oven for 8 to 12 minutes or until the cheese is evenly melted.

Cut into 4, 6 or 8 pieces and serve.

Alfredo Sauce

- 4 tablespoons butter
- ¼ cup garlic, minced
- 2 cups onions, diced
- ½ cup flour
- 2 tablespoons chicken base (solid, not stock)
- 4 cups milk
- 2 cups heavy cream
- 8 ounces Parmesan cheese, grated
- ¼ cup fresh parsley, minced
- 2 teaspoons white pepper
- Salt to taste

In a large pot, heat butter over medium heat. Add garlic and onions and cook until clear. Add the flour and solid chicken base and cook for 2 to 3 minutes, stirring constantly to avoid burning flour.

Slowly add the milk and cream and bring to a simmer.

Reduce heat to low. Slowly add the cheese and stir until it is all melted.

Add parsley, white pepper and salt. Makes 7 cups.

Pantry Purged for Healthier Lifestyle

May 16, 2001

Wanda Strother

When Wanda Strother decided it was time to change her family's eating habits several years ago, she didn't mess around.

She purged her pantry of all the white stuff — white bread, refined white flour, white rice, white sugar. Next she looked for food with dyes and preservatives. Then out went processed foods in packages.

"When my children were little I was into cooking healthy and was in La Leche League and everything," Strother says.

"Then as they got older and started playing ball at Hope Mills, we were living in the van and grabbing fast food between games and practices."

Michael is 24 and lives away from home. Adam graduated from East Carolina University and is living at home and son John is 15 and a student at South View High School.

Strother says her sons and her husband, Mike, have slowly adapted to a healthier way of eating and cut back on fast foods.

"We went from white to whole wheat bread and they fussed at first," she says.

"But my husband is a wonderful sport and will try new things. I used to send him to the store for milk, and he would come home with a two-liter Pepsi and a big bag of Dorito chips. He doesn't do that anymore."

For snacks she likes to prepare a dish of raw vegetables with a healthy dip.

Carrot or Zucchini Cake

- 2 cups whole wheat flour
- 2 teaspoons baking powder
- 1½ teaspoons baking soda
- 1 teaspoon salt
- 2 teaspoons cinnamon
- ¾ cup oil
- ¾ cup honey
- 4 eggs
- 2 cups grated carrots or zucchini
- 1 cup unsweetened, crushed pineapple, drained
- ½ cup chopped nuts

CREAM CHEESE FROSTING:

- 8 ounces softened cream cheese
- 1 teaspoon vanilla
- 8 tablespoons butter, softened
- 2 to 4 tablespoons honey
- ½ cup chopped nuts (optional)

Preheat oven to 350 degrees. Mix dry ingredients in a large bowl. Add oil, honey, and eggs; mix well.

Stir in remaining ingredients.

Turn into three greased and floured 9-inch layer pans, or a 9-by-13-inch pan. (Dust pans with wheat germ for extra nut flavor).

Bake at 350 degrees for 35 to 40 minutes. Cool a few minutes in pan; turn out and thoroughly cool on racks.

Fill layers and frost with Cream Cheese Frosting.

Beat cream cheese and butter until fluffy.

Beat in honey to taste. Add vanilla and nuts.

Keep refrigerated.

"We do eat chicken and fish, but I don't cook red meat any more," she says. "If they want it, they get it when we eat out. Once in a while I might cook a pork roast."

Mrs. Strother likes to cook brown rice, dry beans and soy beans. She grows herbs and likes to use the fresh ones in salads and other dishes.

"I don't put a lot of spices in my food and I cook simple things," she says.

For desserts, Strother says she might make muffins with honey in the winter. "And we are big fruit eaters," she says. "We each eat four or five fruits a day."

Strother says her healthier diet and more exercise have kept her blood sugar level in a normal range. She lost her father and her brother to diabetes and knows it is important for her to watch her diet.

She is a distributor for a vitamin and food-supplement company and likes to teach others about healthy eating. She shares recipes and health tips with friends every other week when they get together for a health-foods luncheon.

"It is kind of like a ministry to help others," she says.

– Alice Thrasher

Lentil Rice Casserole

- ¾ cup uncooked lentils, green or red
- ½ cup uncooked long-grain brown rice
- ¼ cup instant minced onion or 1 small chopped onion
- 3 cups water with 1 tablespoon chicken broth
- ½ teaspoon basil leaves
- ¼ teaspoon oregano leaves
- ¼ teaspoon thyme leaves
- ¼ teaspoon garlic powder
- ½ cup grated tofu or cheddar cheese (optional)
- Fresh minced parsley (a handful) to garnish

Blend together all ingredients except tofu or cheese and parsley in a casserole dish.

Cover and bake for 2 to 2½ hours at 300 degrees.

During the last 20 minutes may top with the grated tofu or cheddar cheese.

Just before serving, stir to blend in the melted tofu or cheese.

If desired, garnish with the fresh minced parsley.

Yield 4 to 6 servings.

Pinto Bean Salad

See photo in center of book

DRESSING:

Mix and set aside

- 3 tablespoons olive oil
- 1½ tablespoons Balsamic vinegar
- 2 cloves garlic, finely chopped
- ⅛ teaspoon chili powder
- ½ teaspoon oregano

SALAD:

- 2 cans (15 ½-ounce size) pinto beans, rinsed and drained
- 1 green bell pepper, seeded and chopped
- ½ red onion, chopped
- 20 black olives sliced and drained

Mix well and place on a bed of dark green lettuce.

Note: Sprinkle feta cheese on top, if desired.

Also good when stuffed in a whole wheat pita bread.

The Zemas Make Cooking a Whole Family Affair

June 25, 2003

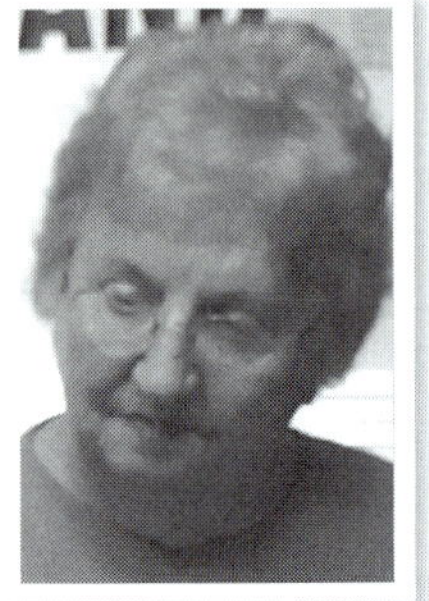

Irma Zema

Okay, time for a quick geography lesson: the name comes from Poland via Czechoslovakia. The cooking style comes from western North Carolina via Ohio.

And the family comes from all over courtesy of the U.S. Army.

Add it all together, and you have the cooking talents of Irma Zema. An Ohio native, she grew up cooking food near and dear to the hearts of Southerners, then had to learn European cooking when she married.

"My husband's family was from Europe, and they knew how to cook. In fact, Joe makes pierogi every Christmas.

"I love them, but honestly, I'll never make them. It's too time-consuming, and just too hard to do all that work by hand. It takes him two days."

Instead, she likes to produce home-style Southern cooking, the legacy of her mom's family in western North Carolina. The family moved to Fayetteville when Joe was in the 82nd Airborne Division, then stayed after his retirement.

"The kids grew up here, even though their dad got deployed quite a bit," Zema said. "This was home to them."

One of those children, daughter Linda Zema, helped raise the others while their mom worked. She watched her mom in the kitchen, eventually surprising her with a full dinner one evening.

"I just watched her and sort of picked it up that way," Linda said.

"She's learned a lot," Irma added.

Both Zemas say they like to cook a variety of foods.

"I like to try cooking foreign food, new recipes and the good old favorites," Irma said. "And the good thing is my husband will eat just about anything.

"We like eating at home, too. Maybe once a week he'll take me out to take a break. But I enjoy cooking. It's not a chore to me. It's fun."

Among her favorite dishes are a great Scottish chocolate cake ("It's an old family recipe") and cooking with eggplant.

"The first time I cooked fried eggplant, I worried that my kids wouldn't even eat them," she said. "They gobbled them up."

Linda adds her specialty — country-fried steak.

"I had to learn to cook okra, too, but I still don't like to eat it," she said. "Unless it's fried. Just don't like that slimy sensation."

Is there anything else they won't eat?

"My dad's oatmeal," Linda said between laughs. "I don't know how they taught him to make it in the Army, but it's just awful!"

– Chick Jacobs

Fried Eggplant

- 1 egg
- ¼ cup milk
- ½ cup flour
- ½ cup cornmeal
- Cooking oil (Zema prefers Crisco)
- 1 eggplant
- Salt and pepper to taste

You will need a large frying skillet, a medium mixing bowl, a plastic bag, and a slotted spoon or spatula for cooking and removing the eggplant from the skillet.

Pour approximately 2 inches of oil into the skillet. This will cover the eggplant cubes, once cooking begins. Heat the skillet while putting your ingredients together. Cook on high to keep the eggplant from getting soggy, but turn the heat down if burning begins.

In the mixing bowl, beat egg with milk. Peel the eggplant and slice into 1-inch slices, then cut slices into cubes. Place the cubes in the mixing bowl, dipping in the egg-milk mixture.

In the plastic bag, add the cornmeal, flour, salt and pepper to taste. Shake the bag to mix. Take a few cubes out of the bowl at a time, shaking off excess milk, and drop them in the bag. As soon as the skillet is very hot, remove the cubes from the bag, shaking off excess flour mixture, and drop into the skillet. Cook to golden brown, stirring to make sure they are thoroughly cooked.

With a slotted spoon or spatula, remove the cubes and place on a paper towel, allowing excess oil to drain. Within 30 seconds, move from towel to a serving dish.

Grandma Anna's Czechoslovakian Cookies

- 6 egg yolks
- ½ teaspoon salt
- ¾ cup sugar
- 3 tablespoons sweet cream
- 2 cups all-purpose flour
- ¾ cup shortening
- ½ teaspoon lemon extract

You'll need: cookie sheet, mixer, spoon, egg separator, rolling pin, cookie cutter, baking brush and sieve.

Preheat oven to 375 degrees. Separate eggs and drop yolks into hot salted water. Cook yolks until hard cooked and press through sieve. Sift flour and salt.

Cream the shortening and sugar until light and fluffy. Add egg yolks and lemon extract, then blend in cream and dry ingredients.

Roll out dough ⅛-inch thick and cut into desired shapes. Place on greased baking sheet and brush tops with beaten egg whites. Sprinkle with colored sugar or ground nuts, if desired. Bake for 6 to 8 minutes.

Polish Sausage and Cabbage

- 1 package kielbasa sausage, sliced
- 1 small head of cabbage, sliced
- 1 small potato, peeled and diced
- 1 stalk of celery, sliced
- 1 carrot, sliced
- 1 large onion, sliced
- 14-ounce can of chicken broth
- ½ teaspoon caraway seed
- Salt and pepper to taste

Place the sliced cabbage in a crock pot. Toss in the vegetables with salt, pepper and caraway seed. Add onions and sausage. Cover the crock pot and cook on low for 6 to 8 hours. If you're in a hurry, cook on high for 2 to 4 hours.

Italian Background Inspires Dishes

April 20, 2005

Jennifer Carter

For Jennifer Carter, cooking is a connection to Chicago, where she grew up, and her Italian background.

"Every now and then I get homesick," she said. After moving to the South, she missed the foods she grew up with, so she decided to learn how to make them herself.

For example, she was used to cakes that were filled with fruit and iced with whipped cream. "We hardly ever used buttercream," she said. When she couldn't find the kind of birthday cakes she wanted, she started making them herself. Then she decided to branch out from baking and make other things from her childhood.

One favorite family recipe is Italian-style potatoes. The potatoes are cooked in a baking dish with Italian sausage and green peppers. "Everybody loves them," she said.

The recipe came from her grandmother, and different family members modified it over the years, adding the sausage and tweaking it in other ways.

Carter, who is married and has two children, is passing on her skills to the next generation. She lets her daughter, who is almost 5, and her 7-year-old son help her in the kitchen, and they do simple recipes together.

Although she likes to re-create the flavors she grew up with, she simplifies the recipes, sometimes using jarred spaghetti sauce, for example, but adding her own seasonings to make it taste homemade.

"Just because it comes from a jar or from a box doesn't mean it has to taste like it," she said.

When Carter gets together with friends, she makes a point of bringing a dish that they may not have tried before. She said people sometimes think her recipes sound strange but end up loving them.

On the other hand, when she moved to the South, she was confronted with foods she hadn't seen before.

Easy Chicken Marsala

About 6 boneless, skinless chicken breasts, or chicken tenderloins (enough to feed 4 or 5 people)

Olive oil

1 bottle white cooking wine or Marsala cooking wine

Fresh mushrooms, cleaned and sliced

3 green onions, cleaned and chopped

Salt and pepper to taste (Jennifer Carter uses about 2 good pinches)

Pasta noodles

With meat tenderizer, pound chicken to ¼- to ½-inch thickness.

Heat skillet with olive oil, just enough to lightly coat bottom of skillet.

Cook chicken until cooked through and lightly brown.

Remove chicken from pan. Put one teaspoon of olive oil in skillet and saute onions and mushrooms, adding the salt and pepper.

Add bottle of wine and cook until the alcohol is cooked out, usually about 5 to 6 minutes.

Serve chicken over pasta, and pour the wine sauce over top.

She recalls thinking, "What is barbecue?" In her experience, barbecue was a verb, not a noun. Although she was skeptical at first, now she tells her family members that they have to try barbecue when they come down for a visit.

Carter doesn't just stick to making foods she grew up with, though; she tries recipes from her many cookbooks and collects recipes she sees on television. She also likes to buy gadgets and appliances for the kitchen.

The kitchen is her favorite room in the house, she said. And as for cooking: "I love it."

– Cathryne Meeks

Italian-style Potatoes

1 stick of butter

Italian seasoning

2 cloves of chopped garlic (add more to taste)

Potatoes, washed and cut into small pieces (skin can be left on if desired)

2 green peppers, cut up

1½ pounds of Italian sausage, cooked and drained

Mozzarella cheese (optional)

Preheat oven to 350 degrees.

In a small saucepan, melt the butter and add to it the garlic and Italian seasoning.

Place potatoes, Italian sausage and green peppers in a baking dish.

Stir to ensure they are mixed well.

Pour butter mixture over potatoes and mix well.

Bake until the potatoes are tender, approximately 1 to 1½ hours.

Optional: Top with mozzarella cheese for the last 5 minutes of baking.

Fruit-filled Birthday Cake

1 box store-bought cake mix and all ingredients listed on back of box

Fresh fruit (bananas and strawberries work best)

Cool Whip or homemade whipped cream (1 cup of heavy cream and ¼ cup of sugar, whipped until peaks form)

Vanilla wafers, crushed

1 can of vanilla frosting (use food coloring to dye the vanilla frosting any color you want)

Lightly grease and flour a pair of 10-inch cake pans.

Prepare cake mix as directed on box. Equally divide cake mix into the pans and bake as directed. When done, place cakes on a rack until completely cooled.

Place whipped topping on top of one layer, then place sliced fruit on topping. Place the second cake layer on top, and frost with the remaining whipped cream.

Place crushed vanilla wafers all along the sides of cake. Use the colored vanilla frosting to decorate and write your message on top of the cake.

Husband Inspires Rediscovery of Cooking

March 15, 2006

Deborah Carr

There was a time when Deborah Carr didn't do so much cooking. That is, until she remarried and became Mrs. Bryan Carr.

"He encouraged me to rediscover the art of cooking," Carr said.

It was a good thing for Bryan and Deborah's two grown sons. Now cooking has become her passion. Carr is known as "The Bonbon Queen" to the people who work at Bleecker GMC on Raeford Road, where her husband is the sales manager. She makes bonbons for them, 100 at a time.

"I just love to watch the expressions on people's faces when they bite into one of the bonbons. I don't really care for them myself–too rich for me–but those people out there do.

"I just have a good time with it. I love cooking because it makes people happy. It's a nice little bridge that brings people together."

The couple belongs to a supper club that meets once a month.

"We just sit around the table eating and having a little wine, and just talk forever."

Carr says her husband calls her a "social butterfly," but he is her biggest fan.

"He's tall and skinny, but he loves to eat. I have to watch myself, or I'll spend my whole paycheck on cooking," says Carr, who is the supply technician for McNair Elementary School.

Her mother, Beulah Huntsinger, was well-known as a good cook, she says. "She was the kind of cook that at a homecoming people would say, 'Miss Beulah, what did you bring today?'"

Her father, Billy Huntsinger, was also a good cook and liked to make desserts.

"It was funny seeing them both in the kitchen

Heart-stopping Corn and Bacon Chowder

- 6 to 8 slices of bacon
- ¼ to ½ cups each of finely diced celery, onion, green pepper and carrots
- 2 tablespoons fresh parsley
- 1 (10-ounce) can cream corn
- 1 (10-ounce) can white shoepeg corn
- 2 or 3 diced potatoes
- ¼ teaspoon paprika
- Salt and pepper to taste
- 4 tablespoons flour
- ¼ to ½ stick butter or margarine
- 3 cups each cold water
- 3 cups half and half
- Cheese for topping
- Reserve cup cold water for flour

Fry bacon in pot and remove. Crumble for later. Saute vegetables and seasoning in bacon grease until tender. Pour in 2 cups water and half-and-half and butter. While milk mixture is coming to boil, mix flour in cup water until dissolved. Add slowly to milk mixture. As milk starts boiling, add corn and potatoes and simmer until all is tender. Before serving, stir in crumbled bacon and top with cheese.

cooking together," Carr says. "Every Sunday my mom and dad cooked Sunday dinner after church. At Christmas, we always had a really big spread. Mom and Dad had been cooking all day, and he always made us take a picture of the table before anybody touched anything. He would read the Bible, and then we would dig in.

"I want to give my boys those kinds of memories, and when they have children, I want them to remember those kinds of things, too."

– Melissa Clement

Beulah's Peanut Butter Bonbons

- 28 ounces smooth peanut butter
- 2 pounds confectioners' sugar
- 1 pound soft butter
- 2 to 3 teaspoons vanilla
- Chopped pecans (optional)
- ½ cup graham cracker crumbs (optional)
- Crisco

Note: I suggest buying the graham crackers already crushed. Making them without graham cracker crumbs will give a smoother texture.

Be sure to chill well. The butter in this recipe melts quickly in the warm, melted chocolate.

Cream butter and peanut butter until creamy. Kitchen Aid mixer comes in handy for this. Add vanilla, then confectioners' sugar a little at a time. Add pecans (optional). Incorporate well.

Using a melon scooper, scoop out peanut butter mixture and place on cookie sheet lined with wax paper. The melon scooper doesn't make perfectly shaped balls so you will have to roll them in your hands a bit. I suggest using gloves for this part.

Place in refrigerator while you are melting chocolate so they can get firm.

Melt chocolate in a double boiler. Add a bit of Crisco or paraffin wax if you want them shiny.

Take bonbons out of refrigerator. Place one in the chocolate and scoop it out with a fork.

Tap the side of the double boiler lightly so the excess chocolate will fall off. Place back on wax paper. When complete, refrigerate to harden.

Deborah Carr says she has not had luck freezing these if they are made with graham-cracker crumbs. They seem to crumble.

Makes about 100 bonbons.

Oreo Bonbons

1 bag of Oreos, finely crushed

1 package cream cheese

1 package chocolate almond bark

1 package white chocolate almond bark

Crisco

Note: It's best to use food processor to crush Oreos, one row at a time. You will find that this recipe will go much smoother if you have a heavy-duty mixer. If you don't have one, you will need to mix the cream cheese with a regular mixer and transfer to a mixing bowl and do the rest by hand. Also, a melon scooper is the ticket in making all the same size bonbons.

Beat cream cheese until creamy. Gradually add the crushed Oreos and mix until all has been blended, stopping a few times to scrape the sides and bottom of the bowl.

Using a melon scooper, scoop out Oreo mixture and place on a cookie sheet lined with wax paper. The melon scooper doesn't make perfectly shaped balls, so you will have to roll them in your hands. I suggest using gloves for this part. Refrigerate while melting chocolate so they can get firm.

Reserve 2 to 3 blocks of each chocolate for decoration. Melt chocolate separately in double boiler. Add a bit of Crisco or paraffin wax to make bonbons shiny.

Remove half of bonbons from refrigerator. Place one in the chocolate and scoop out with a fork. Tap the side of the bowl lightly so the excess chocolate will fall off. Place back on wax paper. When complete, refrigerate to harden.

To prepare decoration on the top, place reserved blocks of white chocolate in a zip-lock bag with a bit of Crisco. Microwave until melted. Be careful not to overheat. Snip a little off the corner of the bag and drizzle over chocolate-covered bonbons.

Repeat above directions using other half of bonbons, covering with white chocolate. Sometimes the white chocolate doesn't always cover the darkness of the Oreo, so you may want to let the ones you plan to dip in white chocolate sit in the refrigerator a little longer. Drizzle with dark chocolate.

Recipes Inspired by Family's Adventures

MARCH 30, 2005

Holly Bonnizzio

Holly Bonnizzio enjoys exploring different parts of the country and picking up culinary tips from each culture. She then adapts the recipes to suit herself and her family.

She and her husband, Daniel, went to high school together in Kent, Wash., south of Seattle. He has been in the Air Force for 16 years and the family has lived in seven places around the United States.

She says their children, Christine, who is 15, Danny, 13, and Brittany, 10, miss their friends when they move, but they see each move as an adventure. They get to see new sights, meet new people and adjust to new cultures.

They also enjoy being in the kitchen with their mom as she prepares some of the recipes she comes up with. Christine has already learned how to prepare meals whenever her mother is delayed.

Holly shares three recipes with different ethnic backgrounds. The first is Hawaiian chicken with an Oriental flair. It calls for chicken breasts, rice, chow mein noodles and a sweet-and-sour sauce.

The second is a chicken-and-cheese dip with a Southwestern heritage. While dining at a Mexican restaurant, the family enjoyed the chicken-and-cheese recipe. By reading the menu, they figured out the ingredients, which were three kinds of cheeses, onions and green peppers, plus chicken.

The third recipe she shares is gingerbread with a New England background. The recipe calls for the usual ingredients: flour, molasses and spices with a tablespoon of vinegar. Holly and a friend once tried

Holly's Hawaiian Chicken

Chicken breast for each person

Rice (any kind your family likes)

Chow mein noodles (optional)

<u>SWEET-AND-SOUR SAUCE:</u>

3 cups packed brown sugar

6 tablespoons cornstarch

2 (20-ounce) pineapple chunks. Drain and reserve juice.

2 cups chicken broth or reserved pineapple juice

2 cups red-wine vinegar

6 tablespoons soy sauce

6 teaspoons ginger

6 cloves garlic

6 tablespoons water

Add brown sugar, chicken broth (or pineapple juice), red-wine vinegar, soy sauce, ginger and garlic to a saucepan. Stir mixture until heated through.

Add cornstarch to water and mix well. Add mixture to saucepan, and stir until bubbly and thickened. Divide sauce into 2 equal portions.

Add pineapple chunks to one half of the sauce. The other half will be used to marinate the chicken.

Marinate chicken in sweet-and-sour sauce. Grill chicken breasts, and use the leftover sauce during grilling to baste chicken.

Make enough rice for each person.

Put a small amount of rice on each plate, then add chow mein noodles (optional) and a whole (or cut-up if desired) chicken breast on top.

Spoon some sauce from pan over plate.

different gingerbread recipes and sampled them. Each time, the one containing vinegar won out. She doesn't know why.

Holly is not the only Bonnizzio who cooks. When Daniel is not deployed, he often makes his own style of pizza on Saturday nights, when the family enjoys playing board games together.

In Kent, Holly grew up close to her grandparents, who gardened. She learned not only how to cook but how to preserve the fresh food by canning and freezing. Today, her children get into the act by helping Bonnizzio put up fresh foods. Holly says she enjoys seeing the rows of jars on the kitchen shelves.

Bonnizzio said her family never buys canned spaghetti sauces. After visiting the farmer's market in Raleigh, they bring home fresh tomatoes and make their own sauce, and can it along with corn and beans. They also search for fresh peaches, blackberries, strawberries and blueberries to turn into jam.

It's always a culinary adventure when the Bonnizzio family travels.

– Melissa Clement

Chicken and Cheese Dip

1 pound mozzarella
1 pound cheddar
1 pound Monterey jack
1 medium onion
1 medium green pepper
Oil
1 pound chicken breasts
Southwest-style seasoning

Grill chicken breast using Southwest-style seasoning, or use Tyson pre-cooked chicken.

Shred all cheese.

Saute onion and green pepper in a little oil until tender, add chicken, and then slowly add cheese a little at a time.

After all cheese has been added and has melted, keep the dip on a low temperature, stirring occasionally.

Serve with tortillas or chips.

Holly's Famous Gingerbread Cookies

4½ to 5 cups flour
2 teaspoons baking soda
1 cup butter
1 cup sugar
1 cup molasses
1 teaspoon each of cinnamon, cloves, ginger
¼ teaspoon salt
1 egg, beaten
1 tablespoon vinegar

Sift all dry ingredients; set aside.

Mix butter and sugar until smooth.

Heat molasses to boiling; pour over butter/sugar mixture.

Add vinegar; mix together and let cool.

Add egg to cooled mixture.

Fold in dry ingredients until well blended.

Cover and chill overnight (or a minimum of 5 hours).

Roll out to a ¼-inch thick and cut into cookie shapes with cutters.

Bake at 375 degrees for 8 to 10 minutes.

Clyde Blends Two Cultures Through Cooking

March 23, 2005

Margaret Clyde

Margaret Clyde learned to cook on a wood stove in a town near Greenville, S.C., called "Travelers Rest." It was so named because in the old days stage coaches paused there for a rest before attempting to climb the nearby mountains.

She remembers how hard it was to control the heat of the stove, but when the family got an electric stove, they burned everything because it got so hot so quickly. She remembers drawing water from the well, roasting potatoes on an open fire and warming toast over a fire using a long fork.

Today Margaret cooks wonderful meals in a thoroughly modern kitchen, turning out dishes such as baked potato soup, cider pork chops and scones.

Scones were not what she grew up eating. It was not until she was widowed and married a widower that she became familiar with British foods such as scones.

She met her Scottish second husband while teaching an upholstery class at Fayetteville Technical Community College, a position she held for 20 years. That's where she met Archibald "Scotty" Clyde. Scotty grew up in Glasgow, Scotland, and later joined the Army and retired in Fayetteville.

Margaret and Scotty spent their honeymoon in 1986 touring Scotland, and still go back every year or two to visit his relatives.

In Scotland, Margaret learned to love some of the dishes she says are very simple and nourishing. One of her favorites is scones, which can be cooked with a variety of grains, spices and fillings such as raisins or cheese to make them sweet or spicy. Margaret uses

Baked Potato Soup

- 4 large baking potatoes
- ⅔ cup butter or margarine
- 6 cups milk
- ¾ teaspoon salt
- ½ teaspoon pepper
- 4 green onions, chopped
- 12 slices bacon, cooked, crumbled
- 1¼ cups shredded cheddar cheese
- 1 carton sour cream, 8 ounces

Wash potatoes and prick several times with a fork.

Bake at 400 degrees 1 hour or until done. Let cool, cut potatoes in half lengthwise and scoop out pulp.

Melt butter in a heavy saucepan over low heat.

Add all-purpose flour, stirring until smooth.

Cook 1 minute, stirring constantly.

Gradually add 6 cups milk.

Cook over medium heat, stirring constantly, until mixture is thickened and bubbly.

Add potato pulp, salt and pepper, 2 tablespoonfuls green onions, ½ cup bacon and 1 cup cheese.

Cook until thoroughly heated.

Stir in sour cream.

Add extra milk, if necessary for desired thickness.

Serve with remaining onion, bacon and cheese. Makes 10 cups.

treacle in her recipe. Treacle can be light or dark. Molasses is a dark treacle. Syrup is a light treacle. Either can be used.

Scones can be cooked in the oven or on the stove top. When Scotty was growing up, his family cooked scones over a coal fire on hot bricks or on a cast-iron griddle inside the fireplace probably about the same time when Margaret was cooking her toast over an open fire in South Carolina.

Margaret says that while growing up in South Carolina, rice was the staple food, but in Scotland, Scotty says potatoes were the standard fare and when there was cooking going on there was always a pot of potatoes boiling. That's where Margaret got the recipe for baked potato soup, which is made with milk, sour cream, crumbled bacon and cheese.

Another of the couple's favorite dishes is cider pork chops with vegetables, strictly a Southern dish, she says, in which the chops are marinated in cider to tenderize them, and sherry is added for flavor. Then she adds vegetables, especially root vegetables, to make a one-pot meal that is fast and easy.

–Melissa Clement

Cider Pork Chops with Vegetables

4 to 6 pork chops
2 cups cider
¼ cup sherry
2 onions, halved
8 new potatoes, quartered
1 turnip, cubed
2 carrots, sliced
¾ cup milk
2 tablespoons flour
¼ teaspoon nutmeg
¼ teaspoon salt
¼ teaspoon pepper
¼ teaspoon thyme

Rub pork chops with thyme, salt and pepper mixture.

Brown chops on each side.

Remove chops. Put cider and sherry in pan.

Return chops to pan. Add vegetables.

Cook 45 minutes or until tender.

Add milk, flour and nutmeg.

Bring to boil and cook two minutes.

Treacle Scones

1 cup plain flour
⅛ teaspoon salt
1 teaspoon baking soda
1 teaspoon cream of tartar
1 tablespoon margarine
2 tablespoons sugar
1 teaspoon ground ginger
½ teaspoon ground cinnamon
½ teaspoon mixed spice
1 tablespoon melted treacle (molasses or thick syrup)
6 tablespoons milk

These can be baked either in an oven or on a griddle.

Sieve the flour, salt, soda and the cream of tartar.

Cut in the margarine and add sugar.

Mix to a stiff consistency with the treacle and milk and turn on to a lightly floured working surface.

Knead lightly and, if it is to be baked in oven, roll ½ thick, or if to be baked on the griddle, ¼ thick.

Cut into 8 pieces, place on a baking-tray and bake 10 to 12 minutes in an oven heated to 400 degrees, or place on a moderately hot griddle.

Bake 3 to 4 minutes on the first side, and when brown, turn and bake 5 to 6 minutes on the second side.

Cool on a wire tray if they are oven scones and in a towel on the tray if they are griddle scones.

Can't Beat the Old Family Favorites

May 30, 2001

Linda Tillman

Linda Tillman says she grew up on venison.

"When we could choose the meal for our birthday, I would like little venison chops," she says.

Her father, Reginald Barton, liked to deer hunt and kept the family supplied with venison in the freezer to cook year round.

"I cook a lot of venison now because Scott is such a big hunter," Linda says. She says her mother, Zula Barton, taught her a lot about cooking venison.

Linda says her son, Scott, and her husband, Warren, like her sweet and sour venison recipe.

Scott is a rising senior at Elon College and likes to cook venison at his apartment now.

"He likes to grill and do a lot of different rubs," Linda says.

Linda and Warren joined a gourmet supper club after moving back to Linda's hometown from the Atlanta area in 1992.

"I love cooking for company," Linda says. "I like to do a lot of different things."

She says her husband is a good sport about trying new dishes.

"He has broadened his likes tremendously. He was strictly a meat and potatoes man when we got married."

Even though she likes to experiment with new recipes, Linda has some old favorite ones handed down from relatives that she says can't be beat.

One of them is a recipe for sweet potato pie that she got from her grandmother, the late Hattie McFayden.

"When she gave me the recipe, she gave it as a little of this and a little of that," Linda says. "When she died I found an old Wurlitzer Centennial Cookbook sent out in 1856 and it had the recipe in it."

Another family favorite is a recipe for barbecue sauce from Warren's mother, Ophline Tillman of Swainsboro, Ga.

"She is a good cook and every time we go see her, I say 'I never knew a pork roast could taste so good.' "

– Alice Thrasher

Sweet and Sour Venison

1 cup vinegar
1 cup brown sugar
½ cup soy sauce
1 teaspoon ginger
1 tablespoon olive oil
1½ teaspoons chopped garlic
1 teaspoon salt
½ teaspoon black pepper
2 pounds venison

Marinate about two pounds of venison, cut into bite-sized pieces, in the refrigerator up to 24 or 36 hours to take out some of the gaminess and tenderize the meat.

Brown meat in a skillet on top of the stove with a small amount of oil.

Pour reserved marinade over browned meat and simmer in a covered skillet about 45 minutes, until meat is done.

Thicken sauce with flour or cornstarch.

Serve over rice.

Makes about six servings.

Mema's (Ophline Tillman's) Barbecue Sauce

1 quart ketchup
1 pint vinegar
4 tablespoons brown sugar
1½ tablespoons salt
2 sticks butter or margarine
2 teaspoons red pepper
Juice of 2 lemons
¾ cup Worcestershire sauce
¼ cup mustard
1 tablespoon black pepper

Simmer until butter melts.

Keeps for months in the refrigerator.

Recipe can easily be halved.

Hattie McFayden's Sweet Potato Pie

1 large (29-ounce) can sweet potatoes, drained
⅓ stick margarine, melted
¾ cup brown sugar
⅓ cup white sugar
1 teaspoon cinnamon
¼ teaspoon ground cloves
1 tablespoon flour
½ teaspoon nutmeg
¼ teaspoon ginger
2 eggs, beaten
¼ teaspoon salt
1 can evaporated milk
2 uncooked pie shells (not deep dish)

Combine ingredients and mix with electric mixer or in a food processor until very smooth.

Sprinkle a little sugar over pie shells and pour in the filling.

Sprinkle a little more sugar over the top.

Cook at 400 degrees for 30 to 35 minutes.

(If cooking pie in a convection oven, check after about 22-25 minutes.)

She Has Expanded Her Tastes Through Travel

July 27, 2005

Wendy Foley

Wendy Foley is a major in the 8th Psychological Operations Battalion (Airborne). She has been in the Army for 19 years, and one of the things she likes most about the Army is being able to travel and learn about other cultures.

Although she is trim, she says, "I definitely like to eat. I've been all over the world and tasted different food. When you come back home, you want to be able to cook those dishes. I learned to cook a Capris salad in Italy. I learned to make Vietnamese spring rolls in Vietnam, Thai curry soups in Thailand, dim sum in Hong Kong and falafel in the Middle East."

In Germany she learned to make spaetzle. That's where she learned to love to cook, she said.

"When you are deployed or overseas, you bond much stronger with others. The Army is a band of brothers. I would get together with other lieutenants, and we would cook and exchange recipes."

Once or twice a month she and friends would get together and prepare dishes to raise money for fun trips for the families of the battalion.

Wendy grew up in Portland, Maine. As the oldest of six children, she had a lot of responsibilities and took a leadership role. This included cooking. Even with relatives who were lobster fishermen, she said, seafood was expensive, and their staples were pasta and potatoes. On Sundays the family had a pot roast cooked with potatoes. When seafood was available, it was always baked or broiled, never fried like in the South.

Being a New Englander, she shares her Boston baked beans recipe. She also likes Mexican dishes. Her chili recipe is white and is made with chicken. It includes white beans, sour cream and cheeses, and it has a bit of a bite from green chilies and cayenne pepper.

Although these may be some of Wendy's own favorites recipes, she does not make them for her daughter, Mary Claire, who is 3 years old. What she likes to eat most in the world is peanut butter and jelly sandwiches.

– Melissa Clement

Salsa

- 10 to 12 Roma tomatoes, chopped
- 1 cup chopped onion
- 1 jalapeno, chopped and seeded
- 1 clove of garlic, minced
- 1 tablespoon lime juice (or lemon juice)
- 1 tablespoon chili powder
- 3 tablespoons vinegar
- 3 tablespoons olive oil
- 1 tablespoon sugar
- 1 bunch of cilantro, chopped (the more the better)
- Salt, pepper, red pepper to taste

Mix tomatoes, onions, jalapeno, garlic and cilantro in a medium to large bowl. Add all remaining ingredients and mix. Enjoy with tortilla chips or on top of Mexican dishes.

Spinach Enchiladas

- 10 corn tortillas (I sometimes substitute flour for a change)
- 1½ pounds fresh, trimmed spinach (or 2 packages of frozen spinach)
- 3 tablespoons olive oil
- 1 small to medium yellow onion
- 2 cloves of garlic
- 1 tablespoon chili powder
- 1 tablespoon cumin powder
- 1 teaspoon black pepper
- ½ teaspoon salt
- ¼ teaspoon cayenne pepper
- 2 cups Swiss cheese, grated

SAUCE:

- 1 cup sour cream (may use light, but not fat-free)
- 1 can of chopped green chilies
- ½ clove of garlic
- ½ teaspoon of cayenne pepper

In a large skillet, saute onion, garlic and spinach in olive oil. Add chili powder, cumin, salt, pepper and cayenne and saute until liquid is gone.

Brush each tortilla with oil, and spread a heaping tablespoon of grated cheese and then a heaping teaspoon of the spinach mixture. (Some of the cheese will be left over. Set this aside.) Fold one end of the tortilla over the filling, and then roll it up. Continue with all tortillas.

Lightly oil a large, shallow casserole dish and arrange enchiladas seam side down.

Make sauce by stirring all sauce ingredients and remaining Swiss cheese in a medium sauce pan. Heat on low until warmed through. Pour over enchiladas, cover, and bake at 350 degrees for 25 minutes. Uncover for last 5 minutes.

White Chicken Chili

See photo in center of book

- 3 cups of chopped chicken-breast meat
- 3 (15-ounce) cans white beans or great northern beans
- 2 (14.5-ounce) cans chicken broth
- 1 tablespoon olive oil
- 1 large onion, chopped
- 4 cloves of garlic, crushed or minced
- 2 jalapenos, minced
- 1 (4-ounce) can chopped green chilies
- 2 tablespoons ground cumin (more if you prefer)
- 1 teaspoon chili powder
- 1 teaspoon dried oregano
- 1½ teaspoons ground cayenne pepper
- 1½ cups shredded Monterey Jack cheese (may use light cheese, but not fat-free)
- 1 block of cream cheese (may use light cream cheese, but not fat-free)
- 2 cups sour cream (may use light sour cream, but not fat-free)
- 1 bunch of cilantro

Heat oil over medium heat and add onions and garlic. Saute for approximately 8 minutes or until onions are golden. Add chicken and saute for another 5 minutes.

Add everything else except beans, cilantro and Monterey Jack cheese. Bring to a quick boil.

Immediately reduce heat to low. Add beans and cheese and simmer for approximately 15 minutes. Sprinkle cilantro on top of individual servings. This is delicious with sweet cornbread.

Boston Baked Beans

- 16 ounces dry navy beans
- 4 cups hot water
- 1 tablespoon olive oil
- 1½ teaspoon salt
- 1 medium onion, chopped
- 1 cup brown sugar
- 1 cup dark molasses
- 1 teaspoon dry mustard
- 3 slices of bacon (preferably cooked)
- 1 teaspoon cinnamon
- 1 teaspoon nutmeg
- 1 teaspoon black pepper

Wash beans and place in a pot, covered with water. Soak overnight.

Drain beans. Put hot water and all ingredients into a Dutch oven or an electric slow cooker. Cover and cook on high for 3 hours. Stir once an hour.

Reduce heat to low and let simmer another 4 hours. Remove cover and cook another hour or until beans are browned. Add water to pot if liquid level is not covering beans.

ABOVE: Green Beans with Garlic.
Mike Dubnansky / Pg. 230.
Photo by Cindy Burnham

RIGHT: Horseradish Whipped Potatoes.
Lib Wilson / Pg. 173.
Photo by Cindy Burnham

FAR RIGHT: Tiramisu Fondue and White Pizza.
Richard Kugelmann / Pg. 109.
Photo by Marc Hall

PRECEDING PAGE: Chinese Fried Rice.
Lee Moeller / Pg. 227.
Photo by Cindy Burnham

ABOVE:
White Chicken Chili.
Wendy Foley / Pg. 128.
Photo by Rachael Santillan

RIGHT:
Pinto Bean Salad.
Wanda Strother / Pg. 111.
Photo by Cindy Burnham

FAR RIGHT: Jollof Rice and Fried Plantain.
Dr. Comfort Okpala / Pg. 211.
Photo by Raul Rubiera

ABOVE: Spinach Cranberry Salad.
Joy Van Hout / Pg. 79.
Photo by Cindy Burnham

RIGHT: Fresh Tomato and Mozzarella Salad.
Mike Dubnansky / Pg. 230.
Photo by Rachael Santillan

FAR RIGHT: Seared Red Snapper and Tomato-Lime Vinaigrette .
Lib Wilson / Pg. 173.
Photo by Rachael Santillan

ABOVE: Tuscan-style Chicken Pasta.
Rick Hamlet / Pg. 193.
Photo by Rachael Santillan

RIGHT: Linguine with Red Clam Sauce.
Rick Hamlet / Pg. 193.
Photo by Rachael Santillan

FAR RIGHT: Sushi.
Etsuko Martin / Pg. 93.
Photo by Rachael Santillan

ABOVE: Waffles.
Lorette Hollinshed / Pg. 203.
Photo by Rachael Santillan

LEFT: Zwiebelkucken (Onion Pie or Cake).
Elke Caesar / Pg. 31.
Photo by Cindy Burnham

FAR LEFT: Fruit Salad.
Norma Maness / Pg. 88.
Photo by Rachael Santillan

ABOVE: Toffee Chip Cookies. *Eileen Rettig / Pg. 8. Photo by Rachael Santillan*

LEFT: Pistachio Chocolate Chip Cream Pie. *Betty Parker / Pg. 107. Photo by Cindy Burnham*

ABOVE: Mamma's Pecan Pie.
Elaine Bryant / Pg. 29.
Photo by Rachael Santillan

LEFT: Date Bars.
Lorette Hollinshed / Pg. 202.
Photo by Rachael Santillan

FAR LEFT: Shaw's Boardinghouse Coconut Pie.
Elaine Bryant / Pg. 28.
Photo by Rachael Santillan

FOLLOWING PAGE: Luscious Lemon Pie with Raspberry Sauce.
Jane Horrocks / Pg. 65.
Photo by Rachael Santillan

Farm Life Was Foundation for Love of Cooking

April 26, 2006

Cynthia Helmick

Cynthia Helmick grew up on a farm in Northwest Kansas. Her parents were Czechoslovakian from Moravia and Bohemia, so they cooked ethnic foods that she still loves and cooks today.

On the farm, she learned to cook early in life, being the oldest of six children. By age 7 she was making cereal, washing produce from the garden and mixing up cookies. Her mother enjoyed working outside in the garden but did not care for household chores, so Helmick took over the cooking as well as the housekeeping as she got older.

On a farm, there is always lots to do, such as putting up vegetables for the winter and making bread, but she says there was always plenty of good food. Since it was the way she grew up, she did not realize she was doing hard work.

One of the recipes she shares is for kolaches, which she describes as something like croissants or Danish pastries, sweet dough with a fruit or cream filling. Her mother's recipe calls for mashed potatoes as well as egg yolks, yeast, shortening, sugar and flour.

Each kolache is made about the size and shape of an egg. Her mother put poppy seeds inside or filled them with a sweet cream-cheese filling or fruit. Her mother made a paste with a little flour, sugar and shortening and crumbled it on top of fruit filling. She also made sweet dumplings with plums inside and covered them with sweetened cream cheese. Helmick says using jelly, jam or cherry pie filling is the easiest way to make kolache filling.

As a child, she learned to cook simple dishes and she still chooses simple recipes. Since her husband had a heart attack, the couple has given up eating red meat and sticks to chicken, turkey and fish.

Another of the recipes she shares is crusty honey whole-wheat bread. When her mother made bread, she used sugar and kneaded it by hand. Today, Helmick uses the same recipes but substitutes honey for sugar and uses a mixer with a dough hook for mixing. She buys active dry yeast in jars rather than in packets for the sake of convenience.

One of Helmick's favorite recipes is piquant cocktail meatballs. She learned to make it after attending a party at Fort Riley, Kan., when her husband, who served in the military, was stationed there. Instead of using hamburger meat, she uses ground turkey. The sauce is made with the unusual combination of chili or picante sauce, lemon juice, ketchup, brown sugar and a can of jellied cranberry sauce. When she makes the meatballs, she is always asked for the recipe.

– Melissa Clement

Kolache

½ cup sugar

2 packets dry yeast

½ cup soft shortening

¾ cup very warm potato water (saved from cooking the potatoes)

1 teaspoon salt

1 cup mashed potatoes

4 egg yolks

2 tablespoons water

4 cups all-purpose flour

Cream sugar, shortening, salt and egg yolks well.

Dissolve yeast in potato water.

Add potatoes and yeast to creamed mixture.

Add 1½ cups of the flour.

Beat on low speed and mix 10 minutes.

Add rest of the flour.

Let rise in warm place till double in size, about 1½ hours.

Punch down.

Using a tablespoon, make dough into balls almost the size of an egg and place on a well-greased pan.

Let the dough-balls rise again.

Using a teaspoon and your fingers, gently form a hole in the center of each ball of dough.

Fill with filling of choice and bake at 350 degrees for 15 to 20 minutes until bread is very light brown.

A jelly roll pan will hold 2 dozen kolaches.

The hole in the dough will shrink a bit during baking so make it about 1 inch or so.

Fillings: jams, jellies, pie filling, sweetened cream cheese.

Mother always topped her Kolache with a crumbly mixture of sugar, flour and shortening before baking.

The cream-cheese filling has no real measurements. I usually soften it in the microwave and add sugar to taste and a bit of milk util it is of a thick, pudding consistency.

For the crumbly topping, again there are no real measurements.

Start with cup sugar. Stir in flour and shortening a teaspoon at a time and mix until crumbly. Place about 1 teaspoon on each kolache.

Piquant Cocktail Meatballs

2 pounds hamburger or ground turkey

2 tablespoons soy sauce

1 egg

1 teaspoon salt

Pepper to taste

⅓ cup dried parsley (optional)

1 cup cornflake or bread crumbs

Chopped onion to taste

FOR SAUCE:

1 (12-ounce) bottle of chili or picante sauce

1 tablespoon lemon juice

⅓ cup ketchup

1 (16-ounce) can jellied, whole-berry cranberry sauce

2 tablespoons brown sugar

Combine the above ingredients and form into meatballs.

Use a rounded teaspoon per meatball.

Place the meatballs on a broiler pan and cook under the broiler until done.

Combine sauce ingredients. Place sauce and meatballs in a crockpot and heat through.

Crusty Honey Whole Wheat Bread

1 cup milk

2½ cups whole-wheat flour

1 cup water

2 packets of active dry yeast

½ cup honey

1 egg

2 tablespoons butter or margarine

1 tablespoon salt

4½ cups all-purpose flour

Heat milk, water, honey and butter to 120 degrees. (If you can hold your finger in it, the mixture is warm enough.)

In a large mixer bowl, combine 1 cup whole-wheat flour, 2 cups all-purpose flour, yeast, egg, salt and warm milk mixture.

Mix with dough hooks for 3 minutes.

Gradually add remaining whole-wheat flour and enough all-purpose flour to form a stiff dough.

Knead with dough hooks until smooth and satiny (about 4 minutes).

Place in a greased bowl and let the dough rise until it doubles in size.

Punch down and divide into 2 equal parts.

Shape into loaves and place in 2 greased 9-by-5-inch loaf pans.

Cover and let rise until double.

Bake at 375 degrees for 10 minutes. Reduce heat to 350 degrees and bake for 30 to 35 minutes.

Cool on a rack after removing from pans.

Please note baking times and temperatures, or else the bread will be doughy in the center.

Family Adopts Nationwide Cuisines

April 10, 2002

Karen Weaver

Karen Weaver grew up as a true California girl, the fourth generation of Californians. Before she married her husband, Cregg, (pronounced Craig) she didn't know barbecue was a noun.

Cregg is a native of Lexington, N.C., and knows what real Lexington barbecue is. He barbecues almost every evening they are home. Everything from fish to pizza goes on the grill.

There was always good food at the Schaffer home. She said they are outdoors people and were constantly grilling everything. Her dad, Brooks Schaffer, created his own outstanding marinade. It has a little bit of sweet stuff and a little bit of sour stuff.

Her grandmother Florence Schaffer made great curry.

Grandmother Florence wrote books on nature and floral design and was a graduate of UC Berkeley.

She was also what Karen lovingly calls "a kind of health nut" who ate sardines, whole grains and fruit sludge. She ground apples, oranges, bananas, pits, peels, stems and all, in a food processor.

Karen says at the time it was pretty scary stuff. Karen spent summers at her old 1915 cabin in the Sierras as a child.

The curry recipe was one Grandmother Florence adapted from Karen's great-aunt who was a missionary in Malaysia.

Karen's grandmother Evelyn Wynne was a voice and piano teacher. She always had a huge box of See's candy in the refrigerator.

She was famous for her lemon meringue pies, divinity, angel food cake and apple cake. Karen says the apple cake is a delicious moist heavy cake, which travels great. She usually frosts it when she gets to where she is taking it.

Florence's Curry

2 pounds lamb (usually use leftover meat: you can use chicken or beef), lightly browned

3 Granny Smith apples, chopped

3 onions, chopped

2 (or more) cloves garlic, crushed

2 tablespoons flour

2 tablespoons curry powder

1½ teaspoons powdered ginger (this is what makes curry hot. Adjust to taste)

1 14-ounce can broth (any kind)

1 teaspoon lemon juice

1 cup dry red wine

TOPPINGS

Chopped peanuts

Chopped green onions

Chopped hard-boiled eggs

Raisins plumped in hot water

Sliced bananas

Pineapple chunks (this one is a must. Sounds wacky but really tastes good)

Major Grey's Chutney

Bombay duck pappadums

Mix ingredients and heat and thicken for about 45 minutes. Serve on a bed of rice. Serve toppings in little bowls and let guests add to taste.

She was a graduate of the University of the Pacific. In the 1920s she and Karen's grandfather would herd their horses from San Joaquin Valley to the Sierras for the summer. She wishes she had a few of the recipes from their treks.

Karen's mom, Patricia Schaffer, is also a terrific cook. She will be visiting in the next week and adores the regional cuisine. Especially Cregg's barbecue.

– Melissa Clement

Brooks' Chicken Marinade

4 ounces soy sauce

4 ounces juice (something acidic like orange juice or pineapple)

¼ cup something sweet (brown or white sugar or honey)

Fresh crushed garlic cloves, to taste

2 ounces oil

3 teaspoons French's yellow mustard

Fresh herbs

Use whatever is in the garden, usually rosemary, oregano or thyme. She rubs them between her hands and throws them in stems and all. Her dad uses a mortar and pestle on dried herbs and that does a lot to bring out the flavor of the herbs. Pour over chicken and leave for a few hours or overnight.

Beef Marinade

5 crushed garlic cloves or to taste

½ cup sliced fresh ginger

½ cup soy sauce

1 cup heavy dry red wine (cheap "jug" burgundy best)

½ cup oil

Pour over beef and marinate overnight.

Evelyn's Apple Cake

2 eggs, beaten

2 cups sugar

2 teaspoons baking soda

¼ teaspoon salt

2 teaspoons cinnamon

1 teaspoon vanilla

2 cups flour

4 cups sliced Granny Smith apples

½ cup oil

1 cup nuts (optional)

FROSTING

3 cups powdered sugar

12 ounces cream cheese

6 tablespoons butter (optional)

2 teaspoons vanilla

Sprinkle with nuts

Mix cake ingredients.

Pour into a 9-by-12-inch greased and floured pan and bake at 350 degrees for 1 hour. This cake tastes even better after it sits a day. It is a very sturdy, dense, moist cake so it travels well.

For frosting, mix all ingredients. You can take the frosting along separately or frost when cake is cool.

Haymount Resident Continues to Create Cuisine

July 28, 2004

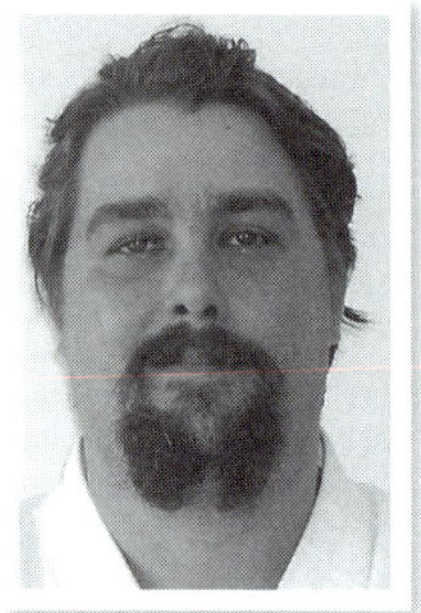

Joe English

Joe English has spent a lifetime cooking. The 29-year-old Haymount resident grew up on a farm in Michigan and spent a year in North Charleston, S.C., before moving to Fayetteville.

"I remember helping my mother make a giant chocolate chip cookie for my brother's birthday when he was 3 years old," he said.

Greg English, 27, who lives in Fayetteville, said what he remembers about his childhood is his brother seemed to always be in the kitchen cooking with their mother.

"I'll never forget Mom began working 50 hours a week. So at age 15, I was cooking for the family," the Chili's cook said.

But English didn't have to cook for his two sisters because they were grown and out of the household.

"Mom would leave a list of what I was supposed to cook. I remember the first time I cooked squash, I had to call my mother for directions. It was easier than I thought," he said with a laugh.

English, who is named after his mother, Jolene, still calls his mother in Michigan from time to time to ask her how to cook a certain dish. "It's just a way to have it taste just like Mom would make it."

Since moving to the Cape Fear region, English usually cooks small meals for him and his brother. However, for the past two years, English has cooked entire Thanksgiving and Christmas meals for anyone he knows who can't make it home for the holidays.

"If anyone has a chance they should try to cook and taste a fried turkey," he said while holding his pet ferret.

Other favorites English likes to cook are chili, beef tips and noodles, angel food cake, apricot candies and oatmeal cake.

But he doesn't cook chili in the summertime, because he feels spicy foods and hot weather don't always go together.

English owns a crock pot and a multi cooker in which he loves to cook his chili or pot roast. "When I put the pot roast in the crock pot, eight hours later it has marinated and is ready to be picked up with a spoon," he said.

Although an oatmeal cake may sound strange to some people, to the brothers it's great. "It's so delicious, no words can explain it," Greg said.

"I have never had a person that didn't enjoy my oatmeal cake," English added.

The reason he's such a good cook, he feels, is because of the recipe book his mother has made and given to all her children.

It has very detailed recipes and is dedicated to her kids. Next to the recipe is the year she first made the dish.

The book is designed for the kids to send her their own recipes so she can add it to the book for the family to share.

"She takes her cooking seriously. I guess that is why I had a good teacher," English said.

— Ealer Wadlington III

Apricot Candies

¼ pound dried apricots
1 cinnamon stick
⅓ cup sugar
½ cup water
1 teaspoon crushed pistachio nuts
1 lemon peel-pinched
2 ounces of Hersheys Bittersweet Chocolate

Put lemon peel, cinnamon stick, sugar and water in a saucepan, and bring to a boil. Stir constantly; when sugar is dissolved turn heat down for 3 minutes. Put apricots in for 6 to 8 minutes until tender. Put apricots on rack to cool. Melt chocolate in bowl, place in microwave. Dip ½ of the apricots, sprinkle with nuts and place back on rack to cool for about 20 to 30 minutes. Put in airtight container with wax paper placed between the layers.

Oatmeal Cake

1 cup oatmeal
1 cup boiling water
½ cup of margarine
½ cup of flour
1 teaspoon baking soda
1 teaspoon ground cinnamon
½ teaspoon salt
½ teaspoon nutmeg
1 cup sugar
1 cup lite Brown Sugar packed
2 eggs beaten
½ cup mayonnaise or Miracle Whip

In a large bowl combine oatmeal, water and margarine. Then set the mixture aside for 10 minutes. In another bowl, mix together flour, baking soda, cinnamon, salt and nutmeg. Set aside. Add sugar, brown sugar, eggs and mayonnaise to cereal mixture and mix together. Add flour mixture to large bowl and mix well. Pour into greased 9-by-13 inch pan and bake at 350 degrees for about 45 minutes. To check doneness of cake, take a toothpick or knife and insert it into the middle of the cake and remove. If the toothpick or knife comes out clean, then the cake is done.

Beef Tips and Noodles

2 pounds beef tips
½ stick butter or margarine
1 pound egg noodles
½ pound mushrooms (optional)
3 tablespoons Worcestershire sauce
2 tablespoons garlic (granulated)
1 teaspoon black pepper
4 quarts water
2 tablespoons cornstarch
½ cup water

In a large skillet combine mushrooms, beef tips, butter, garlic, pepper and Worcestershire sauce. Cook until beef tips are done. In a 6-quart pot, bring 4 quarts of water to a boil. Add egg noodles to boiling water and cook 6 to 8 minutes. Stir frequently. Drain water from cooked pasta and rinse with warm water. Put noodles back into pot. Strain meat and mushrooms leaving the grease in the skillet. Add meat and mushrooms to the noodles. To make gravy, take 1 cup of water, add to grease and bring to a boil. Add cornstarch, ½ cup of water and stir constantly until thick. Remove from heat. Add gravy to the beef tips, noodles and mix together.

A Self-proclaimed Cookbook Addict

July 13, 2005

Linda Coons

Linda Coons calls herself a "cookbook addict." She owns more than 400 cookbooks and keeps buying more. She particularly likes to pore over antique cookbooks because the recipes are unique and the writing archaic.

"Folks back then had so little to work with and yet they created these wonderful recipes,"she says, "and you look at it and you say, 'How in the world did a woman in the 1890s create these wonderful dishes when they had so little to work with?' How did they know the right chemistry to make that cake rise? They must have just baked it and prayed."

When she finds an interesting recipe Coons records the name and page number on a card. After trying it out she may or may not save it by filing it in her recipe box. She keeps it near a huge kitchen cabinet where she stores her favorite cookbooks.

Linda has one cardinal rule about cooking from recipes.

"Follow recipes exactly like they are written," she says. "If you start messing with them, you are not going to have good results. Those recipes have already been tested."

If you don't like a certain spice, say cinnamon, you can leave it out or substitute another spice, she says, but don't mess with the body of a recipe like the amount of flour.

Coons grew up in Fayetteville and learned to cook from her mother, Pearl Stevens, and her grandmother, Hettie Bass, who lived in Iron Hill in Columbus County. Both were "the best cooks on earth," she says.

The first thing Linda cooked was biscuits at age 10. "It was a nightmare. I destroyed the kitchen and you could have knocked somebody out with those biscuits."

That was when her mother and grandmother promised to teach her how to cook, and they did.

After she married Philip Coons, they lived in Hawaii, where he was stationed with the military. There she found her recipe for yam–or sweet potato–bread. It came from a small 1973 newspaper.

"You never know where the best recipes in the world are going to crop up," she says.

Her peanut apple squares recipe came from a 1939 recipe that came with a stove made by Frigidaire.

"Grandmas's Chew Bread" was in a church cookbook put out by seniors who lived on an island near Wilmington.

"I love church cookbooks. They contain a lot of family recipes handed down from generation to generation."

–Melissa Clement

Yam (Sweet Potato) Bread

- 4 eggs
- 1 cup cooking oil
- 3 cups sugar
- 1½ teaspoons salt
- 1 teaspoon cinnamon
- 1 teaspoon nutmeg
- 3 cups flour
- 2 teaspoons baking soda
- 1 cup mashed yams
- ⅔ cup water

Mix together eggs, oil, sugar, salt, cinnamon and nutmeg.

Add flour, soda, yams and water. Blend well.

Put in 4 small rectangular bread pans or two bundt pans.

Bake at 350 degrees for one hour or until done. Yields 3 to 4 loaves or 2 cakes.

Peanut Apple Squares

- ¼ cup butter
- 1 cup sugar
- ½ cup peanut butter
- 1 egg
- 1¼ cups all-purpose flour
- 1 teaspoon baking soda
- ½ teaspoon salt
- ½ teaspoon cinnamon
- ¼ teaspoon nutmeg
- 1 cup applesauce

Cream butter. Gradually add sugar, beating well. Add peanut butter and egg; beat well. Combine flour, soda, salt cinnamon and nutmeg. Add to creamed mixture, alternating with applesauce, beginning and ending with flour mixture.

Pour into greased 8-inch pan. Bake at 350 degrees for 40 minutes. Cool in pan for 10 minutes.

Grandma's Chew Bread

- 1 16-ounce package light brown sugar
- 4 eggs
- 2 cups all-purpose flour
- ½ teaspoon salt
- 1 teaspoon vanilla
- 1 cup chopped pecans

Combine sugar and eggs in a heavy saucepan, stirring well.

Cook over medium heat, stirring constantly until sugar dissolves.

Remove from heat. Add remaining ingredients, stirring well.

Bake in 10-by-15-by-1-inch pan.

Bake at 400 degrees until golden brown.

Woman Gets the Hang of Cooking Later in Life

July 12, 2006

Celia Gainer

As a cook, you might say Celia Gainer was a late bloomer. She was born in California into a large family. Her mother was a great cook, but it didn't all rub off on Celia.

"In my first year of marriage, I managed to burn a pan of water and ruin my first meatloaf," she says. "None of my family ever considered me a great cook, and quite frankly, I agreed, but I kept on trying."

Then one night after dinner, her 5-year-old son, John, told her it was the best meal ever.

"The meal consisted of Campbell's tomato soup, saltine crackers and milk. I hugged him and thanked him and at that point began to get more serious about meals."

She says it was lucky for John that he had an Aunt Carolyn, the family's best baker of pies and cakes, and an Aunt Marilyn who married a terrific cook, Uncle Bob, known for his lasagna. But Celia kept on learning.

"One Easter I made the whole meal, and everyone came, nephews, nieces included. The meal was a success even though my rabbit cake looked like a groundhog instead of a rabbit."

In 2002, Celia moved to Fayetteville from California to be near her Special Forces son and his wife and children. Since she has been here, she has learned to cook some Southern recipes that she will take back with her when her son retires and returns to California. She may prepare the recipes she shares with us. They are buttermilk-ranch chopped-chicken salad, filled strawberries and spice-rubbed rib-eye.

Every Sunday after church, she cooks a meal for her family, and then they play board games together. Her grandchildren are particularly fond of the stawberry shortcake and cheesecake she makes.

"Several months ago, my sister Marilyn and her husband came out to visit and raved about my chili and cake and were amazed the recipes were in my head and 'spur of the moment' creations. They even took several pieces of cake for the road. I had finally arrived."

– Melissa Clement

Buttermilk-ranch Chopped Chicken Salad

1 cup buttermilk ranch dressing

1 pound chicken, cooked and chopped

1 cup celery, chopped

1 cup cucumber, chopped

1 cup red pepper, chopped

1 cup green pepper, chopped

3 green onions, chopped

Salt to taste

Pepper to taste

Lettuce

Croutons

Cheddar cheese, shredded (optional)

Combine first seven ingredients and mix thoroughly. Adjust seasoning with salt and pepper. Place onto lettuce-lined plates and top with croutons and shredded cheddar cheese, if desired. 4 servings.

Spiced-rubbed Rib-eyes

2 tablespoons corn oil

¼ cup Mexican seasoning blend

1 teaspoon hot salt

4 boneless rib-eye steaks

In a bowl, stir together corn oil and seasoning. Sprinkle hot salt on both sides of each steak. Brush seasoned oil over the steaks. Grill or broil to your preference.

Filled Strawberries

6 ounces cream cheese, at room temperature

½ teaspoon pure vanilla extract

1½ tablespoons confectioners' sugar

12 strawberries

¼ cup sliced almonds

Whip cream cheese until slightly fluffy. Add vanilla extract and confectioners' sugar. Trim tops and bottoms of strawberries to level. Use a small melon baller to scoop out strawberries. (If you want to avoid wasting the scooped-out strawberry middles, you can add them to the cream-cheese mixture.)

Fill a pastry bag fitted with a ½-inch star tip with cream cheese mixture. Fill the berries until the mixture brims over the tops.

Toast the almonds in a 350-degree oven until golden brown. Arrange on top of filling.

Cook Counts on Large Groups

November 16, 2005

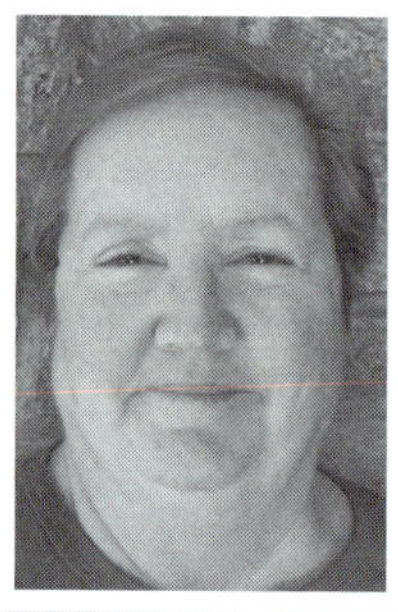

Charlene Gause

When accountant Charlene Gause moved to Toccoa, Ga., with her husband, Jim, in 1986 she couldn't find a job. There was one opening at the Toccoa Conference Center for a night cook.

"I had never cooked anything more than a meal of a family, but the director liked my enthusiasm and trained me," she said. "It made me feel good to get the meals all prepared and ready to eat. I felt as if I had found my calling and have been preparing meals for large crowds since 1986."

Maybe her skill as an accountant helps her take family-size recipes and increase the ingredients to feed several hundred people at Haymount United Methodist Church every Wednesday and Thursday and snacks on Sunday after church services. She also prepares meals and banquets for special conferences, ministries, interfaith hospitality events and summer camps.

Gause will be around today helping the United Methodist Women prepare lunch during their bake sale. The money the women raise will be used for local and outreach missions. The sale begins at noon.

While you are at the bake sale, you might want to have lunch and try the ham-and-cheese croissants and cream of broccoli soup, which will be available for lunch from noon to 1:30 p.m. The price is $4. You do not have to be a member of the church to attend the bake sale or any of the meals served at the church.

Cakes, pies, muffins, cookies and casseroles, as well as holiday gifts and handmade crafts, will be for sale, along with jars of homemade tomato-and-basil dressing. The bake sale will be open today until 7 p.m.

Gause is responsible for the evening fellowship meal served each Wednesday from 5 to 6:30 p.m. The price is $5, and you must have reservations.

Every Thursday Gause and others prepare a luncheon which runs from noon to 1:30 p.m. and costs $2 to attend. No reservation is required.

Gause shares the cream of broccoli soup that will be served today, along with lemon ice box pie and tomato-basil vinaigrette dressing.

The lemon pie–you know it has to be old to be called "ice box"–was her mother's recipe. It's made with whipped topping and lemonade concentrate. The dressing is easy to make and good, she says.

Haymount United Methodist Church is at 1700 Fort Bragg Road.

– Melissa Clement

Cream of Broccoli Soup

- 1 cup chopped onion
- 1 cup margarine
- 1 cup flour
- 1 quart chicken stock
- 20 ounces chopped broccoli
- 1 quart milk
- Salt and pepper to taste
- Grated Swiss or cheddar cheese, optional

Saute onions in margarine. Add flour and stir until smooth. Slowly stir in chicken stock.

Add broccoli and simmer briefly.

Add milk and heat to serving temperature. Add salt and pepper to taste. Stir in cheese, if desired. Yields 10 servings.

Lemon Ice Box Pie

- 2 (9-inch) graham-cracker pie shells
- 1 large container of Cool Whip
- 1 (12-ounce) container of frozen lemonade concentrate (or any fruit blend you may wish), thawed

Mix the Cool Whip and the lemonade with electric mixer.

Dip into pie shells and place in freezer overnight.

Tomato-Basil Vinaigrette

- 2 cups red wine vinegar
- 3 cups canned diced tomatoes (use equal parts of tomatoes and juice)
- 1 pack Classic Italian dressing mix
- 1 tablespoon crushed basil
- 4 cups salad oil

Pour vinegar and tomatoes with juice into a bowl. Add Classic Italian mix and basil.

Mix at a high speed for 2 minutes while slowly adding oil. Chill.

Makes 32 2-ounce servings.

Musician Has Adventures in Cooking

February 8, 2006

Barbara Hudgens

Anyone who knows Barbara Hudgens can tell you she is a great cook, but it took her a while to become one, she said. She never cooked much before marriage because her mother, grandmother and maid were all good cooks, and she was assigned the dishwashing chore.

"I did more eating than cooking," Hudgens said with a laugh. "I did not know how to do any cooking except fancy recipes. I tried a crabmeat casserole cobbler from a Pillsbury Bake Off. It is no longer in my repertoire.

"When I first got married I was still in school and inept at cooking," she said. "For Christmas, my husband had a choice of a turkey or a ham from his office. I chose the ham because I thought it would be small and easy to cook, but it turned out to be a 20-pound ham. I had nothing but a cookie sheet to bake it on, and it buckled. You can imagine how long it took two people to get rid of a 20-pound ham."

Recently Hudgens was cooking a pork tenderloin. The recipe called for port wine, and when she added the second bit of wine, it caught on fire.

"Maybe the oven was too hot, but my grandchildren call it my pork flambeau recipe," she said. "It tasted good, but I was afraid the house would go down with it."

The only other food problem she has ever had is making biscuits. Hudgens said she has tried every recipe known to man, and her biscuits still come out hard as a rock.

She credits cookbook author Beth Tartan, who is a food editor and columnist for the *Winston-Salem Journal*, with inspiring her to become the excellent cook she is today.

Hudgens reads books, magazines and newspaper articles and says she is addicted to the Food Network. She loves to cook, even if it isn't the kind of food she grew up eating.

She fondly remembers growing up five miles from Winston-Salem, where her father was a Realtor. He had a large garden where he grew vegetables and fruit trees. He kept pigs, chicken and cattle, and also was a hunter, so the family always had plenty of good food. Hudgens especially remembers her Moravian mother's apple and blackberry pies, old-fashioned churned ice cream, homemade grape-leaf pickles in a slow cooker and sourwood honey with combs to chew on.

In college, she majored in music and was the organist and choir director at St. James Lutheran Church in Fayetteville for many years until she retired. Musician Terry Jordan calls her the "St. James emeritus organist."

– Melissa Clement

Carrot Soup with Thyme and Fennel

¼ cup (½ stick) butter or margarine

1 pound carrots, chopped

¾ cup onions, chopped

¾ cup leeks, chopped (white and pale green parts only)

2 garlic cloves, chopped

½ teaspoon chopped fresh thyme

¼ teaspoon fennel seeds

5 cups or more canned low-salt chicken broth

Melt cup of butter in large saucepan over medium-low heat. Add carrots, onions, leeks, garlic, thyme and fennel seeds. Stir to coat. Cover, cook until onion is transparent while stirring occasionally, for about 15 minutes.

Bring broth to simmer and partially cover. Simmer until carrots are very tender, stirring occasionally for 40 minutes. Cool slightly. Working in batches, puree soup in blender. Return to pan. Season with salt and pepper. Can be made one day ahead, cool slightly; cover and chill.

Bring soup to simmer. Ladle into bowls. May sprinkle with additional thyme.

Cabbage Potato Soup

1 quart water

2 teaspoons salt

2 teaspoons chicken bouillon granules

1 medium onion, chopped

4 potatoes, peeled and quartered

½ medium head of cabbage, shredded

1 tablespoon butter

Pepper, to taste

In a large saucepan, bring water, salt and onions to a boil. Add chicken granules and potatoes and cook until tender, about 15 minutes.

Mash potatoes in pot. Add cabbage and butter. Bring to a boil. Simmer 10 to 15 minutes, stirring occasionally until cabbage is tender. Season to taste with pepper.

Vegetables Aspic Salad

1 3-ounce package lemon Jell-O

¾ cup boiling water

½ cup cold water

¼ cup cider vinegar

1 14-ounce can tiny green peas, drained

1 14-ounce can French-cut green beans, drained

1 tablespoon chopped onion

½ cup chopped celery

¼ cup chopped olives

1 diced medium cucumber

Green pepper, chopped (optional)

Salt and pepper to taste

Dissolve Jell-O in boiling water for 2 minutes. Add cold water and vinegar, then spices and vegetables. Chill until firm.

Serve with dressing, made with cup mayonnaise, cup sour cream and 1 tablespoon horseradish. Mix well and chill.

Couple's Tastes Influenced by Travel

January 18, 2006

Dotty Lowell

Dotty Lowell grew up in Pennsylvania with a Pennsylvania Dutch heritage. Her family lived on a farm with plenty of poultry and livestock and ate a basic meat-and-potato diet. Her husband, Neil, came from the same background, but Lowell said his service in the Air Force changed his eating habits.

When Lowell's husband was stationed in Germany, the couple spent years traveling all over Europe and Scandinavia, where Lowell picked up different recipes and her taste in food began to change. Soon after Neil Lowell's retirement, they traveled to Australia and New Zealand.

"In Pennsylvania, we grew up on mostly German food," Dotty Lowell said. "Neil's experiences opened my world to food. He is more inquisitive than I am. I learned about the different kinds of exotic fruits in warm countries, vegetables and other food I had not been exposed to."

When they traveled to Thailand, Burma, Hong Kong, India and Laos, Lowell developed a taste for the hot-and-spicy foods she likes to cook today.

In Hungary in the 1980s, a friend gave her the recipe for Hungarian goulash.

Lowell developed the recipe for Zippy Meatballs on her own using frozen meatballs, two jars of chili sauce, one jar of grape jelly and 2 tablespoons of chipotle peppers in adobe sauce. Talk about hot.

Aunt Ada's black walnut coffee pudding is quite another thing. When she hosts dinner parties, friends ask her to cook the unusual dish. The recipe calls for milk, strong coffee, sugar and an egg. The ingredients are cooked together and cooled before the black walnuts are mixed in.

Once, when Lowell added the walnuts while the dish was too hot, the oil melted into the mix and made it too runny. To save the dish, she added Cool Whip. It turned the pudding into a kind of mousse and that was delicious, she said.

Lowell is not sure where the couple's next adventure will be, but wherever it is, it will surely yield a bounty of recipes.

– Melissa Clement

Emmi's Hungarian Goulash

- 1 pound pork cut in 1-inch cubes
- 1 pound beef cut in 1-inch cubes
- 2 tablespoons oil
- 2 onions, coarsely chopped
- 2 cups boiling water
- 2 red or green peppers, coarsely chopped
- 7 tablespoons Hungarian paprika powder
- 2 large cans of chopped tomatoes
- Salt and pepper to taste

Brown the meat in the oil. Remove to slow cooker. Add onions to oil and saute until lightly browned. Remove to slow cooker. Saute the peppers slightly and add to the slow cooker. Add paprika and stir.

Heat tomatoes in microwave until very hot. Add tomatoes, boiling water, salt and pepper to the slow cooker and cook for 5 to 6 hours. Serve with spaetzle noodles or regular noodles.

Aunt Ada's Black Walnut Coffee Pudding

- 2 cups milk, scalded in double boiler
- ½ cup sugar
- 3 tablespoons cornstarch
- ½ teaspoon salt
- 1 cup strong coffee
- 1 egg, slightly beaten
- ¼ cup sugar
- ½ cup black walnuts

Mix ½ cup sugar with cornstarch and salt. Pour scalded milk over mixture. Add coffee and return the mixture to the double boiler. Cook until thick.

Mix egg with ¼ cup sugar. Add a little of the hot mixture to the egg mixture.

Add the egg mixture back into the hot mixture and cook for another 5 minutes. Let the mixture cool for 10 to 15 minutes before adding the chopped nuts. If you want a mousse-like dessert, fold in Cool Whip. Garnish with chocolate curls.

Zippy Meatballs

- 5 pounds frozen meatballs
- 2 jars of chili sauce
- 1 (8-ounce) jar of grape jelly
- 2 tablespoons chipotle peppers in adobe sauce

Put all ingredients in a slow cooker. Cook for 4 hours or until heated through. Serve with toothpicks.

For a milder version, use chipotle sauce instead of peppers.

Sisters Carry on Relatives' Recipes

December 22, 2004

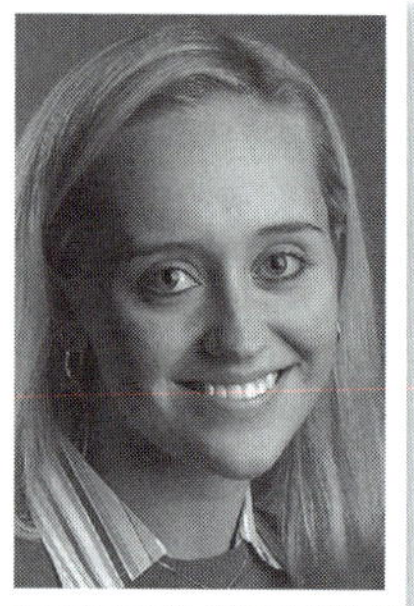
Jessica Meoni

"White chocolate raspberry truffles, chocolate chip cookie dough with ice cream, chili, roast beef sandwiches, pasta — any kind of pasta with sauce." Jessica Meoni rattles off things when asked what she likes to cook and eat.

Her sister, Jennifer Meoni, adds chicken salad, deviled eggs, cheese fries, handmade biscuits, macaroni and cheese and potato salad.

"We've been at it since we were about 5 years old, says Jessica, who is 16 years old and a junior at Terry Sanford High School. Jennifer is 14 and a freshman.

When they were very young, their grandmother picked them up after school while their mother, Sarah Kennedy, a teacher, was working. Grandmother Marie Futrell taught them to cook.

"She used to say, 'If you can read, you can cook,"' says Jessica. "We spent a lot of time cooking with her."

"We can cook anything if there is a recipe," says Jennifer.

Jessica likes Italian food best. Her father, Mark Meoni, comes from an Italian family, and their great-grandmother, the late Mary Lomma, immigrated from Italy. She wrote her recipes in a book by hand and that's what Jessica uses for some of her Italian dishes.

"She cooked pure Italian food and we devoured it," Jessica says. " When she cooked, it smelled so good that dogs even came in. We loved the huge family get-together."

Jessica likes to watch a TV cooking show called "Everyday Italian." When she was in the 10th grade she researched Italian food as a project and made Strawberry bruschetta and rosemary focaccia for the whole class.

Jennifer prefers to cook old-fashioned Southern fare like she learned from grandmother Futrell.

"The best things you can make that's Southern is pecan pie," she says. "Sweet potatoes — you cook them in a toaster oven and they taste awesome. Ant logs — you get celery (stalks) and put peanut butter in them and raisins on top, that's ant logs," Jennifer says.

– Melissa Clement

Apple Cranberry Casserole

3 cups unpeeled apples

2 cups raw cranberries

¾ cup sugar

FOR TOPPING:

1 cup uncooked oatmeal

⅓ cup flour

1 stick butter or margarine

½ cup brown sugar

½ cup chopped nuts

Preheat oven to 350 degrees.

Line casserole with apples and cranberries.

Sprinkle ¾ cup sugar over them.

Melt 1 stick butter or margarine.

Add rest of topping ingredients to saucepan.

Mix together and spread on top of apples and cranberries.

Bake at 350 degrees for one hour.

Ciambeletto

- 1 cup shortening
- 1½ cups sugar
- 1 pinch salt
- 4 eggs
- 3 cups flour sifted, leaving aside 6 tablespoons from the sifting
- 1 cup milk
- 1 lemon rind, grated 4 teaspoons Anisetta
- ½ teaspoon anise seeds

ICING:

- ½ cup milk
- ½ cup powdered sugar
- 3 tablespoon flour
- ½ cup shortening Crisco
- ½ teaspoon Anisetta or lemon flavoring
- 1 teaspoon colored candy for decoration

Pour in a greased oval dish.

Bake at 375 degrees for ½ hour. Reduce temperature to 350 degrees and cook for ½ hour more.

Boil all of ingredients besides the candy in a pot until thick. Pour over bread and put candy on top.

Special Easter Cheese Bread

FOR YEAST:

- ½ pound flour
- 2 eggs well beaten
- 1 cup lukewarm milk or 1½ cups water
- 1 cake yeast

FOR BREAD:

- 5 pounds flour
- 1 orange rind
- 3 tablespoons salt
- 4 tablespoons pepper
- ½ teaspoon ground cloves
- 2 pound Italian grated cheese (Locatelli)
- ½ quart milk, warm
- 3 tablespoons Crisco
- ½ pound butter
- ¼ teaspoon allspice
- 2 dozen well-beaten eggs

Make yeast first by mixing all of the yeast ingredients together. Let rise. When risen, pour in with ingredients.

Mix everything thoroughly together with yeast mixture.

Let rise, then knead again, and let rise.

Grease 6 pans. Make six loaves, and put them in the pans to rise again.

Put them in the oven at 300 degrees for around 1 hour, or until nice and brown all around.

Beat yolk of an egg and brush loaves with yolk.

When bread has cooled, wrap it and put it in the refrigerator.

Pecan Pie

- ¾ cup sugar
- 2 tablespoons flour
- 3 eggs, beaten lightly
- 1 stick butter, melted
- 1 cup light Karo syrup
- 1 tablespoon vanilla
- 1 cup pecans, coarsely chopped
- 1 deep dish pie shell

Mix sugar, flour, and beaten eggs.

Add butter, syrup, vanilla, and pecans.

Pour into unbaked pie shell.

Bake at 325 degrees for 60 minutes. Remove after 60 minutes even if pie doesn't look done.

Farm Life Cultivates a Love for Cooking

June 28, 2006

Kathleen Nichols

Kathleen Nichols is a good cook. She had an excellent teacher. She was taught by her mother, Narsisia McCormick, who is now 102 years old. Until she was 100, she cooked Sunday dinners for her family. Those meals included fried or baked chicken, corn, okra, greens and cakes. For the past two years she has been in a retirement home, but she still can "do for herself."

As a child in Angier, Nichols says her mother helped with farming duties and tended her own vegetable garden. Until her mother was in her 90s, she still worked in her garden, and Nichols helped her can and put up vegetables.

Growing up on a farm, Nichols, along with her two sisters and three brothers, would get up early and help prepare breakfast before they went to school. Her mother made sure the three girls learned how to cook. Nichols says that both her parents insisted their children eat healthy food. They were not allowed to eat too many sweets, although her mother baked chocolate and coconut cakes around the holidays. Like most mothers at the time, her mother insisted the children eat whatever was put before them.

By the time Nichols was in high school, she knew the farm and community did not hold much opportunity for her.

"I had a vision that I wanted to do something with my life," she says.

She moved to New York City to live with relatives and attend high school. After high school, she attended a city college. After college, she worked in a hospital and later was employed by an advertising agency. Then she accepted a job with AT&T and kept it until retiring in 1998, when she moved to Fayetteville to live near her mother.

Kathleen is a lifetime learner. As soon as she arrived in Fayetteville, she started looking around for something that would be a learning experience. She found classes in quilt-making, and today she is an active member of the Cape Fear Quilting Guild and prepares potluck dinners for its Sunday-afternoon quilting sessions. Some of her specialties are eggplant Parmesan, lasagna and spaghetti, Italian dishes she learned how to make in New York.

She likes to cook Southern foods such as stuffed cabbage and fried chicken. Nichols reads cookbooks and recipes, and when she is really stuck with cooking questions, she calls her sister, who is a former chef.

"I try to eat healthy and always keep fruit in my house," she says. "When I feel good, I just cook and take food to my family or ask people to come and eat with me."

– Melissa Clement

Bean Salad

- 1 can French-style string beans
- 1 can small, young, tender garden peas
- 1 can white shoepeg corn
- 4 stalks celery, chopped
- 1 medium onion, chopped
- 1 small jar pimientos
- ½ bell pepper (chopped)
- 1 cup sugar
- ½ cup salad oil
- ½ cup white vinegar

Drain beans, peas and corn. Mix other ingredients, then pour in other vegetables. Mix well, cover and store in the refrigerator overnight. Will keep for days.

Eight Minute Light-n-Fruity Pie

- 1 (3-ounce) package Jell-O gelatin, any flavor
- ⅔ cup boiling water
- 2 cups ice cubes
- 1 (8-ounce) container Birdseye Cool Whip Non Dairy Whipped Topping, thawed
- 1 cup diced fruit (optional)
- 1 (9-inch) graham-cracker crumb crust

Completely dissolve gelatin in boiling water, stirring about 3 minutes. Add ice cubes and stir constantly until gelatin is thickened, about 2 to 3 minutes. Remove any unmelted ice.

Using wire whip, blend in whipped topping, then whip until smooth. Fold in fruit; chill if necessary until mixture will mound. Spoon into pie crust. Chill 2 hours.

Woman's Interest in Cooking, Baking Started Early

April 27, 2005

Shay Owen

Shay Owen comes from a family of good cooks. There is a saying in the Bill Booth household that Betty, Shay's mother, could cook an old shoe and make it taste good. Shay Booth Owen takes after her mother, and so does Shay's brother, Johnny Booth.

"My brother and I used to sit in the kitchen on stools and just watch my mother cook and learn from watching. She would let us help her. The first things I made were biscuits and cookies."

Today Shay works at Cape Fear Valley Health System in Information Services and Technology. She is also working toward a master's degree. She still takes time to cook for her husband, Tim Owen, her nieces and nephews and her godchildren.

"I always enjoy cooking. I like trying new recipes and like to read recipe books to find out what my family likes, but I don't like complicated recipes. I like something easy that tastes good."

She says she combs through cookbooks and watches cooking shows on television to get ideas.

"The presentation of food, how you put it on the plate is important. If I was serving a tart, I would heat it first and then put a dollop of whipped cream on it and a mint leaf. You want it to look as good as it tastes."

Recently when Shay had surgery on her jaw, she couldn't eat anything but grits. Tim cooked the grits and took them upstairs to her, but she had to keep sending him downstairs to get salt, then for pepper and then again for butter.

"Later when I had surgery again, he had learned his lesson and brought it all up at one time. He was wonderful. The moral of that story is that he had learned that cooking is a little more complicated than he thought."

She shares her recipe for Shay's chicken, which is her husband's favorite. It was given to her by Tim's mother, Mary Owen. Sandy Reynolds gave her the recipe for yummy caramel tarts. Sandy is the wife of Shay's boss, Randy Reynolds.

The third recipe is what she calls her Chapel Hill cake. She found the recipe in a cookbook, and after she had surgery at Chapel Hill, she was so fond of the doctor and nurses that she made them the cake and took it to them.

Shay enjoys cooking, and her friends and family are glad she does.

– *Melissa Clement*

Chapel Hill Cake

4 eggs
½ cup sugar
¾ cup Mazola oil
½ pint sour cream
1 teaspoon vanilla
1 cup chopped nuts
1 package Duncan Hines butter cake
1 teaspoon cinnamon
5 tablespoons brown sugar

Grease and flour tube pan.

Mix eggs, sugar and oil. Add sour cream, vanilla and nuts. Add cake mix and beat well.

Pour half of batter into tube pan. Sprinkle with cinnamon and brown sugar. Add rest of batter. Bake at 350 degrees for an hour.

Shay's Chicken

4 boneless, skinless chicken breasts
4 strips of bacon
Pam cooking spray
1 2-ounce jar of dried chipped beef
1 10-ounce can cream of mushroom soup
1 cup sour cream

Roll a strip of bacon around each chicken breast and secure. Soak chipped beef in water for 3 minutes and drain. Spray a baking dish with Pam. Layer bottom of dish with dried beef, overlapping. Place bacon-wrapped chicken breasts in the dish. Mix cream of mushroom soup and sour cream. Pour over to cover chicken. Cover dish with tin foil and bake at 350 degrees for 45 minutes. Uncover and bake for 15 more minutes.

Yummy Caramel Tarts

FILLING:
2 sticks margarine, melted
2 cups light-brown sugar
1 cup sugar
2 teaspoons plain flour
2 teaspoons corn meal
1 teaspoon vinegar
1 teaspoon vanilla
4 tablespoons milk
4 eggs

SHELLS:
Individual tart shells, unbaked

Mix all ingredients for the filling. Pour into tart shells. Bake 30 minutes at 350 degrees.

Woman's Club Uses Her Culinary Skills

June 20, 2001

Ginger Powers

When Ginger Powers was a little girl growing up in Haymount, she loved to cook.

Her first attempt at cooking was a success.

The recipe she used is called "One Egg Cup Cake."

She still has her mother's old-fashion original recipe, which calls for fewer eggs than we would use today and less sugar.

Older recipes, she says, seem to call for less sugar.

"I still use that recipe and cook the cupcakes on my birthday."

When her daughter, Bland Sky, was growing up she made the cupcakes for her on her birthday and now she makes them for her daughter, Taylor, who is 5 years old.

Today Powers puts her culinary skills to work at The Woman's Club, a part of Heritage Square on Dick Street.

She is a longtime member and one of a team of members who raise money for the organization by catering wedding receptions, parties, hail-and-farewell functions and bus tours.

They handle four or five a month.

When Ruth Downing, the Heritage Square special events chairman, is contacted about an upcoming event, she contacts five or six members of the committee and plans the menu, giving the clients the price of the dinner per head.

They shop for the food, cook and serve it.

They donate their labor and the pay for the food to the club.

Powers says they try to buy chicken, pork and other meats when it is on special.

One of the most popular recipes is hot chicken salad.

Others include cold chicken salad and pork loin.

Powers sometimes cooks casseroles, four at a time. Members cook the desserts at home.

Desserts are cakes, pies and cookies with ice cream.

The selection is made with consideration to how heavy the meal is.

On holidays the theme is carried out with menus and table decorations.

One of the big events is a bridge party that goes on for two days.

Tour groups from the North seem to love the Southern cooking as well as the Southern accents they hear when they are being served.

They may also be treated to the story of the ghost that treads the house in the stairwell.

– Melissa Clement

Crustless Pecan Pie

20 Ritz crackers

1 cup sugar

2 cups pecans, chopped

3 egg whites, stiffened

¼ teaspoon cream of tartar

1 teaspoon vanilla

Whipped cream

Roll crackers in plastic bag until finely ground. Mix crackers, ½ cup sugar and pecans.

Blend egg whites, cream of tartar, ½ cup sugar and vanilla.

Mix all ingredients together. Put in a pie pan and bake 20 minutes at 350 degrees.

Put a towel over the pie and refrigerate overnight.

Add whipped cream to the top before serving.

Poppy Seed Chicken

1 whole chicken, cooked and deboned

8 ounces sour cream

1 can cream of chicken soup

1 stack of Ritz crackers, crumbled

1 stick of butter, melted

Poppy seeds

Pour soup in 9x12 buttered casserole dish then put the chicken on top of that.

Add the sour cream and crackers in that order.

Dribble butter on top and sprinkle with poppy seeds.

Bake at 375 degrees for 30 minutes.

One-egg Cupcake

1 2-layer size chocolate cake mix

1 8-ounce package cream cheese, softened

⅓ cup sugar

1 egg

1 6-ounce package semi-sweet chocolate bits

Dash of salt

Mix cake according to package.

Fill paper cups ½ to ⅔ full and place in muffin pan.

Mix cream cheese and sugar together. Beat in egg and salt. Stir in chocolate.

Drop one rounded teaspoonful of the cream cheese mixture into each cupcake.

Bake according to the cake mix package directions.

This Cook Makes More Than Desserts

July 11, 2001

Paula Thomson

When Paula Thomson was growing up she liked to bake desserts.

"I never had any desire to cook other things," she says.

She still likes to bake pies and cakes and has a dream of opening a little coffee and dessert shop with her brother one day.

"I really like to read and would like for it to be a place where people could sit and read while they have coffee and dessert," she says.

Now that Thomson has a family of her own, she has branched out from desserts and developed a love of cooking dinners.

Many of the favorite recipes that she and her husband, Jeff, and son Ben like came from Paula's older brother, Mark Crane from Florida.

"Mark is six years older, and when he went away to school he didn't have a meal plan. He cooked in his room and developed an affinity for good food and wine.

"I love it when he comes home and we try interesting things."

Paula has been the financial secretary at Snyder Memorial Baptist Church for three years and says she doesn't have enough time to cook as often as she would like.

"Both of us work all day," she says. "When I take a vacation, I like to stay at home so that I have plenty of time to try new things."

She and Jeff met in a Sunday school class at Snyder and got married six years ago. They are both involved in a drama ministry there and sing in the choir.

"We made an agreement when we got married that if she cooks, I'll clean the kitchen," Jeff says. He is the manager of Bell's Seeds in downtown Fayetteville and likes to grow tomatoes and peppers in the backyard of their home in Cottonade.

Jeff says he was used to good cooking. His mother is Patty Thomson, who retired this year from running her home-based Patty Cakes business for many years.

"Mama is a good cook and cooks just about anything," he says.

Jeff and Paula both love spicy foods. One of their favorite dishes is a squash bisque that she says her son finds too hot.

"The older he gets, the more spicy stuff he likes." She's hoping he'll try it one day.

– Alice Thrasher

Curried Mixed Vegetables

- 3 cups mixed vegetables
- ⅓ cup Velveta cheese (cubed)
- 2 tablespoons milk
- 1 tablespoon butter
- ¼ teaspoon curry powder

Cook vegetables approximately 7 to 10 minutes. Drain. Mix together cheese, milk and butter. Heat and stir until cheese is melted. Season with curry powder, salt and pepper. Combine with vegetables and heat.

Marinade for Pork Tenderloin

¾ cup lemon juice

½ cup soy sauce

6 tablespoons honey

2 shallots, coarsely chopped

2 large cloves garlic, halved

2 bay leaves, crumbled

2 teaspoons salt

2 teaspoons pepper

1 teaspoon mustard powder

½ teaspoon ginger

4 pork tenderloins, approximately 12 ounces each.

Puree first ten ingredients in blender.

Pour marinade over pork in zip-lock bag and marinate overnight in the refrigerator.

Pour off marinade into a small saucepan.

Grill the pork — char the outside first — then turn down the heat to cook.

Cook until 150 to 160 degrees internal temperature; about 20 to 25 minutes.

Before roast is done, start boiling down the marinade.

Cook it down until it's a nice consistency and serve with sliced tenderloin.

Squash Bisque

2 small acorn squash

½ cup onion, minced

1 red bell pepper, seeded and finely diced

¼ cup dry white wine

1 cup orange juice

½ teaspoon ground coriander

1 teaspoon fresh ginger, grated

¼ teaspoon cayenne pepper

¼ cup nonfat plain yogurt

1 teaspoon oil

2 cloves garlic, minced

2½ cups chicken stock

½ teaspoon ground cumin

¼ teaspoon dry mustard

½ teaspoon salt

¼ teaspoon white pepper

Preheat oven to 350 degrees.

Split squash in half lengthwise, leaving in the seeds (to help the squash steam more quickly due to moisture content).

Line a baking sheet with aluminum foil and spray the foil with Pam.

Place the squash flesh side down onto the foil and bake until soft, about 40 minutes.

Scoop out squash seeds and discard.

Scoop flesh from shells and mash well; set aside and discard shells.

In a large stock pot heat oil. Add onion and sauté over medium heat until onion is soft.

Add garlic, bell pepper and wine and cook for five minutes. Add reserved squash, stock, juice, cumin, coriander, ginger, mustard, salt, cayenne and white pepper.

Bring to a boil, lower heat, cover and simmer for 35 minutes.

Puree soup in blender about a third at a time. Add back to pot over simmer.

Temper the yogurt with some of the soup and then blend into the pot. Taste for seasoning and serve hot.

Stew Made of Venison or Beef a Crowd-pleaser

March 6, 2002

Susie McFadyen

Susie McFadyen and her husband, Bill, like to entertain at their home in Eastover.

Whether it's music-company executives from Dallas, relatives or friends, Susie handles it all in stride, Bill says. "We tend to be more casual," Susie says.

Bill helps out by providing venison and other wild game. He does some cooking, too.

"He makes a great teriyaki sauce he learned to make when he was living in Hawaii, and he makes an excellent venison jerky," Susie says.

"We eat what he kills."

Venison and other meat is stored in a freezer for year-round meals.

One of the family's favorites is Eegee's Stew, a slow-cooking dish made from venison or beef tips. The McFadyen's children, Maggie, 3½, and Jamie, 2, like it because they like rice, Susie says.

"It's named for my best friend, Eegee Williams, who moved to Alabama," she says.

"It's our standard, when I don't know what else to cook. I keep the ingredients on hand all the time."

Susie and Bill were married seven years ago. He is from Fayetteville and works in the music store his family owned for many years. She grew up in Greenville and learned from her mother, Pauline Hudson, how to grow vegetables and can and freeze them.

She cans tomatoes and field peas and makes homemade preserves from strawberries and blackberries growing in her garden. "We will have blueberries this year to make jelly," she says.

When it's time to make one of her favorite salads, Susie only has to walk out the door of the screen porch to gather the lettuce. She grows various kinds of lettuces and salad greens year-round. "There's usually some onions in the dirt somewhere," she says. "In the summer I have a big summer garden."

"With my salads I try to include some kind of toasted nuts — pine nuts, walnuts or whatever I have on hand," she says. "I just barely toast them in butter. I add a little feta cheese or mozzarella and either go with tomatoes or fresh fruit."

She says her favorite salad is made with half Romaine and half mescaline mix. "We grow our own mescaline, but it is a lot spicier than the kind in the grocery store," she says.

Susie says another secret to her salads is the dressing she keeps on hand. She mixes a package of Good Seasoning Italian dressing with balsamic vinegar and uses part olive oil and part vegetable oil.

Another favorite recipe she likes to make for her family or for entertaining guests is guacamole, a dip made from ripe avocados.

"I make it any time I can find avocados that look pretty and are a good price," she says.

Susie finds time to serve on the board of directors for First School preschool at First Presbyterian Church in Fayetteville and helps teach a religion school class there.

"I love being at home and that I can include my children in working in the garden and other things."

– Alice Thrasher

Eegee's Stew (aka No-Peek-Tips)

2 pounds beef tips or venison

1 can cream of mushroom soup

1 package onion soup mix

1 cup ginger ale

1 can sliced mushrooms

Combine all ingredients in a Dutch oven; stir. Tightly cover top of pot with foil.

Place in 300-degree oven for 3 hours. There is no need to stir or peek. Serve over rice or egg noodles.

Guacamole

2 ripe avocados

4 small Roma tomatoes, chopped

2 tablespoons fresh cilantro, chopped

1 chopped green onion

3 to 4 tablespoons mayonnaise

1 tablespoon key lime juice

2 tablespoons chopped jalapenos

¼ teaspoon cayenne pepper

½ teaspoon salt

Scoop avocado out of rinds with a spoon; mash coarsely with fork.

Add other ingredients and stir just until well mixed.

Let sit a couple of hours in the refrigerator to blend flavors before serving.

Serve with your favorite tortilla chips.

Salad Dressing

1 package Good Seasonings Italian salad dressing mix

Olive oil

Balsamic vinegar

Vegetable oil

Prepare dressing as directed except use balsamic vinegar instead of regular and use half olive oil and half vegetable oil (Olive oil solidifies when cold. The vegetable oil keeps it liquid.)

Retired Chemist Thinks, Bakes Healthy

MARCH 13, 2002

Barbara Olcott

Barbara Olcott and her husband, Tom, are committed to a healthy lifestyle. They are both retired chemists and know what they eat. They are on a high-protein, low-carbohydrate diet.

"The older you get the more sensitive you get to sugar and white flour," she says. "You have to know your own body and have to do what works for you. I was gaining weight because I was eating all the wrong foods for me, although people are all different in their needs. I am sensitive to glucose and have to have a diet real low in starches and sugars."

They concentrate their diets on lean meat, fish, vegetables, nuts and whole grains.

Barbara says she did without bread for three years until she found a store in Hope Mills that sold bread mixes containing whole wheat, soy, black walnuts and graham flour.

Using a bread machine she cooks fresh bread and also bakes bread in the oven. She also makes bread from scratch. When oiling pans for cooking she uses animal fats such as lard, which she thinks is less harmful than butter or margarine. She also uses Teflon-coated pans to cook in and says that any residue that gets in the body from Teflon does not have any effect upon it.

Barbara finds fresh, hearty breads made with whole grains or the pulp of pumpkin go great with hot soups and stews.

She says whole grains are complex carbohydrates and take longer to digest and therefore do not leave you feeling hungry between meals.

Cranberry-Orange Bread

- 2 cups whole wheat flour
- 2 cups unbleached flour
- 1 tablespoon baking powder
- 1 teaspoon baking soda
- 1 teaspoon salt
- ½ teaspoon cinnamon
- ¼ teaspoon nutmeg
- 1 cup packed, brown sugar or Sweet'n Low brown sugar equivalence
- 1 cup Splenda (Sucralose) or white sugar
- ½ cup cold butter or lard
- 1 tablespoon grated orange rind
- 2 large eggs
- 1½ cups orange juice
- 2 cups chopped cranberries
- 1 cup chopped pecans
- ⅔ cup golden raisins

Grease and flour two 9-inch loaf pans. Stir dry ingredients together until well blended. Cut in shortening with knives or pastry blender.

Grate orange on fine side of grater and mix with eggs and orange juice.

Mix liquid into dry ingredients and stir just until flour is wet.

Fold in cranberries, nuts and raisins.

Pour into pans. Allow to rest for 45 minutes in order for leavening process to begin.

Preheat oven to 350 degrees. Bake 55 to 60 minutes until done, or toothpick comes clean when inserted in center of loaf. If using dark pans, cook for less time before testing.

This recipe can be made into 3 medium loaves, 4 small loaves or 6 tiny loaves. Just cook for shorter time. Great for gift giving.

She avoids foods that have a high concentration of sugar, starches, harmful fats and refined products that have nutrients taken out of them.

She says the nation is suffering from obesity, heart diseases and other problems such as diabetes as a result of a steady diet of fast food and an overabundance of sugars and refined carbohydrates. Before birth and as children they are getting too many sugary foods, she says.

The Olcotts not only watch their diet but work out regularly at a spa, swim at least three times a week and compete in senior games.

"It's helps control weight and cholesterol, its anti-aging and heart healthy," she says. "I don't want to die in a wheelchair. I want to keel over when I'm exercising," she says with a laugh.

– Melissa Clement

Cottage Cheese Dill Bread

- 2½ cups whole wheat pastry flour, graham flour or whole wheat flour
- 2 teaspoons baking powder
- ½ teaspoon baking soda
- ¾ teaspoon salt
- 2 heaping tablespoons dried dill weed
- ½ cup olive oil
- ¼ cup honey
- ¾ cup whole milk
- 1 large egg, well beaten
- 1 cup cottage cheese

This batter is very thick, so you may want to make only one batch at a time.

Grease and flour a 9- inch loaf pan with lard and whole wheat flour. If pan is nonstick, just grease.

In a large bowl mix flour, baking powder, soda, salt and dill.

In a saucepan, warm honey and oil, stir until just blended. Remove from heat and stir in milk, egg and cottage cheese. Pour gradually into flour mixture. Beat until just combined.

Scrape into loaf pan. Thump to remove air bubbles. Smooth top with spatula. Allow to rest for 45 minutes for leavening process to begin.

Preheat oven to 375 degrees. Bake for 45 to 50 minutes, until toothpick inserted in center comes out clean. If pans are dark, lessen cooking time.

Graham-Soy Black Walnut Bread

- 2 cups graham flour or whole wheat flour
- ½ teaspoon salt
- 1 cup raisins
- ¾ cup black walnut pieces
- 1 cup soy flour
- ¾ cup molasses
- ½ tablespoon olive oil
- 2 cups whole milk
- 2 teaspoons baking soda
- 1 tablespoon vinegar

Grease two medium loaf pans with lard.

Mix the baking soda and vinegar separately into the milk.

Combine dry ingredients including the raisins and the nuts. Add molasses and oil.

Add the milk mixture to the dry ingredients. Stir until well blended.

Pour into pans. Allow batter to rest for about 45 minutes in order that the leavening action begins.

Preheat oven to 350 degrees. Bake until toothpick comes clean from center to loaf.

If the pans are dark, lower oven to 325 degrees and bake for 40 minutes.

Teen Likes to Improve on Recipes

October 12, 2005

Elyse Russing

Seventeen-year-old Elyse Russing likes to eat at home. Meals are always great there, she said.

"In my home, someone is always cooking something, and so we normally eat there. Every night we sit down at the table and talk to each other without television. My mother loves to bake desserts; my stepdad likes to barbecue outside. I like to cook main dishes. Only my brother doesn't cook."

Elyse was young when she cooked her first dish, scrambled eggs. She remembers how much she liked watching Martha Stewart's cooking shows with her mother on Saturday mornings, and she recalls a trip to Savannah with her family.

"We ate in really nice, expensive restaurants, and I realized how much I really enjoyed eating and making food. I realized I would like to do that for a living. My favorite thing is taking a recipe and trying to make it different and better. I like to challenge myself by cooking gourmet dishes," she said.

She likes to watch the Food Network. Her favorite chefs on television are Bobby Flay and Paula Dean. While in Savannah, she ate at Dean's restaurant, "The Lady and Sons."

Another of her favorites is Alton Brown's show, "Good Eats."

"He makes you understand everything. He goes into details and explains why things are like they are.

"My mother has been a big influence on me. I learned a lot from her. Everything she cooks is from scratch."

A family friend, Colleen Wellons, has also helped Elyse hone her cooking skills. Her father, Loyd Russing, is also a good cook. His mother taught him to cook because she believes men should be able to cook as well as women.

One of the dishes Elyse shares with us is pepper-crusted filet mignon with balsamic fig reduction, developed when the family's fig tree had an over-abundance of figs. For this dish she uses thick steaks, balsamic vinegar, honey, sugar, salt and pepper, and about eight figs.

She also offers her recipe for zucchini fritters with her own brand of dipping sauce. Another recipe is orange-cranberry glazed scones, made using orange-flavored cranberries and an orange glaze.

She attends the Fayetteville Academy and would like to go to North Carolina State University or the College of Charleston and someday own her own restaurant.

– Melissa Clement

Zucchini Fritters with Dipping Sauce

FRITTERS:

3½ cups zucchini, coarsely grated

¾ cup Parmesan cheese, freshly grated

2 eggs, beaten

4 tablespoons unbleached, all-purpose flour

Salt and freshly ground black pepper

Vegetable oil for frying

DIPPING SAUCE:

¼ cup sour cream

½ cup smooth salsa

Cilantro to taste (optional)

Squeeze the zucchini in a dish towel to remove any water. Then combine the zucchini with Parmesan cheese, eggs, flour, salt and pepper.

Heat enough oil to cover the base of a large frying pan. Add 2 tablespoons of the mixture for each fritter, and cook only 3 at a time.

Cook the fritters for 2 to 3 minutes per side until golden. Drain on paper towels.

Set your oven to warm, and put the fritters that are already done on a sheet pan in the oven to keep warm.

For the dipping sauce, place the sour cream and salsa into a mixing bowl. Stir until smooth.

Chop a few leaves of cilantro and add to the mixture. This step is optional and can be left out if you do not like cilantro.

Serve the fritters warm with a spoonful of dipping sauce.

Pepper-crusted Filet Mignon with Balsamic Fig Reduction

6 (5- to 6-ounce) filet mignon steaks, each about 1 inch thick

1½ cups balsamic vinegar

3 tablespoons honey

1 tablespoon sugar

8 figs cut in half

Freshly grated nutmeg

Salt and freshly ground black pepper

Olive oil

Boil balsamic vinegar, sugar and honey in a heavy, small saucepan over medium heat, stirring occasionally, for about 18 minutes, until the liquid is reduced to a cup. If the sauce gets too thick, just thin it out with a little more balsamic vinegar.

Once the mixture has thickened, fold in the figs, being careful not to break them down.

At the very end, add grated nutmeg, salt and freshly ground black pepper.

Meanwhile, rub olive oil on one side of each steak. Cover the same side with freshly ground black pepper, pressing into each steak to form a crust. Sear steaks, pepper side down, on medium-high heat in an oiled skillet. Cook steaks to desired doneness, about 3 minutes per side for medium-rare.

Transfer the steaks to a plate and top with the balsamic-vinegar-and-fig reduction.

Orange-Cranberry Glazed Scones

SCONES:

2 cups unbleached flour, plus more for rolling the cranberries

1 tablespoon baking powder

1 teaspoon salt

⅓ cup sugar

¼ cup unsalted butter, chilled and cut in chunks

¾ cup buttermilk

1 egg

1 cup dried orange-flavored cranberries

ORANGE GLAZE:

2 tablespoons unsalted butter

2 cups powdered sugar, sifted

2 oranges, juiced and zested

Preheat oven to 400 degrees.

In a large bowl, sift together the flour, baking powder, salt and sugar. Mix thoroughly.

Cut in the chilled butter with a fork or a pastry blender. The butter pieces should be coated with flour and resemble crumbs.

In another bowl, mix together the buttermilk and egg and then add them to the dry ingredients. Mix together, but be sure not to overwork the dough.

Roll the dried cranberries in flour to coat. Fold the cranberries into the batter.

Drop a large tablespoon of the batter onto an ungreased cookie sheet. Bake for 15 to 20 minutes or until golden brown. Cool before applying the glaze.

For the glaze, combine the butter, sugar, orange zest and juice over a double boiler.

Once the butter and sugar have melted and the mixture has thickened, remove from the heat.

Drizzle or brush on top of the scones and let them dry.

Cooking Viewed as Skill to Share

April 19, 2006

Vimala Rajendran

Vimala Rajendran, a native of India, visited Fayetteville during the Peace March in Rowan Park on March 18. With a contingent from Chapel Hill, she cooked Indian food for the crowd and talked about her love of cooking her native cuisine for others.

She said she had been intrigued by food preparation since she was a young child making chappaties, Indian whole-wheat flat bread, when she was six years old.

When Rajendran's neighbors in Chapel Hill got a whiff of her food and noticed that her children were rarely sick, they became interested in her cooking. They began calling on her to cook for special occasions.

"I decided to cook for any and all who would want to experience the goodness," she said. "While I don't have a commercial kitchen of my own, I cook up my wandering feasts on location, wherever I am called."

The last 10 years have been busy for Rajendran. She and her children were homeless for a while, but with the help of her community, she turned her life around.

"I joined a church, taught Sunday school, attended conferences for spiritual growth and empowerment and saw my inner strength gradually blossom. Ultimately I was able to give back to a community that had supported me through difficult situations."

Rajendran is one of the founders of Chapel Hill's community-access television station, The Peoples Channel. As a television producer she has created documentaries and serves on multiple Orange County boards and task forces.

"Using my cooking skills to fund-raise for non-profit organizations and valuable community causes became a way of life," she said. "I realized that if I made food service my way of life, my family would never go hungry. In fact, my home has a reputation for feeding anyone who walks in the door."

She shares her recipes for Goan pork vindaloo, but said she uses chicken or tofu instead of pork. Goa is a tiny state on the west coast of India. She says it is famous for its distinctive cuisine, the pork vindaloo being the most well-known. This was served in Fayetteville made with hormone-free chicken or with tofu.

Another of her recipes is jeera rice, which is cumin-flavored buttered rice. The rice was introduced into India by the Moguls and is popular because it is versatile and can be served with almost any curry. It can be cooked with a variety of spices, herbs, vegetables, meats, seafood and poultry.

Her basmati rice is authentic Indian long-grain white rice, which has a nutty flavor and is popular in India. A variety of rice dishes are made with basmati, including gourmet dishes, she said. Another of her recipes is makhani dal. Dal refers to the dry split peas or the cooked soup often served at the functions for which she cooks.

– Melissa Clement

Goan Pork Vindaloo Hot And Sour Pork

- 5 tablespoons oil
- 8 ounces cider vinegar
- 3 pounds lean pork (may substitute cubes of boneless chicken or tofu)

MARINADE

- 1 tablespoon cumin seeds
- ½ teaspoon whole cloves
- ½ teaspoon whole black peppercorns
- 1 teaspoon green cardamom pods
- 2 teaspoons black mustard seeds
- 1 teaspoon turmeric
- 1 teaspoon ground cayenne or bright red paprika
- 1 teaspoon ground cinnamon
- 1 onion, chopped
- 8 cloves garlic chopped or 4 teaspoons garlic paste
- 1-inch piece of ginger chopped or 2 teaspoons ginger paste
- 6 dried red chilies (seeds removed to reduce heat)
- 1 tablespoon tomato paste

Dry roast the cumin seeds, cloves, cider vinegar and black peppercorns in a pan until lightly toasted.

Grind all the marinade ingredients together in a blender, using cider vinegar to liquefy the mixture, until it reaches a thick-paste consistency.

Pour spice paste over the pork and rub the mixture well into the meat. Cover and keep in the refrigerator overnight.

Heat the oil and fry the meat over a medium-high heat until brown.

Add vinegar and cook for 5 minutes on high. Reduce heat and simmer gently for 45 minutes to 1 hour, until the meat is tender. Serve hot with jeera rice.

Jeera Rice

- 2 cups basmati rice
- 3 tablespoons ghee or oil
- 1½ teaspoons cumin seeds
- 2 bay leaves
- 1½ teaspoons salt
- 3 cups hot water
- 2 tablespoons butter (optional)

Wash the rice in lukewarm water.

Drain completely and let it sit.

Heat ghee or oil on medium heat, add bay leaves and cumin seeds and saute for a minute.

Add rice and saute until rice starts to clump together.

Add hot water and salt. Boil until almost all water has evaporated.

Cover and reduce heat to low and cook for another 10 minutes.

The rice should be fluffy.

Serve hot with any curry. Adding a dollop of butter on the hot rice will add flavor, if desired.

Makhani Dal

- 1 cup dal (any split peas or lentils)
- 1 tablespoon cumin powder
- ½ teaspoon turmeric
- 1 teaspoon ground cayenne or paprika
- 6 cups water
- Salt to taste
- 6 to 7 tablespoons butter
- 1 onion, finely chopped
- 1 tomato, chopped into small cubes
- 1 teaspoon ginger, grated
- 2 tablespoons butter
- ½ teaspoon ground cayenne or paprika
- 2 tablespoons heavy cream plus more to garnish

Wash the dal.

Soak for 20 minutes.

Cook dal along with the spices–cumin powder, turmeric, ground cayenne or paprika–and salt in 6 cups of water.

In a pan, melt butter on medium heat.

Add the chopped onion and fry until golden brown.

Add ginger, chopped tomato and 2 tablespoons heavy cream.

Cook for 5 minutes.

Add the cooked dal and mix thoroughly.

Let simmer for a few minutes.

Transfer the dal into a serving container.

Heat 2 tablespoons of butter in a separate pan. When the foam settles, add cayenne or paprika and mix quickly.

Pour over the dal.

Pour heavy cream that you have set aside for garnishing over the dal.

Wagner Hails From a Long Line of Entertainers

January 26, 2005

Jean Wagner

Jean Wagner grew up in Cambridge, England. She says her mother and grandmother were fabulous cooks. Her grandmother learned the art at the school of Cordon Blue and owned a teahouse in Madingley, outside Cambridge. She served afternoon teas with scones, cakes, Victoria Sponge Cake and her most popular dish, Pavlova cake.

Jean smiles when she thinks of the special things her mother and grandmother made such as hot cross buns for Easter, Christmas cakes and chocolate éclairs. Her mother's brandy snaps were rolled up and stuffed full of fresh cream.

"With all those wonderful foods, it's a wonder we weren't as big as the house. In the mornings we had partridge, egg, sausage, fried bread, bacon and fried tomatoes."

Coconut ice was another of her mother's specialties. It was basically sugar made in a tin with white and pink food coloring, sort of a coconut fudge, she says.

She stayed at home, gardened and cooked for her four children.

Her grandparents were known for their lavish parties and were popular in social circles. Her grandfather owned several businesses including a brewery and a pub. Wagner once entertained the idea of starting her own tea room.

The garden her father worked provided the family with vegetables almost year-round including runner beans and a patch of rhubarb. There was also a backyard orchard where they grew apricots and apples.

Her mother had a flower garden and supplied the family with a feast for the eyes with her huge chrysanthemum collections.

Pavlova Cake

- 3 egg whites
- 6 ounces granulated sugar
- ½ teaspoon vanilla
- ½ teaspoon vinegar
- 2 level teaspoons cornstarch
- ½ pint double cream, whipped
- 1 16-ounce can pineapple, peaches or apricots
- Cherries and angelica to decorate

Set oven to 300 degrees.

Draw an 8-inch circle on nonstick paper and place it on a baking sheet.

Beat egg whites until very stiff, then beat in the sugar, half at a time. Beat in the vanilla, vinegar and cornstarch.

Spread the meringue mixture over the circle, piling it up around the edges to form a wall with a sunken middle.

Bake in the center of the oven for about an hour, until firm. Leave to cool. Then carefully remove paper.

Place on a flat plate, pile the cream into the center, arrange the drained fruit on top, and decorate with cherries and angelica.

When the family picnicked, it was on the beautifully kept lawn. They spread a blanket in the back patio near what she calls "a lovely rock garden."

One of her favorite dishes is Bubble and Squeak, which she calls "a poor man's meal." She makes it by cooking mashed potatoes in a frying pan with greens and adding Brussel sprouts.

On Sundays the family dinner was chicken with white sauce, a kind of stuffing, she says, but more liquid than our stuffing. It is made with bread, onion and milk.

Jean, who is self employed, has followed her family's example. Last fall she entertained friends on a Sunday with a costume party and plenty of good food.

"I don't have much time but I love to have people over and see them having a good time," she says.

– Melissa Clement

Sherry Trifle

- Ladyfingers (can use Sara Lee poundcake)
- Raspberry jam
- Raspberry Jell-O
- Sherry (Harvey's Bristol Cream is good)
- 1 can mixed fruit, drained (save juice)
- Package of Bird's custard
- Whipped cream or Cool Whip
- Slivered almonds

Note: There is no exact measurement for the ingredients in this recipe because it depends on the size of the bowl.

Make the Jell-O according to the package instructions, using the juice from the canned fruit instead of water. Allow the Jell-O to cool, but don't let it set.

Make the custard according to the instructions and allow to cool.

In a deep glass bowl, place layers as follows:

Ladyfingers or pound cake.

Sherry, drizzled over cake.

Jam, spread on cake or ladyfingers.

Fruit.

Repeat the layers until all the cake is used. Pour the cooled Jell-O over all; it should fill to the top layer. Place in refrigerator and allow Jell-O to set.

When set, pour custard on top. (By this time, you should have reached the top of the bowl.) Allow to cool thoroughly.

Just before serving, spread whipped cream or Cool Whip on top. Sprinkle with slivered almonds and place a cherry in the middle (from the can of fruit).

If you were in England, you would then serve and pour double cream over your serving.

You can use any canned fruit you want; another way you can make this is with Cointreau (instead of sherry) and mandarin oranges (instead of mixed fruit). Use your imagination!

Yorkshire Pudding

6 ounces plain flour
3 eggs
Pinch of salt
1 pint of milk
Lard

Optional ingredients:
1 pound ground round
English sausages
1 to 2 pounds apples
1 large can apricots

Basic batter: Sift the flour into a bowl with the salt.

Add the eggs and mix.

Gradually add the milk until smooth.

The batter is best made the night before and allowed to sit overnight in the refrigerator.

When you are ready to bake the pudding, place a good dollop of lard in a 9-by-14-inch baking dish, and allow it to melt in a 425-degree oven.

When it is melted, pour in the batter all at once and bake for about 40 minutes.

This will vary according to your oven.

Remove from the oven and cut into about 8 pieces and serve. This is good with gravy poured over it.

Variations:

As another dish, you can add 1 pound of ground round to the batter before pouring it into the pan, or lay some good English sausages in the bottom of the pan before pouring in the batter.

Yorkshire pudding can be served cold, spread with butter and sprinkled with a little sugar.

One can also make popovers in a muffin pan (individual Yorkshire puddings); just put a little dollop of lard in each cup.

As a dessert (use 4 ounces butter instead of lard), peel, core, and slice 1 to 2 pounds (according to taste) of cooking apples and lay in the bottom of the pan, then add batter and bake. You could also use a large can of drained apricots instead of the apples.

Gingerbread Houses a Labor of Love for White

December 29, 2004

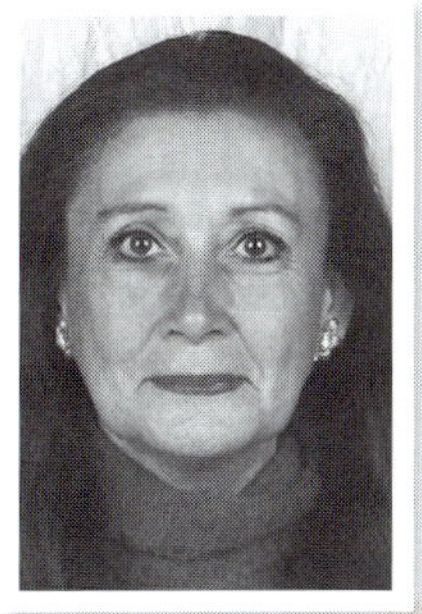
Anita White

Anita White's gingerbread houses are so elaborate you'd think she would need a building permit. They are usually replicas of buildings or houses, not only the exterior but a modified interior including fireplaces, tables, dinnerware, carpets, chandeliers and even the family dog made of marzipan.

When Larry Norris, president of Fayetteville Technical Community College, wanted to surprise his wife, Judy, with a replica of the historic house they have restored, he asked White to make a gingerbread house.

She called it a labor of love after working on it for about six hours a day for two weeks. When she tried to hurry it up, the roof fell in because the egg and sugar mixture used for icing had not hardened enough. Humidity also played a part in the hardening process and she had to keep her kitchen reasonably dry.

The price of the construction materials including candy for the trimmings, tiny toys around the Christmas tree and the marzipan used to create the house was around $100.

The house is wired for electricity with tiny candles at each window, a lighted fireplace, Christmas tree lights, a musical doorbell and a pond outside with running water.

White has been making gingerbread houses since she was a child, but honed her skills and began to teach classes in the art when she was stationed in the Air Force in Germany in the '80s.

While there she replicated the Zweibrucken Palace. The Lord Mayor rewarded her with media coverage and made her an honorary citizen. When it went off display it was sent to an orphanage for the children to enjoy. For the July 4 celebration in Germany she made a replica of Independence Hall with the Liberty Bell.

When creating her first wired gingerbread house she used a lightbulb so powerful that it caught the sugar in the fireplace on fire and caused smoke to come out of the chimney. Her first thought was to quickly make a gingerbread firetruck to put it out. Now she uses tiny Christmas tree lights that don't ignite the interior. Another tip she learned from experience is to measure the kitchen door before you cut the styrofoam base it will sit on.

White uses a Dremel rotary tool that she keeps just for cooking. It has different carving tips for details such as scoring bricks. The bricks on the Norris house were made to look antique by layering different colored icing and letting both colors show through.

She used upside-down ice cream cones for trees, which were coated with green icing and sprinkles. A clear gelatin formed window panes and using a pastry bag with a leaf tip, she made wreaths that were decorated with red candy.

– Melissa Clement

Basic Gingerbread

6 cups all-purpose flour
1 cup sugar
⅔ cup shortening
1 tablespoon ground cinnamon
1 tablespoon ground ginger
2 teaspoons double-acting baking powder
¼ teaspoon salt
1 teaspoon baking soda
1 teaspoon vanilla extract
1 8-ounce container sour cream
2 eggs
6 cups flour

To prepare dough:

Into large bowl measure 3 cups flour and ingredients. With mixer at low speed, beat until well mixed. By hand knead in remaining 2 cups flour to make dough soft. Wrap dough in plastic wrap and refrigerate 2 hours or until dough is not sticky and is of easy kneading consistency.

To roll dough:

Keep refrigerated until ready to use. Working with half a batch at a time on lightly floured work surface with lightly floured hands, knead dough until smooth. Then on a greased and floured 17 inch by 14 inch cookie sheet, with lightly floured rolling pin, roll dough about ¼-inch thick.

To cut and bake dough:

Cut patterns from lightweight cardboard. Using a knife or spatula cut as many pieces as you can from rolled dough, leaving small space between them. Remove scraps and reserve for rerolling. Preheat oven to 350 degrees and bake 20 to 25 minutes or until golden brown and very firm when lightly touched with finger. Remove cookie sheet from oven and cool on wire rack for 5 minutes. Then carefully remove baked pieces from cookie sheet and place on wire rack to cool.

Ornamental Icing

- 1 16-oz package confectioner's sugar
- ½ teaspoon cream of tartar
- 3 egg whites at room temperature
- ½ teaspoon vanilla extract

Combine all ingredients in medium bowl. With mixer blend until smooth, then beat at high speed until very stiff. Makes 3 cups.

Note: Because the icing dries very quickly, make each batch just before you are ready to use it. If you must store for a few hours or overnight, cover tightly with plastic wrap. When using, keep container covered with a damp cloth or paper towel. Mix in food colors as needed. If icing is too thick when using fine tubes, add a few drops of water. For thicker icing, beat in a little extra confectioner's sugar.

Soft Frosting:

Follow above recipe, but beat at high speed only until light and fluffy of spreading consistency.

Construction Tips:

When assembling pieces of house with icing, work with a decorating bag with medium tube. Pipe a line along edge of one wall; press it against adjoining wall and hold in place for several minutes until icing sets. It may be necessary to shave edges with a sharp knife to assure proper fit. Repeat until all walls are joined. Smooth seams with damp cloth. Fill in any extra spaces with more icing. For extra stability pipe icing along seams inside of house, too. Allow house to stand for at least one hour until icing is completely dried.

If you are not planning to eat the house, you can use toothpick nails for sturdier construction. Cut toothpicks diagonally into ½-inch lengths. With real nail or skewer, pierce edge of two pieces to be joined. Inserts toothpick nail into one hole. After applying icing on edge of one piece, put two pieces together with nails in place. If you have leftover dough, make cookies. Decorate with remaining frosting.

Chef Creates Quick, Special Recipe for Friend

April 5, 2006

Lib Wilson

Lib Wilson loves food. She loves to cook it, and she loves to eat it. But she needed a meal that she could cook for others. She needed something that was quick and easy but still really special, so she asked a friend who is a chef to come up with just such a recipe.

He gave her a recipe for seared red snapper with braised baby leeks. It was great, but she prefers onions rather than leeks. Wilson made a few changes in the recipe and now calls it "divine" and "the answer cake," an old saying used by her mother when she had solved a problem.

"It's so quick and easy and can be prepared ahead of time, all but the fish. That's the beauty of it. When it's time to eat, while the guests are sitting at the table pouring the wine, you are in the kitchen pan-searing the fish. The whipped potatoes with horseradish and onions or leeks are already done, and by the time you get them on the plates with the horseradish, it's time to flip the fish and sear it on the other side. You put the vinaigrette on the fish while it's still hot. Then you sit down at the table like the Queen of Sheba."

She has learned not to use extra-virgin olive oil to cook the fish because it is too strong. She uses canola oil. Although the recipe calls for yellow tomatoes in the vinaigrette, she often uses red tomatoes and doesn't put them in until the very end.

Each year, Wilson and her husband, Bob, visit their daughter Lee Wilson Threlfall in Beaconsfield, which is 30 miles west of London. Last year she wanted to impress her son-in-law, so she used this recipe.

"I did good," she says.

While they were there, they went to London to dine at Fifteen, one of the restaurants owned by "The Naked Chef," Jamie Oliver. It is called Fifteen because he wanted to help disadvantaged youth by training them to be chefs, so he took on 15 of them. The program, Fifteen Foundation, has done well, and the food in the restaurant is cooked by the 15 chefs.

That was when Wilson found out that "naked" refers to stripping down food to its essentials to prove that you don't have to dress up dishes or have fancy gadgets to make good food.

Wilson, a six-year survivor of colon cancer, says vegetables are the mainstay of her everyday meals because of the health benefits of fiber. She likes vegetables oven-roasted and steamed and also eats plenty of fruits. Her taste in food is like her taste in music, she says.

"I love all kinds of foods. I've tried everything from antelope to snake. Some of it I really like. I like all kinds of food except liver and oysters. I like all kinds of music too, except rap and hip-hop."

– Melissa Clement

Seared Red Snapper and Tomato-Lime Vinaigrette

See photo in center of book

- 2 ounces lime juice
- 2 tablespoons sugar
- 1 cup diced yellow tomato
- 6 ounces olive oil
- 8 3-ounce filets of red snapper
- 3 ounces olive oil or canola oil
- Salt and pepper to taste

For vinaigrette, combine lime juice with sugar. Slowly add 6 ounces of oil until emulsified. Add tomato. Salt and pepper to taste. Stir lightly to combine.

Just before dinner, heat skillet to medium-high and add 3 ounces of oil.

Season snapper with salt and pepper. Sear snapper filet skin-side down until golden brown.

Flip and finish cooking flesh-side down.

Braised Baby Leeks and Caramelized Onions

- Baby leeks, 1 per serving
- ½ cup chicken stock
- 2 ounces white wine
- Salt and pepper to taste
- 2 sweet onions, sliced and separated into rings
- 1 tablespoon oil
- 1 tablespoon butter

Leeks: Season stock with salt and pepper. Place leeks in shallow casserole dish. Add wine and stock to casserole dish and cover with lid. Place in 300-degree oven and cook until tender.

Onions: Saute onion in 1 tablespoon oil and 1 tablespoon butter until brown and slightly sticky, about 20 to 25 minutes.

Horseradish Whipped Potatoes

See photo in center of book

- 4 large russet potatoes, peeled
- ½ cup heavy cream
- 4 ounces whole butter
- ¼ cup fresh grated horseradish
- Salt and pepper to taste

Place potatoes in a pot with cold water and cover. Bring to boil. Let simmer until tender.

Heat cream and butter until hot.

Mash potatoes and combine with butter and cream mixture.

Stir in horseradish. Salt and pepper to taste.

Meal assembly: Prepare braised baby leeks or caramelized onions, vinaigrette and potatoes ahead of time.

After searing the snapper, place hot leek or onion on plate and top with ½ cup potatoes.

Place snapper filet on potatoes and drizzle with vinaigrette.

Joy, Ribbons Come From Family Recipes

FEBRUARY 13, 2002

Julie Bromley

Julie Bromley grew up in a household of good cooks who made everything from scratch. No biscuits in a can for grandmother June Boyle. No prepackaged vegetables for Julie's mother, Betsy Bromley.

Good food was important in their household in Wellington, Ohio. Julie learned all the tricks hands-on from her relatives and from her family's favorite cookbook, "The Joy of Cooking."

Julie and her mother even competed at the Lorain County Fair in the cooking division, winning in several categories, including third for a cream cheese pound cake.

Julie's friends say she deserves multiple blue ribbons for the bounty of fabulous desserts and dinners she cooks for them. She is a travel agent at Fort Bragg and between work and her church, the Division Memorial Chapel on Fort Bragg, she has plenty of opportunities to try out new recipes and use the old familiar ones she learned at home.

Baking is her hobby, and for Valentine's Day she makes a red velvet cake from a recipe that has been passed down through her family for generations.

She also celebrates Valentine's Day with heart-shaped tarts filled with cherries.

She likes to make and preserve jams and jellies and decorate cakes. Each holiday she makes decorated cookies using cookie cutters for the occasion, shamrocks for St. Patrick's Day, Santa for Christmas. Other occasions call for umbrella cookies for a rainy day in April and cookies cut like soldiers for military events.

She watches cooking shows, but takes most of her inspiration from reading cookbooks and magazines. She collects antique cookbooks and has a prized 1900 Czechoslovakian cookbook she had translated into English.

Baked desserts are her favorite, but she also cooks meat and potatoes and is known for her spaghetti with meat balls, a recipe she got from her mother and "tweaked it a little," after a lot of "experimentation" with her friends, who serve as her taste testers.

– Melissa Clement

Snickerdoodle Cookies

- 1½ cup butter or margarine
- 1 cup sugar
- 1¼ teaspoon baking soda
- 1 egg
- 1½ teaspoon vanilla
- 1½ cups flour
- 2 tablespoons sugar
- 1 teaspoon cinnamon

Cream in mixer: butter or margarine and baking soda. Beat until combined.

Beat in egg and vanilla.

Stir in flour. You may chill this dough if preferred.

Combine 2 tablespoons sugar and 1 teaspoon of cinnamon.

Take dough and form 1-inch balls and roll in cinnamon/sugar mixture until coated.

Place on baking sheet and bake at 375 degrees for 10 to 11 minutes.

Let cool on wire rack.

Cream Cheese Pound Cake

- 1½ cups butter (no substitute) room temperature
- 6 eggs, room temperature
- 2⅓ cups sugar
- 1 package (8 ounces) cream cheese, room temperature
- 3 cups all-purpose flour
- 1 teaspoon vanilla extract

In a large mixing bowl, cream butter and cream cheese.

Gradually add sugar, beating until light and fluffy, about 5-7 minutes.

Add eggs, one at a time, beating well after each addition.

Gradually add flour. Beat until blended.

Stir in vanilla.

Pour into greased and floured 10-inch tube pan.

Bake at 300 degrees for 1½ hours or until cake tests done.

Cool in pan 15 minutes before removing to a wire rack.

Red Velvet Cake

- ½ cup shortening
- 1½ cups sugar
- 2 eggs
- 2 ounces of red food coloring
- 2½ cups cake flour (sifted)
- 1 teaspoon salt
- 2 teaspoons cocoa
- 1 cup buttermilk
- 1 teaspoon vanilla
- 1 teaspoon baking soda
- 1 teaspoon vinegar

FROSTING:

- 3 tablespoons flour
- 1 cup milk
- 1 cup sugar
- 1 teaspoon vanilla
- 1 cup shortening (white, not butter flavored)

In mixer, cream shortening, sugar and eggs until fluffy.

Add food coloring and mix well.

Sift together cake flour, salt and cocoa.

Mix buttermilk and vanilla. Add alternately with flour mixture into creamed mixture.

Mix together baking soda and vinegar and add to mixture.

Bake at 350 degrees for 30 minutes or until cake tests done.

FROSTING:

Combine flour and milk in small saucepan over medium heat until thickened. Let cool completely. Cream together shortening, sugar and vanilla. Add cooled flour/milk mixture. Blend well.

Cooking Used as Tool for Teaching

July 26, 2006

Lynn Sweeney

Lynn Sweeney adds an unusual twist to preparing food. She uses it as a learning tool.

She calls it "teachable moments." One such opportunity came when her daughter, Kyra, then 9, had a friend sleep over. When they decided to make a packaged cinnamon cake for breakfast, Sweeney asked them to learn to spell "cinnamon" before they could eat it.

"During the measuring and mixing process, those two 9-year-olds tested each other until they both had it down pat," she said.

Kyra, now age 11, and Shannon, who is 8, were making pumpkin muffins when she suggested they double the recipe. Without much help, they learned to figure the measurements by using fractions.

Food budgeting was another lesson. Sweeney asked them to plan, shop and prepare a meal for their family of four for no more than $8. They also had to use the government's pyramid guide for nutrition to ensure they would be getting a balanced diet. That gave them a lesson in reading packages for ingredients and also figuring out the cost per ounce to find the best buys.

Sweeney and her husband, Dan, also let their children order for themselves when they go to restaurants so they will learn to speak loudly and clearly to adults. The girls ask waitresses whether they serve nonfat or whole milk, the soup of the day and what brand of macaroni and cheese they serve.

"By allowing them to order for themselves, we help develop their confidence and poise as well as assure they will eat what is served."

Sweeney also likes to expose her children to a variety of foods from different cultures.

"As we studied ancient civilizations, I prepared falafel and tabouli and then asked them to spell it. As we studied Spain, I prepared gazpacho. Days after we ate gazpacho, my 8-year-old was reading a book where the characters all sat down for a meal of gazpacho. She was thrilled to know what they were talking about. Times like that make cooking for my family a real joy. I love the fact that we sit down together as a family at dinner time seven days a week. It's one of the best parts of my day."

– Melissa Clement

Pumpkin-Raisin Mini-Muffins

1¼ cups flour
⅔ cup sugar
1 tablespoon baking powder
1 teaspoon cinnamon
⅛ teaspoon salt
1 egg
1 egg white
½ cup low-fat milk
¼ cup vegetable oil
½ cup canned pumpkin puree (not pumpkin pie filling)
1½ teaspoon vanilla
½ cup golden raisins

In a large bowl, mix the flour, sugar, baking powder, cinnamon and salt. In a second bowl, mix the egg, egg white, milk, oil, pumpkin puree and vanilla. Add the wet ingredients to the dry ingredients, and stir only until moistened. Do not over mix. Stir in raisins.

Spray mini-muffin tins with vegetable cooking spray. Spoon batter into prepared tins, filling each section full. Bake 12 to 14 minutes, until a toothpick inserted in the center comes out clean. Makes 24 mini-muffins.

Tilapia with Brown Sugar Carrots

4 tilapia fillets
3 tablespoons extra virgin olive oil
1 cup pan searing flour
1 (16-ounce) bag of mini carrots
¼ cup unsalted butter
⅓ cup brown sugar
1 tablespoon honey

Spread flour in a shallow dish and coat both sides of the tilapia. Heat the olive oil in a large frying pan over medium-high heat. Cook tilapia for 3 to 5 minutes on each side, turning only once until the fish is golden brown and cooked throughout.

For the brown-sugar carrots, heat butter in a medium frying pan over medium-high heat. Stir in carrots and saute for 5 minutes. Reduce heat to medium-low and cover. Continue cooking until carrots are fork tender, around 5 to 7 minutes more. Stir in the brown sugar and honey. Serve immediately.

Suggestion: Serve with packaged couscous, a quick and easy to prepare pasta that offers a change from spaghetti.

Cooking Fits Into Active Lifestyle

April 13, 2005

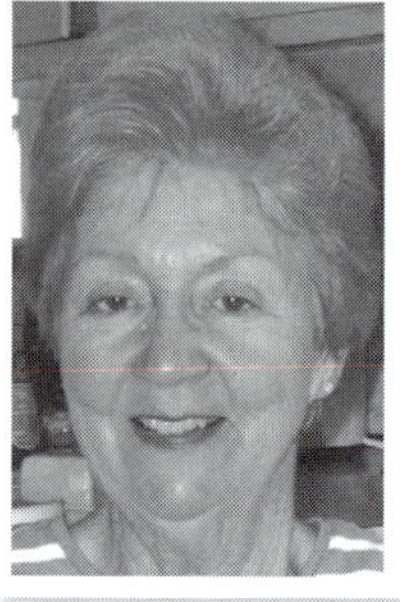

Mary Lou Turlington

Mary Lou Turlington says she likes to stay active. Between golfing, working in her yard, taking care of her family and cooking, she said, "I'm busier than I've ever been."

Turlington said she has done a lot of cooking in the 47 years she and her husband, Mac, have been married. The Turlingtons are longtime Fayetteville residents and have three sons. One, John, is an ordained Baptist minister who lives in Georgia, and their other two sons, Neil and Daley, live in Fayetteville and work in the family auto-supply business.

Turlington said her family is big on meat and potatoes. She is constantly cooking beef, chicken, potatoes and rice, but she said she makes sure they have vegetables in every meal. She also said she likes old-time cooking, including ham hocks, cabbage and turnip greens.

Turlington, who is originally from Dunn, said she likes to experiment with her cooking. She said she loves to bake, especially breads.

Turlington considers herself a small-town girl and has stayed active by playing sports since she was young. She said she was on the basketball team in high school, and she even was on the synchronized swimming team while she was in school at the Woman's College of the University of North Carolina at Greensboro. She is a member of Highland Country Club and plays golf on a regular basis.

Turlington said she has been teaching her 8-year-old granddaughter, Elizabeth, how to cook. She said Elizabeth told her that when she grows up, she's going to teach her children how to cook the way her "Oma" taught her.

Turlington offers up a handful of favorite recipes. One is her chicken pot pie, which she says is a lot of work but is well worth the effort. "It's delicious," she said.

She said one of her husband's all-time favorite recipes is her nut roll.

"I used to take it to Mac when he was playing football at Carolina," she said. "His teammates used to fight over it."

– Paige Maxwell

Chicken Pot Pie

- 2 cups chicken, cooked and cubed
- 2 tablespoons chicken fat
- ½ cup chopped celery
- ½ cup chopped onions
- 3 tablespoons flour
- 1½ to 2 cups chicken stock
- 2 small potatoes, peeled and cubed
- ½ cup sliced carrots
- Pie crust
- 2 cups plain flour
- 10 tablespoons shortening
- ½ teaspoon salt
- 5 tablespoons ice water

Stir chicken into chicken fat and saute gently.

Add in celery and chopped onions and saute.

Sprinkle 3 tablespoons flour over the top of celery and onions. Cook slowly.

Stir in chicken stock gradually.

Add potatoes and carrots and cook until tender.

For pie crust, mix ingredients together well and form into a ball. Roll out flat to desired thickness.

Grease the bottom of a 7½-by-11-inch casserole. Pour the mixture into the casserole and cover with pie crust.

Bake at 350 degrees until crust is brown.

Asparagus Casserole

- 1 large can Leseur garden peas
- 1 large can asparagus tips
- 2 cups sharp or mild cheddar cheese
- 1 can of cream of chicken soup

In a 7-by-9-inch casserole, layer ingredients in the following manner: asparagus, garden peas, 1 cup cheese, cream of chicken soup and 1 cup cheese. Bake at 350 degrees until bubbly.

Nut Roll

- 1 cup raisins
- 1 cup evaporated milk
- 1-pound bag marshmallows
- 1-pound box graham-cracker crumbs
- 2 cups chopped pecans

Set aside ¼ cup of graham-cracker crumbs.

Heat milk in a saucepan.

Add marshmallows and allow to melt.

In a large bowl, combine graham-cracker crumbs, raisins and pecans.

Slightly cool marshmallow mixture and add to bowl.

Mix together with hands.

Form 2 long rolls and roll in remaining ¼ cup graham-cracker crumbs.

Traveling Cook Works Wonders With Beans

DECEMBER 26, 2001

Della Kernodle

When Della Kernodle was living in the country in Guilford County, she says, her family ate a lot of beans. She learned to spice up the beans a bit and came up with a casserole with pinto beans, chili powder, ground beef and tomatoes that became a favorite.

The recipe starts out with dried pinto beans, but Kernodle says the casserole can be made with cooked pinto beans as well.

"Sometimes if you cook a pot of pinto beans and you don't want to eat beans again, it's a good way to use the leftovers," she says.

Kernodle says she doesn't cook as much as she used to when her two sons and her daughter were growing up.

After her husband, J.F. Kernodle, died she moved to Fayetteville in 1989. She lives with son Mark and his wife, Carol, and spends time with her son James in Charlotte and daughter, Laura Hawkes, near Greensboro.

"And I like to travel a lot,' she says.

She went to China last year on a tour with a friend and is going to Russia in June. She likes to try new foods when she travels.

She worked in food services bookkeeping with the Guilford County School System and Guilford College before going to work at the University of North Carolina at Greensboro. She earned an associate's degree in institutional food management and was the assistant food director for UNC-G in the early '60s.

"I gave it up when we moved back to the country and I didn't want to commute," she says.

Another favorite recipe of her family is for a banana-split dessert.

The recipe came from an *Ideals* magazine for children's parties.

"My children love it," she says. "I used to keep it on hand in the freezer. Being in the country, people would drop in and I would serve it with a cup of coffee."

After moving to Fayetteville, Kernodle became active at Gardners United Methodist Church and volunteers at the Stanton Hospitality House for Cape Fear Valley Medical System.

Some of her favorite recipes are included in a church cookbook published by the Gardners United Methodist Women.

She has a big collection of cookbooks.

"I could spend all afternoon reading cookbooks," she says.

– Alice Thrasher

Squash Casserole

2 cups cooked summer squash

1 cup chopped onions

¾ cup margarine

2 eggs

1 cup evaporated milk

2 cups saltine cracker crumbs

1 cup grated cheddar cheese

Salt and pepper to taste

Wash squash, slice them and steam them until tender, but not mushy. Spray baking dish with vegetable spray or spread margarine in bottom. Divide cracker crumbs in half.

Combine 1 cup of crumbs with other ingredients and spread in baking dish. Spread rest of crumbs on top.

Bake at 375 degrees for 45 minutes.

Favorite Casserole

- 1 cup dried pinto beans
- 5 cups tomatoes
- 1 cup chopped green pepper
- 1½ cups chopped onion
- 2 cloves garlic, minced
- 1 to 2 tablespoons butter
- 1 pound ground chuck, cooked and drained
- Chili powder, to taste
- 1 teaspoon pepper
- 1½ teaspoon salt
- ½ cup parsley

Wash beans and then place them in a pot. Cover them with water and soak overnight.

Simmer in same water until beans are soft, ½ to 1 hour.

Add tomatoes and simmer 5 minutes.

Saute green pepper, onion and garlic; add to bean mixture and simmer 5 minutes.

Add butter and simmer another 5 minutes.

Add the cooked and drained ground chuck and simmer 5 minutes more.

Add remaining ingredients. Simmer 1 hour, with the lid off for the last half hour. Skim off the grease.

Serves 4 to 5.

Note: Can also be made with two cups cooked pinto beans (reduce cooking time if you use cooked beans). Della Kernodle uses ¼ cup chili powder, but says that may be too spicy for some people.

Banana Split Dessert

- Graham cracker crumbs
- 3 to 4 bananas
- ½ gallon Neapolitan ice cream
- 1 cup chopped walnuts
- 1 cup chocolate chips
- ½ cup softened butter
- 2 cups powdered sugar
- 1½ cups evaporated milk
- 1 teaspoon vanilla
- 1 pint whipping cream, whipped and chilled

Cover an 11-by-15-inch pan with graham cracker crumbs.

Slice bananas over crumbs.

Slice ice cream ½-inch thick and place slices over bananas.

Sprinkle with nuts.

Place in freezer until firm.

Melt butter and chocolate chips over low heat.

Add sugar and milk; cook until thick, stirring constantly. Cool and pour over the frozen mixture.

Chill whipped cream. Add ¼ cup powdered sugar and the vanilla; pour over all. Freeze.

Serve in slices or squares.

Serves 25.

Still Cooking Favorites for Friends, Family

December 5, 2001

Lucy Lytch

Lucy Lytch, who is 79, remembers her first cooking experience. She was 8 years old and living on her family's farm in Dillon County near Florence, S.C.

She was too small to reach the table and stove so her father made a wooden box for her to stand on. He fastened rubber to the bottom to keep it from sliding.

She and her mother cooked on a wood burning stove. She said it was hard to keep to an even temperature.

Her first lesson was how to make biscuits.

"Later my mother told me they were the worst things they ever tried to eat but at the time she told me they were delicious. But I improved fast."

She improved so fast that she has been known as a terrific cook ever since. For 16 years she prepared breakfasts and dinners for Highland Presbyterian Church, retiring in 1983.

At first she cooked only one dinner a month with the aid of two helpers. Later, the Wednesday night dinners were held weekly. To prepare for Thanksgiving breakfasts at Highland she had to get up at 5 o'clock in the morning.

She also catered church weddings, often staying up until 2 o'clock in the morning preparing the food.

Now she cooks for her four children, six grandchildren and four great-grandchildren when they come to her home for dinner. Her children are especially fond of the dressing she makes at Thanksgiving. For that

Bread Dressing

STEP ONE

4 cups white medium, ground corn meal

½ teaspoon baking soda

1 teaspoon salt

4 eggs

1 cup vegetable oil

Add water as needed until well mixed

STEP TWO: BROTH

2 packs chicken backs and necks

1 large onion

1 pork chop

STEP THREE

6 chopped boiled eggs

3 chopped onions

1 can cream of celery soup

1 cup Pepperidge Farm Herb Dressing Mix

6 crumbled biscuits or toasted loaf bread

Step 1: Pour mixture into well-greased black iron skillet. Cook on medium heat — brown on both sides. Cool.

Step 2: Cover with water and boil until done. Strain broth.

Step 3: Crumble cook bread and add the ingredients above.

Mix well and add broth until mixture is soft and juicy.

Pour into large baking pan.

Bake at 350 degrees until done. Top will be brown. Cooking time about 60 minutes.

she saves and freezes her homemade biscuits. She also makes cornbread in a skillet on top of the stove and cooks a broth from chicken backs and necks and a pork chop.

Her chocolate layer cakes are another favorite of family and friends. She uses sour cream in the batter and cream cheese in the chocolate frosting.

Liver pudding is one of her more unusual dishes and a favorite of her family. It is made with fresh pork liver to which she adds onions and spices and medium ground corn meal.

Lytch says commercial liver pudding has too much cereal in it for her taste. To make good liver pudding the weather must be very cold, she says.

– Melissa Clement

Layer Cake with Chocolate Frosting

CAKE:

- 2 sticks of butter
- 3 cups sugar
- 6 eggs
- 8 ounces sour cream
- 1 teaspoon vanilla
- Sift together:
- 2⅔ cups plain sifted flour
- ¼ teaspoon baking soda
- 1 teaspoon salt

CHOCOLATE FROSTING:

- 1⅔ boxes confectioner's sugar
- 5 rounded tablespoons Hershey's Cocoa
- 1 stick melted butter
- 3 ounces softened cream cheese
- 1 teaspoon vanilla

Beat butter, add sugar slowly, one cup at a time until fluffy.

Add eggs, one at a time — don't overbeat eggs.

Add flour mixture, ½ cup at a time alternating with sour cream. Begin and end with flour.

Add vanilla.

Preheat oven to 350 degrees.

Bake 25 to 30 minutes in 3 round layer cake pans which have been greased and floured.

Chocolate Frosting: Mix until spreadable. Use canned milk if frosting needs to be thinned.

Liver Pudding

- 8 pounds fresh pork liver
- 4 pounds fresh pork fat
- 3 pounds Autry Brothers medium ground, white corn meal
- 3 pounds onions
- 5 ounces rubbed sage
- 4 tablespoons crushed red pepper
- Black pepper and salt to taste

Wash liver and fat. Put into large pot and cover with water and boil until well done. Take liver and fat out of broth. Cool. Grind liver, fat and onions with food grinder.

Preheat oven to 350 degrees.

Put meal into 9-by-13 pan and parch until lightly brown — stir frequently.

Mix meal with liver, fat and onions. Use some of the broth to mix ingredients. Add salt, black pepper, sage and red pepper. Mix thoroughly.

Put into loaf pans within inch of top of pan.

Bake in preheated 350-degree oven until liver pudding is brown on top.

Recipes From Abroad Make Themselves at Home

JULY 10, 2002

Peggy McDuffee

Peggy McDuffee and her husband, David, have been able to sample foods from other countries during their tours abroad with the Army and through their travels.

"I like to eat most everything," Peggy says. "I like gourmet foods and just plain old country cooking — especially in France and Turkey."

They traveled to China last year for a two-week tour and plan to take a cruise around Norway this year.

Some of the dishes that they liked have become favorites, and Peggy likes to serve them to relatives and friends.

David served in the Army in the Signal Corps for 10 years and became a stockbroker after he and Peggy decided to make Fayetteville their home in 1963. He was manager of the former E.F. Hutton office for years and retired from his second career 10 years ago.

During their Army days they lived in Turkey and France. Among the dishes Peggy likes to make is an eggplant chickpea casserole that she says is similar to one that her maid cooked in Turkey in the 1960s.

She grows small Japanese eggplants in her own small vegetable garden plot in Haymount, along with herbs to use in cooking. She grows oregano, thyme, basil and rosemary.

"I cook a good bit," Peggy says. "Three or four times a week. Some meals are as simple as a pork chop on the grill. I enjoy cooking and enjoy having people over to eat with us."

Peggy says she and her husband like lamb and grill lamb chops a lot, also. She has a recipe for a marinade that she uses for lamb or beef.

"We started out in Turkey using it for lamb, but it is just as good on beef," she says.

She says her older daughter, Linda, loves the marinade. Linda was born in France and now lives in Asheville. Daughter Susan was born in Turkey and now lives in Augusta, Ga. Son David Jr. was born in Maryland and lives in Wilmington.

Peggy marinates the meat, then makes shish kebobs on the grill. She alternates pieces of meat with pieces of raw onion, red and green peppers, cherry tomatoes and sometimes preboiled new potatoes.

"We use our gas grill year round," she says. She likes to put olive oil on sliced eggplant, along with salt and pepper and balsamic vinegar, and cook it on the grill.

Peggy grew up in western Maryland in Hagerstown, at the foothills of the mountains. David is from Henderson. She says when she and David got married her grandmother told her how to make potato salad.

A lot of the other cooking skills came through trial and error, she says.

In France, she learned to make potato salad a different way and it has become a favorite dish. She says some of her friends who are Lebanese like to make the potato salad and put mint in it.

"When we went to France I learned to make leek soup and salad dressing. I still prefer vinaigrette. I use balsamic vinegar a lot and use olive oil. I don't fry things any more."

Peggy keeps a big scrapbook of favorite recipes. "And I get a lot of recipes off the Internet and everywhere else," she says.

When they are traveling, she says they eat out a lot.

"And after we have been traveling, the first thing I want when we get home is meatloaf."

– Melissa Clement

French Potato Salad

8 to 10 small new potatoes

¼ cup chicken broth

¼ cup fresh chives, chopped

DRESSING:

½ teaspoon dry mustard or 1 teaspoon Dijon mustard

2 tablespoons white vinegar

⅓ cup olive oil

Garlic salt and pepper

Boil potatoes until tender. Peel and cut into quarters and while still warm, add chicken broth and allow to sit about 5 minutes.

Potatoes will absorb most of the broth. Sprinkle with chives and toss with dressing.

Whisk vinegar, mustard, salt and pepper together. Slowly whisk in the olive oil. Taste and add seasonings if necessary.

Eggplant and Chick Pea Casserole

1 can (15½ ounces) chick peas (garbanzos)

Olive oil

2 medium-sized eggplants — washed, but not peeled, and cut into 2-inch cubes

3 medium-sized onions, sliced thin, separated into rings

3 teaspoons salt

Fresh ground pepper

5 or 6 ripe tomatoes, chopped or 2 cans chopped tomatoes, drained

1¼ cups water

¼ cup lemon juice

Heat some olive oil in a skillet until almost smoking.

Drop the eggplant cubes and cook for about 5 minutes until they are lightly browned.

Transfer to a 9-by-14-inch casserole dish and spread out evenly.

Add onions to oil left in skillet (adding more if necessary) and saute until they are lightly browned (don't burn) about 8 to 10 minutes.

Spread the onions on top of the eggplant and put a little olive oil on top.

Sprinkle with salt and pepper.

Scatter the chick peas on top and then the tomatoes. Add a little more salt and pepper.

Mix water and lemon juice and pour over the top.

Bake at 400 degrees about 40 minutes until bubbly and vegetables are tender.

Cool and serve at room temperature with pita bread. Serves at least 6.

Peggy McDuffee's Grandmother's Potato Salad

Dressing:

2 tablespoons mustard

4 tablespoons sugar

Thin with mayonnaise

Cook 4 or 5 medium potatoes until tender. Cut up while hot and put butter, salt and pepper on the hot potatoes.

Cool and add any other ingredients you like and toss with the dressing.

Can add: celery, onions, green and black olives, bacon bits, chopped, hard-boiled eggs, etc.

Marinade for Lamb or Beef Shish Kebobs

1 clove garlic, crushed

1 tablespoon Worcestershire sauce

⅓ cup red wine vinegar

1 tablespoon minced onion

¼ cup chili sauce

¼ cup water

½ teaspoon oregano

½ teaspoon thyme

Mix ingredients and marinate meat in refrigerator for one hour or more.

Put large cubes of meat on skewers with onion and green pepper between each piece of meat. (Can use other vegetables, such as cherry tomatoes and parboiled new potatoes, as well.)

Mix leftover marinade with ½ cup chili sauce and bring to a boil. (The bringing to a boil step is important for food safety after using the marinade sauce, Peggy McDuffee says.)

Brush on meat while grilling. Thin even more with water and serve with meat and grilled vegetables.

Cold Weather Means Soups for Cook

JANUARY 9, 2002

Laura Whisnant

When cold weather hits and an occasional snow covers the ground in Fayetteville, Laura Whisnant knows what to cook.

"To me, there's nothing better than a cup of hot soup on a cold day," the retired schoolteacher says.

"I love soup and could make it every night of the week when it gets cold. There is no comparison to homemade soup and the kind that you get out of a can."

Two of the favorite soups that Whisnant and her family like are barbecue bean soup and hearty minestrone. The barbecue bean soup has small pieces of ham and the minestrone can be served with cooked and drained Italian sausage, if desired.

She cooked a big pot of the barbecue bean soup last week to serve on New Year's Day, a tradition at her home on Lenox Drive. "I always use the ham bone from Christmas dinner," she says.

Whisnant says the soup recipes are not original, but she has adapted them a bit by substituting her special herbed vinegars for regular vinegar. "It just adds a little extra zip," she says. "It is real subtle, but it makes a difference."

The soups freeze well, although the pasta or potatoes in the minestrone may get pretty soft when reheated, she says.

She grows herbs in pots on her patio and in the backyard garden. She washes the clipped herbs and combines them with white vinegar or wine vinegar. She lets the vinegar sit for several months and then strains it before bottling it. She gives the vinegar to friends and sells it at her church's annual holiday bazaar every year.

Whisnant likes to cook for a crowd — whether it's for her husband, Donald, or other family members; her circle at Westminister Presbyterian Church or the Nguyen Vietnamese family of five children she has grown close to for nearly 20 years. She got to know the family when they first came to Fayetteville and Thuy Nguyen, now 26, was in the second grade.

This year only one of the Whisnants' three daughters could be home for Christmas. Crystal Whisnant came over from Southern Pines. Daughters Ellen Abernathy of Morganton and Sherri Spichiger of Bowling Green, Ky., didn't get to come home.

Whisnant says she always gets a request to make her potato casserole for Christmas Day dinner. It is a hearty casserole with cheese that could be good for a cold winter meal as well. "We had 15 or 16 for Christmas dinner this year," she says.

A hearty dessert that she makes a lot for church suppers is an apple torte, made with cream cheese. "It is almost like a cheesecake," Whisnant says.

She likes to bake, but has had to adapt recipes since her husband was diagnosed with diabetes two years ago.

Now that the holidays are over, she says they will have to get back to their routine of walking in the mall for an hour every morning.

"He has been doing real well and is going off his medication next week," Whisnant says.

– Alice Thrasher

Hearty Minestrone

- 1 tablespoon olive oil
- 1 pound potatoes, peeled and diced (about 2½ cups)
- 3 medium carrots, peeled and diced
- 3 medium ribs celery, diced
- 1 medium onion, thinly sliced
- 1 medium red bell pepper, cored, seeded and diced
- 2 cloves garlic, crushed
- 3 10½-ounce cans chicken broth
- 1 bay leaf
- 2 16-ounce cans red kidney beans, rinsed and drained
- 2 16-ounce cans whole tomatoes in puree, coarsely chopped
- 1 10-ounce package frozen peas
- 2 tablespoons freshly grated Parmesan cheese
- 1 tablespoon balsamic or red wine vinegar (Laura Whisnant uses red wine vinegar, flavored with rosemary, sage, bay, basil and garlic.)
- ¼ to ½ teaspoon crushed hot red pepper
- Salt to taste
- Thin shavings of Parmesan cheese (optional)

In 4-quart saucepan over medium heat, heat oil; add potatoes, carrots, celery, onion, red bell pepper and garlic; cook, covered, about 10 minutes until vegetables are almost tender, uncovering to stir occasionally.

Stir in chicken broth and bay leaf; bring to boil. Reduce heat to low; simmer, covered, about 10 minutes. Add kidney beans, tomatoes, peas, grated Parmesan, vinegar, crushed red pepper and salt; cook about 5 minutes longer, or until heated through.

Remove bay leaf before serving. If desired, serve soup garnished with thin shavings of Parmesan cheese.

(Note: Laura Whisnant sometimes substitutes tiny pasta shells for potatoes. Also, you can brown and drain Italian sausage and add a small amount to completed soup.)

Grated Potato Casserole

- 1 cup milk
- 3 eggs
- 1½ teaspoons salt
- ⅛ teaspoon pepper
- 1 cup cubed cheddar cheese
- 2 tablespoons softened margarine
- ½ green pepper, cut up
- 1 small onion, quartered
- 4 medium potatoes, pared and cubed

Preheat oven to 350 degrees. Grease 1 quart casserole. Put all ingredients in blender container in the order listed; cover and run on high speed just until all potatoes go through the blades — (do not over blend, texture should be similar to that of grits). Pour into casserole and bake 1 hour.

Barbecued Bean Soup

- 1 pound dry pinto beans (2½ cups)
- 8 cups water
- 4 medium carrots, finely chopped
- 1 cup chopped onion
- 1 meaty ham bone or 2 smoked ham hocks (about 1 pound)
- ¼ cup chili sauce
- 2 tablespoons brown sugar
- 1 tablespoon salt
- 2 tablespoons Worcestershire sauce
- 2 tablespoons prepared mustard
- ¼ cup vinegar (Laura Whisnant uses vinegar flavored with rosemary or sage)
- 1 (16-ounce) can tomatoes, cut up

In a Dutch oven, combine beans and water. Bring to boiling. Simmer 2 minutes.

Remove from heat; cover and let stand 1 hour (or soak beans in water overnight) do not drain. Stir in carrots, onion, ham bone, tomatoes, salt, vinegar, chili sauce, sugar, Worcestershire sauce and mustard. Bring to boiling; reduce heat. Cover and simmer 2-3 hours or until beans are tender.

Remove ham bone or hocks; cool slightly. Remove meat from bones and dice. Return to soup. Mash beans slightly if desired.

Makes 8 to 10 servings.

Bavarian Apple Torte

CRUST:

- ½ cup margarine
- ⅓ cup sugar
- ¼ teaspoon vanilla
- 1 cup all-purpose flour

FILLING:

- 1 (8-ounce) package cream cheese, softened
- ¼ cup sugar
- 1 egg
- ½ teaspoon vanilla

TOPPING:

- ⅓ cup sugar
- ½ teaspoon cinnamon
- 4 cups peeled, thin apple slices
- ¼ cup sliced almonds

Cream margarine, sugar and vanilla. Blend in flour. Spread dough onto bottom and 2 inches high around sides of 9-inch springform pan.

Combine softened cream cheese and sugar, mixing until well-blended. Add egg and vanilla; mix well. Pour into pastry-lined pan. Combine sugar and cinnamon; toss with apples. Spoon apple mixture over cream cheese layer; sprinkle with nuts. Bake at 450 degrees, ten minutes. Reduce oven temperature to 400 degrees; continue baking 25 minutes. Cool before removing rim of pan. Serves 8 to 10.

Blueberries a Specialty for Farmer's Wife

August 17, 2005

Ellon Carter

Ellon Carter knows her blueberries. She and her husband, Buck, own the popular pick-your-own blueberry farm in Vander, open each year in July and August.

I went to the farm to meet the Carters, who live in a neat home beside Clinton Road. We sat on the enclosed back porch, and she pulled out her box stuffed with recipes on time-worn cards.

For more than 30 years, the Carters have operated the strawberry and blueberry pick-your-own farm, and customers have shared plenty of recipes with her, Ellon says.

The blueberry bushes, just little switches the first year, were set out in 1974 and '75 and were ready for picking two or three years later. Pollinated by bees, they have grown tall over the years and continue to produce abundant crops.

When the blueberries first bloom, they are sprayed, but as the berries are growing, no more spray is used, the Carters say.

Ellon says the best way to freeze blueberries is to pick out the stems, put the berries in freezer bags and freeze without washing. They can be washed just before they are used. Never freeze them when they are wet, she says, or they will become soggy. If you must wash them before freezing, they must be dried before they are frozen.

One of her favorite recipes is called Blueberry Dump Cake. The "dump" comes from the process in which you dump a box of cake mix on top of the berries, along with canned pineapple, butter and nuts.

Another all-time favorite is her Blueberry Delight Pie, made with lemon juice, sweetened condensed milk and Cool Whip put into a graham-cracker pie crust.

Ellon makes her dishes not only for her family, children and grandchildren but for shut-ins and for church suppers at Pleasant Grove Baptist Church, where she and Buck are lifelong members.

On a cold winter night, Ellon says, they like to get ice-cold milk, add a little sweetener and vanilla, and pour it over frozen blueberries. But the best way to eat the berries, by far, she says, is right off the bush.

– Melissa Clement

Blueberry Peach Cobbler

- 1 cup butter or margarine
- 2 teaspoons baking powder
- 1 cup plain flour
- 1 cup sugar
- 1 cup sugar
- 1 cup milk
- 2 cups sliced peaches
- 2 cups fresh blueberries

Melt butter in a 9-by-13-inch baking dish and set aside.

Mix together flour, cup sugar, baking powder and milk and pour into baking dish.

In a separate bowl, mix peaches, blueberries and ½ cup of sugar. Stir and pour on top of the ingredients in baking dish. Don't stir. Bake in 350-degree oven for 35 to 40 minutes.

Blueberry Delight Pie

- 1 large or 2 small graham-cracker pie crusts
- 1 cup lemon juice
- 1 14-ounce can Eagle Brand condensed sweetened milk
- 1 cup sugar
- 1 cup chopped nuts
- 1 (18 ounce) carton Cool Whip
- 1 quart fresh blueberries

Stir ingredients gently and pour into crust. Top with nuts. Cover with plastic wrap.

Refrigerate overnight to avoid pie being runny.

Blueberry Dump Cake

- 1 box cake mix
- 1 (26-ounce) can crushed pineapple
- 1 stick butter, melted
- 1 quart blueberries
- 1 cup chopped nuts

Preheat oven to 350 degrees. Grease 13-by-9-by-2-inch baking dish. Wash and drain blueberries. Pour in dish and spread out. Dump cake mix on top of berries and spread over berries. Spread pineapple on top of cake mix. Spread nuts on top. Pour melted butter over nuts. Bake 45 minutes to 1 hour until light brown on top.

Retired Engineer Revs up for Healthy-Cooking Challenge

March 22, 2006

Rick Hamlet

Rick Hamlet is a man who revels in taking on challenges. When this 51-year-old engineer recently took early retirement from DuPont, he wanted to spend more time with his 11-year-old son, Connor, and be able to pursue other interests. He also set about running again. His challenge is to run the Marine Corps Marathon in October. His goal was to lose 20 pounds, so he signed up to be on the Observer's weight loss team.

Hamlet's wife, obstetrician-gynecologist Dr. Gerianne Geszler, is dedicated to fitness and healthy eating, so she gave him sessions with trainers who drilled him on fitness and diet.

His final challenge was to do the cooking for his wife and son.

"Until retiring, my biggest culinary dilemma had been to find the best white wine that went with oatmeal," he says. "I was in a new world."

But Hamlet says he was a man with a plan and a can. His first chore "was to find recipes that were nutritious, so I could get my wife's approval–aesthetically pleasing, so the wife would think I cooked all day–but simple, so I actually wouldn't have to cook all day."

For this he found help not only with the weight loss team, but from Men's Health magazine and the Zoneperfect.com Web site. Still, going to the grocery store was a challenge.

"At times I'd pick recipes that had ingredients that I never knew existed and then challenge myself to find them."

But then there was the manly urge "to go on the hunt," he says.

"Finding the normal stuff was easy, but starting cold, stalking quickly but quietly, not knowing what a cannelloni bean is or where it might be nesting, was a particular challenge the first time.

"Another key to my making the adjustments to the cooking task was in realizing that I didn't have to abandon my primal competitive urges or my desire to use power tools."

One of his first steps was to buy organic chicken from a co-op, combining it with a variety of colorful vegetables. Some of his favorite recipes came from "Men's Health" and "Gourmet" magazine.

He shares his Tuscan-style chicken pasta, linguine with red clam sauce, and Italian sausage with red grapes.

"These recipes have a robust amount of protein to help with repairing muscles from my workouts, as well as helping to suppress my appetite," Hamlet said. "Eating nutritious food is part of the equation, but it doesn't have to be a chore. Having a good recipe and using some creativity in cooking can make the task easier and fun."

– Melissa Clement

Tuscan-Style Chicken Pasta

See photo in center of book

2 ounces penne

2 4- to 5-ounce chicken breasts, pounded to inch thickness

4 baby spinach leaves

1 15-ounce can cannelloni beans, rinsed

Salt and pepper to taste

1 teaspoon olive oil

1 clove garlic, crushed

½ teaspoon dried rosemary, finely chopped

2 heaping tablespoons diced roasted red bell peppers

2 tablespoons grated Parmesan cheese

Boil 1 quart water. Drop in the penne, stir and cook until the pasta is al dente, about 9 to 11 minutes.

While the pasta cooks, sear the chicken in a skillet on medium-high, about 4 to 5 minutes per side, seasoning each side with a pinch of salt and pepper as the other side cooks.

Remove the chicken from skillet and set aside.

Reduce skillet heat to medium. Add spinach, beans, oil, garlic, rosemary and bell peppers. Stir frequently until spinach wilts, about 1 or 2 minutes.

Slice chicken. Toss it with drained pasta and spinach- and-bean mixture. Top each serving with 1 tablespoon cheese. Makes 2 servings.

Linguine with Red Clam Sauce

See photo in center of book

1 (15-ounce) can diced tomatoes with chili peppers, undrained

3 (6-ounce) can baby or minced clams

12 ounces linguine, cooked according to directions

Basil and oregano, to taste

½ (2-ounce) can anchovy fillets, minced

Saute garlic in oil or butter in a large skillet.

Dump in the tomatoes with chili peppers, including the liquid in the can, and oregano.

Cook for 2 minutes.

Drain canned clam juice into the pan. Cook for 2 minutes.

Add cooked pasta and cook for 1 minute. Stir in the clams, anchovies and basil. Heat through.

Top with grated Parmesan cheese. If you're not an anchovy fan, leave them out.

Italian Sausage with Red Grapes

2 tablespoons olive oil

2 pounds sweet Italian sausage (about 12 3- to 4-inch links)

2 pounds seedless red grapes, stemmed

¼ cup balsamic vinegar

Salt and pepper to taste

Heat olive oil in a 12-inch heavy skillet over moderate heat until hot but not smoking.

Cook sausages, turning over once until well browned, about 8 minutes total.

Add grapes and cook, stirring occasionally, until sausages are cooked through and grapes are softened, 10 to 12 minutes.

Stir in vinegar. Salt and pepper to taste.

From Soup to Sweets, She's Got the Recipe

March 31, 2004

Jennifer Britt

When the Haymount United Methodist women start cooking, it's hard to decide where to start buying.

Jennifer Britt has a logical suggestion: try a little of everything.

"There are so many good cooks in this church, it's impossible to say what's best," she said. "There are some wonderful pies, cakes, cookies, all sorts of things. And you've got to check the 'bread of life' table."

Britt, a longtime member of Haymount United Methodist, will have some of her favorites in today's fund-raiser beginning at noon. But she doesn't concentrate only on sweets. Look for her turkey-taco soup when the sale kicks off at the church. It's a recipe from her mom, Shirley Jenkins, of Fairmont.

"It's a great recipe," she said. "It's easy, and you can freeze it to use later. It's one of our family favorites, especially with our son, Tyler, playing baseball. We have some late dinners."

Like many cooks, Britt started by watching her mom and grandmother in the kitchen. But, Britt notes, she really didn't do much cooking until she got married.

"We moved to Fayetteville in 1980 when Carl got a job here," she said. "I think every bride has that story about a casserole that didn't work. Certainly I do, but since then, I've learned a lot."

She's also developed a system for revamping recipes she's collected. In each cookbook, she notes changes she's tried and the family reaction.

"Some the kids love and Dad doesn't, some are great, some just say never again," she said.

Unfortunately, when people ask her for a recipe, she has to double-check the changes she's made.

"All my cookbooks are written in, little notes all over them," Britt said. "It can get confusing."

There's no confusing her recipe for crepes and strawberries, though. "It's a great treat this time of year, when strawberries are ripe," she said.

"Some people are intimidated by crepes, but once you get the hang of it, it's really easy."

Her other recipe is for a surprising strawberry and spinach salad.

"The lime juice helps offset the sweetness in it," Britt said. "It's another easy recipe that really works well.

– Chick Jacobs

Strawberry-Spinach Salad

- 10 ounces fresh spinach, torn into bite-size pieces
- 2 cups fresh, sliced strawberries
- ½ cup dairy sour cream
- ¼ cup honey
- 2 teaspoons lime juice
- ⅛ teaspoon ground cardamom or nutmeg
- Shredded coconut

Gently toss the spinach and strawberries in a salad bowl and refrigerate. In a small bowl, combine all other ingredients except coconut until well blended. Cover and refrigerate to blend flavors. Toss salad with dressing. Garnish with shredded coconut.

Crepes

3 eggs
1½ cups milk
1⅓ cups all-purpose flour
½ teaspoon salt
1½ tablespoons vegetable oil
Nonstick cooking spray

CREPE FILLING:
8-ounce package cream cheese
½ teaspoon vanilla
3½ cups sliced strawberries
1½ cup confectioners' sugar
8 ounces Cool Whip

Combine ingredients in blender and process for a minute. Refrigerate for one hour. Spray cooking spray in bottom of 10-inch or 6-inch non-stick pan. Place over medium heat until oil is just hot, not smoking. Pour about 3 tablespoons of batter in the pan. Tilt the pan to evenly distribute a thin film. Cook for one minute, then lift edge of crepe to test doneness, flip and cook for another 30 seconds. Place crepes on a towel to cool. Layer with wax paper. You may freeze them for up to a month.

Filling: Combined softened cream cheese, sugar and vanilla. Fold in Cool Whip. Fill crepe with cup cream cheese mixture and cup strawberries. Fold and top with cream cheese mixture and fruit. Should fill 12 to 15 crepes.

Strawberry Cake

2 cups strawberries, capped
1 cup sugar
1 cup all-purpose flour
½ cup milk
1 stick butter

Melt butter and mix in other ingredients. Pour into an 8-by-8-inch pan. Cook at 350 degrees for 30 to 35 minutes. Serve warm with fresh whipped cream.

Turkey Taco Soup

1½ pounds ground turkey
1 medium onion, chopped
1 teaspoon salt
½ teaspoon pepper
1 package taco seasoning mix
1 package ranch dressing mix
1 15-ounce package frozen whole kernel corn, thawed
3 cans Original Rotel canned tomatoes (for less spicy, use 1 can original and 2 cans mild Rotel)
1 16-ounce can black beans
1 16-ounce can Great Northern beans
1½ cups water

Brown ground turkey with onions. Drain off fat. Combine all ingredients in slow cooker and simmer for several hours. Serve with sour cream and grated cheese.

Cooking for a Large Group Is Woman's Specialty

July 9, 2003

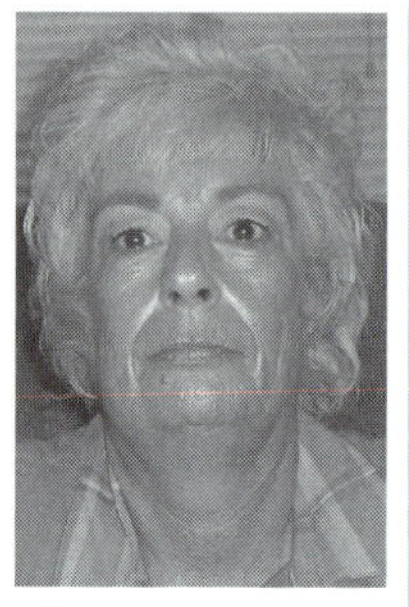

Betty Burkett

Preparing food for a large crowd could be a cumbersome task for some people.

Not Betty Burkett.

She welcomes the opportunity to invite family and friends into her home to share some of her favorite dishes.

"To me it's just as easy to cook for 20 as it is to cook for five," Burkett said. "It's the same thing; you just make more of it."

Burkett put her culinary skills to work a couple of weeks ago when she cooked breakfast for approximately 20 people at her home. The menu consisted of hash brown casserole, banana bread, overnight French toast, oven omelet, grits, biscuits, bacon, country ham, sausage and a variety of fresh fruits.

"Breakfast for a crowd is the hardest thing for people to come up with," Burkett said. "I do enjoy fixing for large crowds. The more, the better."

Of all of the breakfast dishes she enjoys preparing, the hash brown casserole is her favorite, Burkett said.

"Not bragging or anything, but I think it's better than Cracker Barrel's," she said.

Most of the recipes in Burkett's files are easy and designed to feed big crowds. The preparation and cooking time isn't long, either, she said.

"Those casseroles I make the day before, and the next day you just get up and put them in the oven," she said.

Burkett's love for cooking started when she was 4 years old. She had a small electric stove and a set of tiny pots. When her mother prepared dinner for the family she would give Burkett some of the same items to cook in her little pots and pans.

"I would cook when she cooked," Burkett said.

From that point on Burkett has been sold on cooking. She not only enjoys preparing breakfast dishes, but she makes a lasagna that receives rave reviews. She uses a spaghetti sauce recipe, and the lasagna has Italian sausage, hamburger, mushrooms, pepperoni and four to five different cheeses.

"All of my Italian recipes are my own," she said. "It would be hard for me to give a recipe to anybody because I don't measure anything. I try different things. It might not be the same next week."

Oven Omelet

¼ cup butter

18 eggs

1 cup sour cream

1 cup milk

2½ teaspoons salt

1 cup shredded Swiss cheese

½ cup mushrooms

1 cup shredded cheddar

½ cup finely chopped green peppers

3 green onions sliced thin

1 2-ounce jar pimientos, drained

½ cup diced ham

½ cup chopped tomatoes

Additional sour cream and diced tomatoes for garnish.

Heat butter in a 13-by-9-by-2-inch baking dish in a 325-degree oven until melted. Tilt dish to coat bottom with melted butter. Beat eggs, sour cream, milk and salt in a large bowl until blended. Stir in cheeses, onions, green pepper, pimientos, ham, mushrooms and chopped tomatoes. Pour into baking dish. Cook uncovered until omelet is set but moist, about 40 to 45 minutes.

Putting her own spin on recipes has become one of Burkett's trademarks.

"I just like coming up with new dishes and seeing people enjoy what I cook," she said. "I love to share my recipes with people, and I love to find new recipes."

Burkett said people will eat one of her dishes and then go home and try to prepare it from her recipe. They often tell her their finished product doesn't taste like hers.

"It's because you can't substitute," Burkett said. "If the recipe says butter, use butter. If it says mayonnaise, use mayonnaise."

– Jeffery Womble

Hash Brown Casserole

- 6 medium potatoes
- ⅓ cup onion
- ¼ cup butter
- 2 cups shredded cheddar cheese
- 1½ cups sour cream
- 1 teaspoon salt
- ¼ teaspoon pepper
- 1 package crumbled bacon
- 2 tablespoons butter

Cook potatoes in skin. Let cool. Peel and shred coarsely. Over low heat, cook onion in butter. Add cheese and stir until almost melted. Remove from heat and blend in sour cream, salt and pepper. Fold in potatoes. Put in greased 2-quart casserole dish. Top with butter and crumbled bacon. Bake at 350 degrees for 25 minutes. The dish may be made the day before and refrigerated, then baked the following day. If done this way, allow extra baking time.

Banana Bread

- 3 cups flour
- 1 teaspoon baking soda
- 1 teaspoon cinnamon
- ¾ teaspoon salt
- 2 cups sugar
- 3 beaten eggs
- 1 cup oil
- 2 cups mashed bananas
- 2 teaspoons vanilla
- 1 can (8 ounces) crushed pineapple
- ½ cup nuts

Combine the first four ingredients in a medium bowl and set aside. Mix the remaining ingredients in a large bowl. Add dry ingredients and mix. Grease and flour two loaf pans or one 9-by-13-inch pan and pour the batter in. Bake in 350-degree oven for 50 to 60 minutes.

Overnight French Toast

- 1 cup brown sugar
- ½ cup unsalted butter
- 2 Granny Smith apples, peeled and sliced
- 2 tablespoons light corn syrup
- 5 eggs
- 1½ cups milk
- Cinnamon and sugar
- 1 teaspoon vanilla
- Loaf of French bread

Mix butter, brown sugar and corn syrup and heat until mixture becomes syrupy (about five minutes). Pour into lightly greased 9-by-13-inch baking dish. Slice apples and spread in dish in a single layer. Slice bread ¾-inch thick and place on top of apples. Whisk eggs, milk and vanilla and pour over bread. Refrigerate overnight. Let it warm to room temperature for 30 minutes. Sprinkle with cinnamon and sugar and bake 40 minutes at 350 degrees.

Cook's Journey Starts in Hawaii, Leads to Seven Lakes

August 13, 2003

Sandi Carl

Sandi Carl was born and raised in Hawaii on the island of Oahu. Her husband, Bill, grew up in Kaneohe seven miles from her hometown. When Bill joined the Army, she followed him around the world, moving 20 times. Their favorite assignment was Hawaii, of course.

Bill ended up at Fort Bragg, and they retired here, later moving to Seven Lakes where they don't golf but love to take long walks around the lakes.

Sandi and her sister grew up taking part in preparing family meals.

"Hawaii is just such a great place to cook and eat, and some of the best cooks in the world live there," she says.

"Everything seems to center around fellowship and hospitality in Hawaii. Whatever you do, there is always food involved. There's a lot of pot-luck food. It's real easy entertainment. The ethnic makeup of Hawaii leads to a large variety of dishes," she says, so she has a huge store of recipes from which to cook.

"We did quite a bit of entertaining in the military, ranging from small groups to as many as 75 people. I like dishes that can be prepared well in advance so that I can enjoy the party along with our guests."

The Carls still do a lot of cooking. Whenever their two daughters have a party, the couple drive to New Jersey or Virginia to do the cooking.

"Our family calls us 'Meals on Wheels,'" she says.

"My husband is well-known among our children's friends for his Korean bulgoki. His recipe is difficult to pass on since he doesn't measure any of the ingredients. Bill does it by taste."

Sandi Carl says some of her recipes are "embarrassingly easy."

Her Elegant Surprise is made from a tub of Cool Whip, a package of ice cream sandwiches, chocolate sauce and walnuts.

"I've never served it that I didn't have guests ask me for the recipe," she says. "You may use 'lite' versions of the ingredients to cut calories."

Her Party Chicken recipe is made with onion soup mix, apricot jam and Russian dressing, which is sometimes hard to find, she says, but Catalina dressing may be substituted.

Her pasta dish is made with meat or seafood, broth, chicken bouillon, spinach and cream cheese.

– Melissa Clement

Elegant Surprise

- 1 8-ounce tub of Cool Whip
- 1 package of ice cream sandwiches (6)
- Chocolate sauce
- Walnuts

Line a glass dish with half the Cool Whip. Layer the ice cream sandwiches on top. Select an appropriate size dish that will accommodate the 6 sandwiches. Follow with the remaining Cool Whip.

Drizzle chocolate sauce in a zigzag pattern diagonally starting from one corner across entire dessert. Sprinkle with chopped walnuts.

Freeze until ready to serve.

Drizzle chocolate sauce on serving plate. Slice dessert into serving portions, place on plate. A strawberry may be placed next to slice. It looks inviting and will always win praise.

Party Chicken

- 1 envelope onion soup mix
- 1 8-ounce jar apricot jam
- 1 8-ounce bottle Russian dressing
- ½ cup water (put into dressing bottle to use up all)

Combine ingredients and pour over 5 pounds of chicken thighs (I usually skin the thighs to eliminate excess fat).

Bake in a 350-degree oven 1 hour or until chicken is done. Baste at least once during the cooking process.

Serve over steamed rice. The gravy is delicious!

Sue's Pasta

- 1 bunch green onions, chopped
- 2 tablespoons olive oil
- 3 cloves of garlic, minced
- 1 can chicken broth
- Chicken granules (bouillon)
- 1 box frozen chopped spinach
- 1 8-ounce block cream cheese
- 2 cups cooked meat of choice (we love shrimp but have also used chicken or mixed seafood)

Saute green onions in olive oil with garlic. Add chicken broth plus added chicken granules for flavor. Add the frozen spinach and stir occasionally until thawed. Add the cream cheese next and stir until sauce is creamy. Meat of choice is added last. Cook until heated and serve over pasta of your choice.

Recipe can be doubled.

This is a great dish to serve with a tossed green salad and garlic bread.

Culinary Skills Are Being Passed Down

MAY 26, 2004

Arline McNeill

Arline McNeill has been cooking since she was a teenager. As a child she watched her mother in the kitchen and developed an interest in learning to cook herself.

"I just wanted to learn how to cook," she said.

She was the fifth child out of eight in her family, but a love of cooking wasn't something they all gained automatically. "I think I'm the cook in the family," she said.

Now she has been married about 35 years, and her husband and children get to enjoy her culinary skills. She has four sons, a daughter, a daughter-in-law and three grandchildren, and they all live in the area, she said.

McNeill said she has been teaching her daughter and daughter-in-law to cook, and they surprised her with a Mother's Day dinner.

On special occasions, McNeill cooks for a crowd, and her food is home-style Southern fare — collard greens, biscuits, candied yams, field peas, and macaroni and cheese are a few of her dishes. She also likes to prepare fried turkey for holiday dinners, she said. Her desserts include chocolate cake, banana pudding and strawberry pudding, a variation on the traditional favorite. "Instead of using bananas, you use strawberries," she said.

Another dish she is known for is her barbecue meatballs.

With so many years of experience in the kitchen, McNeill doesn't use cookbooks.

"I just get in the kitchen and start," she said.

— *Cathryne Meeks*

Blueberry Pound Cake

1 box butter recipe cake mix

8 ounces cream cheese

3 eggs

½ cup water

½ cup vegetable oil

2 cups blueberries

Mix first 5 ingredients with mixer. Stir in blueberries. Bake in a tube pan for 1 hour at 350 degrees.

Strawberry Delight

1 box vanilla wafers

16 ounces Cool Whip

2 (4-ounce) boxes instant vanilla pudding

2 (4-ounce) boxes wild strawberry Jell-O

2 cups strawberries

½ cup pecan halves

Line a 9-by-13-inch pan with vanilla wafers. Mix pudding as directed on box; mix half of the Cool Whip with it. Prepare Jell-O as directed on box; add strawberries when it stars to jell. Spread pudding mixture over wafers.

Spread Jell-O mixture over pudding mixture. Spread the other half of the Cool Whip over this. Place pecan halves on top.

Good, Simple Food is a Way of Life

February 15, 2006

Lorette Hollinshed

Lorette Hollinshed grew up in the town of Hamilton in Martin County. Her family had a vegetable garden. She says the family enjoyed simple foods such as hot biscuits, potatoes, ham, sausage and pork chops and never cared about gourmet dishes. She remembers eating raw sweet potatoes in the afternoon after school.

Hollinshed graduated from Meredith College in Raleigh with degrees in English, education and psychology. In Raleigh she met her future husband, Vivian Hollinshed, who is a graduate of North Carolina State University. They moved to Fayetteville, his hometown, where she taught school until her children, Marty and Tom, were born.

Their first garden was at the farm of Elliott Harris. While her children were riding their horses, Hollinshed used the time to grow vegetables and flowers. When the children grew up, the Hollinsheds moved their garden to the property where his business, Comtech, is located. They still garden there and like to eat their own fresh vegetables that have been cooked a short time.

Hollinshed is a Master Gardener and a weekly volunteer at the Cape Fear Botanical Garden.

She freezes corn and okra and other vegetables for the winter. Tomatoes are frozen and used for soup and spaghetti sauce. She likes pickled home-grown beets and okra.

One of the couple's favorite dishes is chili con carne.

"It's easy to make, and you use only one pot or skillet," she says. "We like to spoon the chili con carne mix over the fried cornbread patties."

You can also turn it into a kind of Mexican dish by using corn chips with fresh torn lettuce, green onions and grated cheddar cheese, she says.

Hollinshed's split-pea soup recipe came from Belle Hamilton, the mother of Hollinshed's friend Mary Griffins. Hamilton served Wednesday-night dinners at the Highland Presbyterian Church in the late 1970s and early 1980s. Along with the peas, it calls for a ham bone, canned tomatoes, shell macaroni, onions and celery. If there is enough meat on the bone, she says, she doubles the recipe.

Hollinshed also shares her recipe for date bars with chopped nuts. They are cut and rolled in confectioners' sugar.

Her favorite recipes are those she finds in *Southern Living* magazine. Her favorite cooking magazine is *Cooks.*

–Melissa Clement

Split-Pea Soup

- ½ cup green split peas
- 2 quarts water
- 1 ham bone with meat (cured ham, not fresh)
- ¼ cup onion, chopped
- ½ cup chopped celery
- Black pepper
- 2 cups canned tomatoes
- 1 cup small shell macaroni

Soak peas overnight or a couple of hours.

Put peas, water, ham bone, onion and celery in pot and cook on low heat for 2 hours.

Take out ham bone, chop meat and add back with tomatoes and macaroni.

Add pepper to taste.

Cook slowly for 25 minutes.

Date Bars

See photo in center of book

- 3 eggs
- 1 cup sugar
- 2 cups dates, chopped
- 1 cup nuts, chopped
- 1 cup flour
- 1 teaspoon baking powder
- 1 teaspoon salt
- ¼ teaspoon cloves
- ¼ teaspoon cinnamon
- 1 teaspoon vanilla
- Powdered sugar

Beat 3 eggs until light.

Add 1 cup sugar gradually and beat until very light.

Add 2 cups chopped dates and 1 cup chopped nuts.

Sift before measuring 1 scant cup of flour. Re-sift with baking powder, salt, cloves and cinnamon.

Add sifted ingredients to egg mixture with 1 teaspoon vanilla. Beat until well blended.

Put in a lightly buttered 9-by-13-inch pan and bake at 325 degrees for 25 to 30 minutes.

Use a tester in center of pan to be sure they are done.

Cut into small squares or rectangles and roll in sifted powdered sugar.

Hot Raspberry Sauce

- 7 cups raspberries, fresh or frozen (thaw slightly)
- 1¾ cups sugar
- 2¼ cups water
- ½ vanilla bean, split or scraped, or 1 teaspoon vanilla extract
- ¾ cup lemon juice

Combine the raspberries, sugar and water in a saucepan and bring to a simmer over medium heat.

Cook until raspberries are soft, about 15 minutes.

Strain the raspberry mixture through a fine-mesh sieve, pressing against the solids with the back of a ladle.

Discard the raspberry seeds and pour the extracted juices into a saucepan; add the vanilla bean, its seeds and the lemon juice.

Simmer until reduced by one-half over medium-low heat or to the consistency of syrup, 20 to 25 minutes.

Serve warm, or cool and store in the refrigerator for up to 10 days.

Makes 2 cups.

Chili con Carne

- Cooking oil
- 1 large onion, sliced
- 1 large green pepper, chopped
- 1 pound ground beef, at least 93 percent fat-free
- 2 (1-pound) cans red kidney beans
- 1 (1-pound) can tomatoes (2 cups)
- 1 (8-ounce) can tomato sauce
- 1 to 1½ teaspoons chili powder
- 1 teaspoon salt
- 1 bay leaf
- Dash of each cayenne pepper and paprika

Brown onion, green pepper and meat in a little hot fat. (Hollinshed uses olive oil.)

Add beans and other ingredients.

Cover; simmer 1½ hours, adding saved bean liquid or water as needed.

Waffles

See photo in center of book

- 3½ cups all-purpose flour
- 2 teaspoons salt
- ½ cup sugar
- 2 tablespoons baking powder
- 8 large eggs, separated
- 3 cups of milk
- 1 cup butter, melted
- 2 cups hot raspberry syrup

Sift together the flour, salt sugar and baking powder into a large mixing bowl.

Make a well in the center of the dry ingredients.

Whisk together the egg yolks, milk and melted butter in a separate bowl.

Pour the wet ingredients into the well of the dry ingredients, stirring until just combined.

The batter will be slightly lumpy.

Do not overmix.

Preheat waffle iron.

Whip the egg whites to soft peaks and fold into the batter in two additions. Ladle about ¾ cup batter into the waffle iron.

Cook the waffles until they are crisp, golden and cooked through, about 3 to 6 mintues per waffle.

Serve at once with the raspberry syrup.

Makes 8 servings.

French Cuisine Shared With Festival

September 28, 2005

Ginette Moreau

On Sunday at the International Folk Festival, Ginette Moreau stood at the French food booth flipping paper-thin crepes and filling them with sweets.

She was dressed in the traditional costume of the women of Nice, France, called the Nicoise. It includes a black apron over a red-and-white skirt. It is worn with a hat that is flat on top and is decorated with flowers, as is the basket that is carried to represent the many flowers that grow in the region.

You might recognize Ginette, pronounced G-net, as the bicycle rider who crosses Raeford Road almost every morning to walk or jog through Cumberland Memorial Cemetery, where her husband is buried. She jokes that she has already paid for her plot there and might as well enjoy it. She has three sons, five grandsons and one granddaughter.

For 30 years, Ginette worked in civil service in the dental and oral surgery unit and in the operating room at Womack Army Medical Center.

After she retired, she went back to France to visit her twin sister. They toured the Loire Valley together by train. Afterward, she visited her son, daughter-in-law and new granddaughter in Palm Springs, Calif.

Now back in Fayetteville, she volunteers at the Care Clinic and loves to cook for her friends. Most are fellow members of the LaFayette Society and the people she worked with at Womack. They get together often for potluck dinners. She rides her bicycle to nearby stores to buy groceries.

When it is too rainy to walk or ride her bike, she

Coq au Vin

- 1 3-pound chicken
- 6 tablespoons butter
- salt and pepper
- 5 ounces lean bacon
- 15 tiny onions
- 1 bottle of red wine
- 1 clove garlic
- 1 tablespoon flour
- Chopped fresh parsley for garnish

Cut the chicken into pieces.

Heat 4 tablespoons butter in a saucepan and add chicken. Season with salt and pepper and brown the chicken on both sides over medium heat.

Meanwhile, finely dice the bacon and put it in a saucepan of cold water. Bring to a boil and blanch for 5 minutes. Drain.

Peel the onions.

Remove pieces of chicken and keep them hot. Put the onions and bacon in the saucepan and fry for about 10 minutes, stirring frequently.

Return chicken to the sauce pan and add wine. Season with salt and pepper. Add garlic. Cover and simmer 1 hour.

Fifteen minutes before the end of cooking time, work together the rest of the butter and the flour to form a soft paste.

Beat in 2 tablespoons sauce from the chicken, then return this mixture to the sauce pan and stir well.

Serve garnished with chopped parsley.

works out on her exercise bike, but she does not credit her slim figure to exercise alone. She eats the French way. That means eating small quantities of good-quality food served with red wine and cheese. It also means eating slowly without the distraction of television, enjoying the company of friends and conversation, and never eating in her car.

She shares her recipe for the crepes she made as she was growing up in France, the same recipe she used at the Folk Festival. It is made with three tablespoons of either rum, Grand Marnier or Cointreau, which is added only after the batter has been left standing for at least two hours.

She likes to cook the crepes in advance, wrap them in foil and place them in the refrigerator where they will keep for two or three days. The batter, she says, will keep well for 24 hours if stored in a container with a tight lid.

Crepes can be served filled with a variety of meats, vegetables and cheeses for a main course or served as a sweet with powdered sugar, jellies and jams.

She also shares recipes for the traditional quiche Lorraine and coq au vin marnier or chicken in red wine.

– Melissa Clement

Crepes

3 eggs
2 cups flour
2½ cups milk
2 tablespoons oil
Pinch of salt
3 tablespoons rum, or Grand Marnier or Cointreau
3 tablespoons warm water
Butter for frying

Beat the eggs in mixing bowl or blender.

Add flour. Beat until smooth, then gradually knead in the milk, the oil and a pinch of salt.

Leave the batter to stand for at least 2 hours, then add the rum or liqueur.

When you are ready to cook the crepes, thin the batter with warm water so it is runny enough to cover the pan immediately.

Put a pat of butter in a crepe pan or frying pan and heat. Pour a ladle of batter into the pan and tip so the batter spreads thinly. Cook 2 minutes or until golden brown on each side.

Slide the crepe out of the pan and repeat with the remaining batter.

Quiche Lorraine

1 pie crust
3 eggs
½ cup heavy whipping cream
1 cup grated gruyere or Swiss cheese
Salt and pepper
1 pound smoked bacon

Preheat oven to 450 degrees.

Prick the bottom of pie crust with a fork.

Dice the bacon and sprinkle over the bottom of the pie crust.

Break the eggs into a bowl and beat with grated cheese and whipping cream and a pinch of salt and pepper to taste.

Pour this mixture over the bacon in the pie crust.

Bake for 20 minutes and serve hot.

If you like the pastry crisp, bake it unfilled before adding the filling.

Bryant Worked at Becoming a Good Cook

March 16, 2005

Catherine Bryant

As a young bride who, she claims, couldn't boil water, Catherine Bryant certainly had her work cut out for her.

She had just married a North Carolina boy whose mom was a terrific cook. He had a hankering for fried chicken and the traditional side dishes. The results, she admits, were not the best.

"But they were very supportive," Bryant said with a laugh.

Years later, Bryant doesn't have to worry about folks spurning her food. She became known as one of the better cooks at Warrenwood Elementary School, and her cakes have been a hit at Haymount United Methodist Church.

In fact, when the church holds its bake sale this afternoon, look for her cakes to be among the first to disappear.

"I'll probably make a cream-cheese poundcake," she said. "And if I can work up the ambition, I'll make some yeast sweet bread, too. People seem to like those."

Her skill as a cook is more impressive when you consider her background. Raised in Minnesota in a family of good cooks, Bryant says she didn't really do much cooking before college.

"Everyone else in the family was a great cook," she said. "So I just ate. I thought everyone could cook like that."

While in college, she met Bill Bryant, a Fayetteville native. Soon they were married and moving back to his hometown–and his mom's cooking.

"She was an excellent cook, too," Bryant said. "But both she and Bill were very patient with me."

She got a lot of practice with other teachers at Warrenwood. "We experimented on each other," she said. "It was a great way to build confidence."

Many of her favorite recipes can be found in the church cookbook, which will be available at the bake sale. Now retired, she enjoys cooking, but not as much as following N.C. State's basketball fortunes.

"I guess I'll be cooking and trying to watch the TV at the same time," she said.

— *Chick Jacobs*

Creamy Chicken and Potato Soup

- 4 cups diced potatoes
- 1 medium onion, chopped
- 4 tablespoons vegetable oil
- 1½ cups cooked, chopped chicken
- 1 can chicken broth
- 2 teaspoons parsley flakes
- 2 teaspoons salt
- 1 13-ounce can evaporated milk

Heat oil in a Dutch oven or large saucepan. Add potatoes and onions, and stir to coat. Add chicken, broth, parsley and salt. Heat to boiling, then lower heat, cover and simmer until potatoes are tender. Add more broth if needed.

Stir in evaporated milk. Heat until hot, but do not boil.

— "The Best of Haymount" cookbook

Pickled Shrimp

- 1 cup salad oil
- 2 teaspoons sugar
- ½ teaspoon dried mustard
- Dash of red pepper
- 1 pound boiled shrimp
- ¼ cup ketchup
- ¼ cup vinegar
- 1 teaspoon salt
- 2 tablespoons Worcestershire sauce
- 3 medium onions, thinly sliced

In a covered jar or bowl, alternate layers of shrimp and onions. In a separate bowl, mix the other ingredients and pour over shrimp and onions. Refrigerate at least 24 hours.

Stir or shake occasionally. Will keep for several weeks in the refrigerator.

— Pat Clayton

Cream Cheese Pecan Poundcake

- 1½ cups margarine
- 1 (8-ounce) package cream cheese
- 3 cups sugar
- 6 eggs
- 3 cups all-purpose flour
- 1½ teaspoons vanilla
- Pinch of baking powder
- 1½ cups coarsely chopped pecans

Cream margarine and cream cheese. Gradually add sugar, beating with the mixer until light and fluffy. Add eggs one at a time, beating well after each addition. Add flour, vanilla, baking powder and pecans.

Grease bottom of a 10-inch baking tube pan. Bake at 325 degrees for 90 minutes. Cool in pan for 10 minutes.

You may make a glaze frosting for this if you wish, but it's good as it is.

— Virginia Bryan

Everything Cook Does Leads to Healthy Eating

August 15, 2001

Hattie Bryant

Hattie Bryant says, "God gave us one body and I think we are supposed to take care of it."

She is trying to do just that.

Several years ago she began studying healthy eating and trying to encourage her four children and grandchildren to eat a more healthy diet.

The first thing she did was to cut down on the fatty food she and her husband ate. She trimmed meat and cut out using animal fat.

Now she uses only extra-virgin olive oil and canola oil.

She reads about health, takes classes on diet and talks to others about their ideas.

One of the things she has found to be most helpful is learning to read labels.

It's surprising, she says, to find that some of the products you always thought were healthy turn out to be full of salt, sugar and fat.

It is important, she says, to read labels and learn what the different listings that are sometimes confusing actually mean.

She grows vegetables in her backyard garden and serves them in the summer. In the winter she cooks dried beans and eats greens.

In her studies she learned that she should eat more grains.

Although she has been using whole wheat bread for a long time she has now added grits and oatmeal with raisins in it.

She cut out whole milk and uses 1 and 2 percent milk. She cut out caffeine and uses only drip decaf coffee now.

Another push has been to eat more fruit.

Only occasionally does she eat red meat and then she cuts any fat off of it.

Bryant, who is a retired Hoke County special education teacher, says she is still learning by reading and trying new recipes.

Recently she has been experimenting with using honey instead of sugar or a sweetener.

When she serves chicken, she says, she grills or broils it usually, but once in a while she cooks her husband fried chicken because he likes it.

"I don't believe in taking everything away that you have been used to all your life. I believe in eating those things on a limited basis, as a treat. I think if you deny yourself of everything you want you will get to the point you give up on healthy eating."

What she does instead is to take her old recipes and convert them to healthier versions that also taste good.

One she calls delicious is her orange salad with graham crackers and cream cheese.

She has developed a recipe using spaghetti with fresh vegetables and olives that she says is both healthy and tasty.

Another of her family's favorites is her chicken casserole with buttermilk crust.

– Melissa Clement

Spaghetti Salad

1 box thin spaghetti
2 cans three-bean salad, drained
6 miniature carrots, grated
5 or 6 radishes, chopped
Small jar of olives, green or black, chopped
5 Roma tomatoes, chopped
Zesty Italian dressing

Cook spaghetti according to directions.

To make smaller portions of the same recipe, use ½ or ¼ of all ingredients.

Drain cooked spaghetti. Mix all ingredients well, including dressing.

Add dressing as desired.

Orange Salad

2 packages fat-free Jello
2 cups boiling water
1 pint orange sherbet
1 can mandarin oranges
Pineapple (optional)

Dissolve Jello in boiling water. Immediately add sherbet and stir until melted.

Add oranges and 1 can crushed pineapple, if desired.

Pour into 1½ quart mold and chill until firm.

Serve plain or with ambrosia fruit salad.

This recipe may also be used as a dessert.

Chicken Casserole with Buttermilk Crust

Chicken parts, 2 each of legs, thighs or breast, or use a 2½ pound- chicken, boiled. Discard fat.
1 can low-fat cream of chicken soup (undiluted)
2 cups reserved chicken broth
1 garlic clove crushed or 1 teaspoon minced garlic
1 cup plain flour and 1 teaspoon baking powder, or use 1 cup self-rising flour.
1 teaspoon salt
½ teaspoon black pepper
1 cup buttermilk
1 stick, margarine

Cook chicken until tender. Remove meat from bones. Save broth.

Cut chicken into small pieces and place in 13-by-9-by-2 inch casserole dish.

In saucepan, mix and bring to boil reserved chicken broth, soup and garlic.

Pour broth mixture over chicken.

In another bowl, combine butter, pepper, salt, flour and buttermilk.

Mix thoroughly to form batter, pour batter over top of casserole.

Bake at 425 degrees for 25 to 30 minutes or until brown.

Professor Shares Her Nigerian Roots

OCTOBER 19, 2005

Dr. Comfort Okpala

Dr. Comfort Okpala serves up dishes from her native Nigeria.

When the Nigerian Cultural Association celebrated the 45th anniversary of the Independence of the Federal Republic of Nigeria on Oct. 8, the menu was filled with traditional cuisine from Nigeria. The gala also raised money to send medical supplies to Nigeria.

A Nigerian woman's group called the Cultural Dancers planned the menu and made many of the dishes. The dancers also performed the welcoming dance.

Dr. Comfort Okpala helped plan and prepare the dishes. She cooked the baked and curried goat meat and plantains. Originally from Nigeria, she is an adjunct assistant professor at Fayetteville State University and the coordinator of research and assessment at Shaw University.

She shares her recipe for fried plantain. The plantain, a large, firm type of banana, is called a "cooking banana." She also gives us a recipe for Jollof rice, which can be made with beef, chicken, goat, pork, fish or just vegetables.

Another dish that was served at the gala was chinchin, a traditional snack made with flour mixed with sugar, eggs and vanilla. It is rolled up, cut and fried.

African cookies made by Felicia Okeagu contained nuts and special traditional flavors.

Angela Okorieocha made the pepper soup, a hot and spicy dish served with goat meat.

Yams, which are similar to sweet potatoes, are pounded to the consistency of mashed potatoes and called fufu. This was cooked by Esther Okonkwo.

The yam dish is dipped into egusi soup when served. The soup is made with ground melon seeds and vegetables to which meat and fish can be added. It is similar to gumbo and was made by Eugenia Ohadugha.

Fried rice was prepared by Nkechi Kamalu. Uju Egbuna cooked the moi-moi, which is ground and cooked black-eyed peas. The Jollof rice was prepared by Angela Igunbor.

Ruth Jalaoso prepared Scotch eggs, in which eggs are fried with sausage. The dish was introduced into Nigeria by the British during their occupation.

Okpala said these are the dishes she grew up with, and she and her husband still prefer them. Her children like both traditional Nigerian food and dishes from this country. She says the dishes she prepares are healthy. She uses only olive oil for cooking. Since most members of the Nigerian Cultural Association are medical doctors, they are constantly educating other members about healthy eating to lower cholesterol.

Nigerians are able to buy African foods here, and tropical fruits such as pawpaws, bananas and mangos are some of their favorites.

— *Melissa Clement*

Jollof Rice

See photo in center of book

- 2 to 3 pounds chicken or hen pieces
- Olive oil or vegetable oil
- 2 onions (sliced)
- 4 tomatoes (cubed or ground)
- 1 small can tomato paste
- 4 cups of chicken broth
- 1 teaspoon salt (to taste)
- 1 teaspoon cayenne pepper
- 1 teaspoon thyme (optional)
- 1 teaspoon curry powder (optional)
- 2 chicken bouillon cubes
- 4 cups uncooked rice
- 2 cups water, and as needed
- 2 red bell peppers (sliced into small pieces)

Note: This dish is very common throughout Nigeria and other African countries. It can be prepared in a number of ways and can be made with beef, chicken, hen, goat, pork or simply vegetables.

In a large stew pot, brown chicken or hen pieces in olive oil or vegetable oil. Remove meat from pan and set aside.

In the same pan, brown the onions until they are golden.

Add chicken, tomatoes, tomato paste, chicken broth, salt, pepper, thyme, curry and bouillon cubes and bring to a boil, stirring as needed.

Reduce heat, cover and simmer 30 minutes or until the meat is nearly cooked.

Add rice, red bell pepper and additional broth if needed and cook until the rice is tender.

This meal can serve 6 to 8 people and can be served with side dishes such as fried plantain, moi-moi (ground and cooked black-eyed peas) or other vegetables.

Fried Plantain

See photo in center of book

- 5 yellow or ripe plantains
- Cooking oil
- Salt

Note: Fried plantain is one of the favorite side dishes among Nigerians. It can be eaten as an appetizer, a side dish or a breakfast meal. The yellow plantain has a sweet taste.

Put oil in a frying pan and place on stove over medium heat. Remove the skin of the plantains. Slice each plantain into 4 parts lengthwise, then cut into small pieces. Sprinkle with salt to taste. Place in hot oil. Turn plantains until they are golden brown. Remove from the oil and drain. Serves 3 to 5 people.

Fried plantains can be served with Jollof rice, cooked beans or red stew.

Aspiring Writer Improvises With Dishes

May 12, 2004

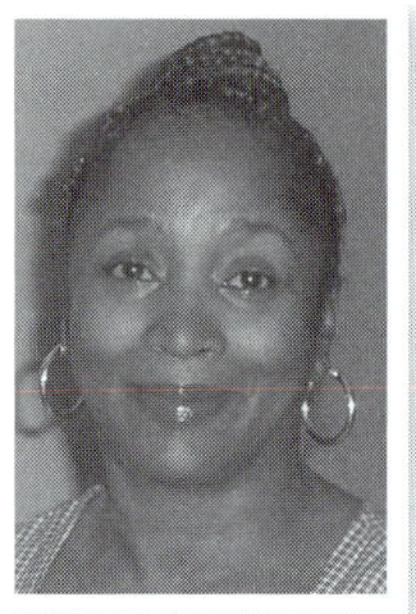
Anita Waller

Anita Waller of Cumberland County likes to cook food naturally. She said it all started in Elizabethtown.

"When I was 12 years old my first meal was hamburger, rice and okra. I used to watch Mom in the kitchen and copy her," she said.

Most of the food for the family of five came straight from the garden or produce store when she was growing up.

Waller would later move to Fayetteville to attend Fayetteville State University. "I didn't learn about fast food until I attended FSU. That's when I was introduced to pizza. I couldn't get enough of it," she said.

After graduating from Fayetteville State, Waller married and traveled with her then military husband.

She was used to using fresh vegetables and fruits but had to improvise when living across the United States. "For example, I had to use baking powder when I didn't have self-rising flour so that the biscuits could rise," she said.

However, when Waller cooks now she doesn't improvise often on her Southern cooking. But she does leave out the fat.

Her three favorite dishes are Carolina oven-fried chicken, cabbage vinegarette and fried-stuffing cornbread.

"My favorite dishes are loved by anyone that tries them. My kids and grandkids can't get enough of my food," she said.

Waller has two daughters and three grandchildren. One daughter has twins, and all are her biggest critics.

The family enjoys her cooking so much that they have asked her to write a cookbook. But for now the cookbook is on hold. After more than 18 years in the Cumberland County school system, Waller is homeschooling her grandchildren and writing her autobiography.

"It will talk about growing up in Elizabethtown. How growing up in a small town taught me about family values," she said. "But I will have to talk about how my love of cooking started there."

— Ealer S. Wadlington III

Carolina Oven Fried Chicken

- 4 chicken leg quarters cut in half, or one whole chicken cut up
- 1 18-ounce bottle of Carolina Treet Barbecue Sauce
- ¼ cup garlic powder
- ¼ cup onion powder
- 2 cups flour
- Butter-flavored Pam spray

Preheat oven to 400 degrees.

Spray baking pan evenly with Pam spray.

Wash and pat dry chicken parts, place chicken in large bowl. Coat chicken evenly with half of the bottle of Carolina Treet Barbecue sauce. Mix dry ingredients in plastic Ziploc bag.

Place individual chicken pieces in plastic bag along with dry ingredients and coat thoroughly. Shake excess flour off chicken and place in baking pan.

Cook until golden brown for one hour.

Cabbage Vinaigrette

- 1 medium head of cabbage
- 2 stems of green onion
- 1 cup white vinegar
- 1 cup vegetable or olive oil
- 1 tablespoon granulated sugar

Cut cabbage and onions together. Wash thoroughly. Heat oil in skillet. Add cabbage and onions. Cook cabbage and onions until tender (about 25 minutes).

Combine vinegar and sugar. Stir into cabbage mixture. Salt and pepper to taste.

Optional: red pepper flakes.

Fried Stuffing Cornbread

- 1 box chicken-flavored stuffing mix (6 ounces)
- 1½ cup yellow cornmeal
- 1 egg
- ½ cup warm water
- 1 cup milk

Mix chicken-flavor seasoning packet with warm water in small mixing bowl. Set aside.

Stir in half of bread crumb mix, cornmeal, egg, and milk until thick (more cornmeal may be added if not thick enough).

Drop into hot oil by spoonfuls. Oil is ready when you drop a very small amount of mix and it bubbles. Brown on each side. Drain on paper towels.

Note: This meal may be served with yellow rice and sliced tomatoes for color and added flavor.

Chicken Salad Recipe Comes to the Rescue

June 14, 2000

Jeneal Harris

When Jeneal Harris was married at age 24, she did not know how to cook.

"If Ken, my husband, hadn't known how to cook we would have starved to death," she says with a laugh. "Ken was the cook. He enjoyed cooking. He would have done all the cooking if he hadn't worked."

The couple was married for 44 years. Ken died two years ago.

Ken learned to cook from his mother and worked in the family grocery store, where he learned butchering. As a student at the University of Florida, he cooked at the campus club while he was a student.

The first Christmas after his death, Jeneal realized she had never cooked a turkey. She went to the market and asked the butcher what she should do. He advised her to try something different, and sold her a pork loin.

"The first time I wanted to entertain, I didn't know if I could do it without him as a back-up in the kitchen."

But her sister, Fay Horne, came to the rescue.

While Harris is not a meat and potato cook, she is well schooled in the art of preparing dishes for teas and parties. She served as president of the Woman's Club of Fayetteville for two years. At their monthly meetings, club members prepare all the food for their luncheons. Last December, she and friends prepared dishes for 60 members.

Some of her favorite recipes for serving at teas are chicken salad that can be served in tiny sandwiches, peach halves, rings of cantaloupe or pastry cups. The chicken salad is placed on a bed of lettuce and a garnish of parsley is added and the dish is served with small wheat crackers.

Cookie recipes are also high on her list of party food. She often bakes cookies for her two grandchildren, who are ages 2 and 3.

Some of her favorite recipes come from a 1973 cookbook by Antoinette Kazmanich Hatfield titled "Food for Fellowship Cookbook."

— *Melissa Clement*

Crispy Cheese Wafers

- 8 oz. sharp cheddar cheese
- 1 stick margarine
- 1 cup flour
- ½ teaspoon salt
- 1 teaspoon red pepper
- 1 cup Rice Krispies

Grate cheese and cream with butter. Sift dry ingredients and add the cheese mixture. Fold in Rice Krispies. Let dough stay in refrigerator overnight. Roll into balls and flatten with fork.

Place on ungreased cookie sheet and bake for 12 minutes at 350 degrees.

Chicken Salad

- 3 cups cooked chicken, diced
- ½ cup celery, thinly sliced
- 2 cups canned pineapple tidbits, drained
- ½ cup slivered blanched almonds
- 1 cup mayonnaise
- 1 teaspoon salt
- Pepper to taste
- 8 peach halves
- Lettuce and parsley

Combine chicken, celery, pineapple and almonds with mayonnaise until completely mixed. Season with salt and pepper to taste. Chill. Scoop onto chilled peach halves. Serve in lettuce cups and garnish with parsley. It may also be served in cantaloupe or honeydew rings.

Sugared Nuts

- 1 stick margarine
- 1 pound pecan halves
- 2 egg whites
- 1 cup sugar
- Dash of salt

Beat egg whites and salt until they form a peak. Gradually add 1 cup sugar while beating until mixed. Add nuts and stir until thoroughly coated with sugar mixture. Preheat oven to 350 degrees and melt butter in roasting pan. Spread coated nuts over melted butter and bake 30 minutes, stirring every 10 minutes.

Peanut Butter Cookies

- 1 box of yellow cake mix
- 1 cup peanut butter
- ½ cup cooking oil
- 2 tablespoons water
- 2 eggs

Bake at 350 degrees for 10 to 12 minutes.

Cook Thankful for Mom's Meals

JANUARY 25, 2006

Leslie Kiewra

Leslie Kiewra says her mother was a really good cook. She says her mother could make the best spaghetti sauce in the world as well as red beans and rice. She cooked from scratch. They lived in Brooklyn and bought fresh produce at the downtown market.

The problem was that Kiewra never fully appreciated her mother's cooking. TV dinners in tinfoil plates were all the rage at the time, and she begged for store-bought meatloaf and canned spaghetti. Today she says she would love to have a chance to thank her mother for all the good things she prepared over the years.

"I feel very guilty to this day. What a gem I had."

Her mother was Irish, and her father's heritage was Italian, German and Scottish, so they ate a variety of foods. Her father was raised in New Orleans, and when the family visited, she ate grits and beans and rice, similar to the recipe she shares. In New Orleans, they shopped at the French Market.

Her mother became a vegetarian after she visited a farm to buy a turkey for a Thanksgiving dinner and saw the bloody carcass. Kiewra is a vegetarian as well.

The biscotti recipe she gives us is a combination of a traditional one and another she found in tofu and soy cookbooks. It substitutes tofu for all or most of the eggs and butter found in other biscotti recipes.

"The lasagna recipe is different every time I make it," she says. "It depends on who will be eating it, what's 'on hand' at the time and the size pan I use. I don't measure unless I'm baking, so the ingredients and amounts will vary in the recipe. I learned how to

Almond-Walnut Biscotti

12 ounces low-fat soft tofu

1 cup sugar or sugar substitute

2 tablespoons vegetable oil

1 teaspoon vanilla extract

1 teaspoon almond extract

3½ cups unbleached flour

2 teaspoons baking powder

½ cup chopped walnuts

½ cup chopped almonds

Blend tofu and sugar until smooth. Add oil and extracts and mix until thoroughly blended.

In a separate bowl, mix flour, baking powder and nuts. Gradually add the tofu mixture to the dry ingredients until combined. Chill mixture until it is easy to handle.

Preheat oven to 325 degrees. Divide dough into 4 equal parts. Roll or pat each part into a log about 2½ by 8 inches. Place logs of dough on a greased cookie sheet and bake for about 25 or 30 minutes. Remove from oven before logs brown.

Lower temperature to 250 degrees. Allow logs to cool slightly. Cut each log on a diagonal into 1-inch slices. Place slices on a cookie sheet and bake again for about 20 minutes, until each slice is slightly brown and hard.

make this almost 40 years ago from a fellow teacher. It's the potluck dish of choice for me because of not having to cook the noodles before assembling the dish saves so much time and mess. I don't mind mess as long as someone else is cleaning up."

On the weekends, Kiewra cooks a variety of vegetables which she eats when she comes home from her job as a Cumberland County school counselor. She loves to read cookbooks and had more than 100 in her collection at one time.

Now that her three children are grown, she doesn't cook as much and doesn't do all the canning and freezing she used to. She recently gave away her canning supplies and instruments. She laughs when she says she also gave away a rusted freezer she bought in 1971, which still works.

"The Smithsonian didn't want it," she says.

— *Melissa Clement*

Lasagna

- Nonstick vegetable-oil spray
- Ricotta, low-fat cottage cheese or soft tofu
- 1 or 2 eggs, or the equivalent of egg whites or eggless product
- Parsley, oregano, Italian seasoning
- Homemade or store-bought pasta sauce
- Regular lasagna noodles
- Fresh or frozen chopped spinach, shredded zucchini or other vegetable
- Shredded mozzarella cheese or soy equivalent
- Parmesan cheese

Note: The amount of the ingredients will depend on the size of the pan.

Preheat oven to 350 degrees. Coat a pan with nonstick vegetable-oil spray.

In a bowl, mix ricotta with eggs. Add seasonings to mixture and set aside.

Layer a small amount of sauce in bottom of pan. Place a single layer of dry, uncooked noodles on top of sauce. Noodles may be broken by hand to fit the pan shape.

Wet each noodle with a small amount of boiling water. Top with a layer of cheese mixture, a layer of vegetables, then a layer of sauce.

Repeat layers, ending with a layer of sauce. Leave room in the pan for expansion.

Add boiling water to the pan until the liquid reaches half way up the side. Cover tightly with foil and bake for 1½ hours or until the noodles have softened.

Remove from the oven and uncover. Sprinkle with mozzarella, Parmesan and additional seasonings.

Return to the oven without the foil for 10-15 minutes, or until cheese is melted.

Let rest for 20 minutes before serving with additional sauce spooned on top.

Red Beans and Rice

- 1 (1-pound) bag small, round dried red beans
- Water
- 1 large onion
- 1 green pepper
- 4 stalks celery
- 2 cloves garlic
- 1 bay leaf
- Tabasco sauce
- Salt
- Pepper
- Smoked tofu, tempeh or other soy product (optional)
- Cooked rice
- Pickled red onions

Wash and pick over beans. Place in a large pot and cover with at least 2 inches of plain water. Soak overnight, while keeping some water covering the beans at all times.

Dice onion, pepper, celery and garlic and saute in a nonstick pan until the vegetables begin to wilt and then caramelize.

Drain soaked beans and return to pot. Add plain water to cover, along with the bay leaf and cooked vegetable mixture.

Optional ingredients may be cooked separately and then added to the beans at this time.

Bring to a boil, lower heat and simmer on low until the beans are soft enough to mash with a fork against the side of the pot. This may take several hours depending on the age of the beans. Remove about half the beans to a bowl and mash with a potato masher. Return mashed beans to the pot and mix. Remove bay leaf and add salt, pepper and Tabasco sauce.

Serve red beans over cooked rice with a garnish of chopped pickled red onions.

She Specializes in Special Events

November 14, 2001

Lynn Clark

In her job as assistant to the president for special events at Methodist College, Lynn Clark gets to pick out recipes and menus for a caterer to cook dishes for dinners and receptions.

"I love to cook, but I don't do as many complicated things as I used to," she says.

Clark grew up in Baltimore and first came to Fayetteville as a student at Methodist from 1968 1972.

She returned in 1985 to work as the alumni director.

Later she was the director of community relations before moving into her current position.

Clark got an early start in event planning. After graduation, she worked for the Chalfonte-Haddon Hall oceanfront resort in Atlantic City, N.J., planning social events and entertainment for guests and conferences.

"It was before the gambling casinos, when the same people would return every year to the large resort," Clark says.

She lived at the resort and enjoyed watching the chefs prepare the foods for the elaborate dinners, holidays and receptions.

She says she learned to cook from scratch around that time.

After she married Sam Clark of Fayetteville, she says she had to learn to cook dishes his family made — dishes like cornbread dressing at Thanksgiving instead of the bread and oyster dressing she had in Baltimore.

Lynn Clark says when she gets a craving for soft-shell crabs, Maryland crab cakes or crab salad, she has to head home to Baltimore to see her father and her brother.

"My husband is allergic to seafood, so I don't cook much seafood," she says.

Other than making her favorite oatmeal lace cookies when she was young, she says she stayed out of the kitchen at home.

She still likes to make the oatmeal cookies from her youth.

"They are my favorite cookies in the whole world," she says. "They get lacy on the top and a smooth glaze forms on the bottom."

Some of Clark's other favorite recipes are entrees and party foods that friends always request her to bring to gatherings and ask for the recipe.

She likes to prepare much of the food for a party ahead of time.

"That's because I like to enjoy my own parties," she says.

– Alice Thrasher

Crab Delight

2½ cups mayonnaise

2½ cups milk

1 pound crabmeat

6 hard-boiled eggs, chopped fine

3 tablespoons green pepper, chopped fine

1 small jar cut pimientos, chopped fine

¼ teaspoon salt

12 slices bread, with crusts, torn into pieces

Shredded cheddar cheese

Crushed corn flakes

Mix mayonnaise and milk; set aside.

Mix crabmeat, eggs, peppers, pimiento, salt and bread. Add milk mixture and mix well.

Pour into a 2½-or 3-quart rectangular casserole dish.

Cover with shredded cheese (just enough to cover).

Refrigerate and cover overnight (or at least four hours).

Take out 1 hour before baking time.

Crush corn flakes on top.

Bake at 325 degrees for 45 minutes.

Yield: 10 to 15 servings.

Mandarin Cranberry Relish

1 can (15 ounces) whole-berry cranberry sauce

⅛ cup red onion, finely chopped (optional)

1 teaspoon fresh ginger, minced, or

¼ teaspoon ground ginger

Dash of nutmeg

1 can (11 ounces) mandarin oranges, drained well

Combine cranberry sauce, onion, ginger and nutmeg; mix well.

Gently stir in oranges.

Chill until serving time.

Serve with turkey, ham or chicken.

Also good on a turkey, ham or chicken sandwich.

Makes two cups.

Oatmeal Lace Cookies

1 egg, beaten

1 cup rolled oats

1 cup sugar

½ cup melted butter

3 tablespoons all-purpose flour, sifted

¼ teaspoon baking powder

½ teaspoon salt

½ teaspoon vanilla

Mix ingredients.

Cover cookie sheets with aluminum foil, shiny side up. Drop batter, six cookies at a time because they spread.

Bake at 350 degrees for 10 minutes.

Slide foil off of cookie sheet. Let cool for 8 minutes on aluminum foil, then peel cookies off foil.

Yield: approximately 3 to 4 dozen cookies.

Olive Sandwich Spread

6 ounces cream cheese, softened

½ cup mayonnaise

1 cup chopped salad olives

2 tablespoons olive liquid from jar

Dash of pepper

Mix together and put in a tightly sealed container and refrigerate.

Can use biscuit cutters to cut white or whole wheat bread for tea sandwiches.

Easy Apple and Yam Bake

1 large can yams (cut), drained

1 can apple pie filling

¼ cup golden raisins (more or less, to taste)

Mix gently with a spoon so that yams are not broken up.

Place in round or square casserole dish and bake at 350 degrees for 25 minutes, or until hot.

Can microwave on high approximately 3 minutes, or until hot.

Yields 6 servings. May be easily doubled or tripled. Preparation time: 4 minutes.

Party Maven Gets Ready for Holiday Festivities

October 29, 2003

Rose Outlaw

Martha Stewart is the maven for entertaining, but Rose Outlaw isn't too far behind.

Take the time when Outlaw attended a function at an eatery, and it closed abruptly, leaving the patrons without a meal. Outlaw invited the entire party to her home and cooked for them.

"I love to do last-minute things," Outlaw said.

Parties are her forte. In just a few weeks her home will be filled with about 125 people for an annual Christmas party. Outlaw has already begun preparing for the festive affair. Her home has begun taking on a holiday look. Greenery with bows hangs above the doorways. Candles are on the table. A Christmas tree with clear lights is up in the den. A DJ has been hired to play the music for this year's event and the one in 2004.

"When you decorate nine rooms with 10 Christmas trees, three outside and two in the garage, you have to plan early," Outlaw said.

Starting this week, she will begin preparing some of the 35 dishes she plans to have on the menu.

"Party foods are my favorites, and I love doing unusual," Outlaw said. "I love to do the country dishes, the black-eyed peas, collards and fatback, but I love party foods."

Outlaw will first cook items that can be prepared in advance and frozen, such as desserts. "A lot of desserts seem to be better to me out of the freezer because of the moisture," she said. Things like fudge and candy are done the day before. Vegetables, meat and shrimp are done the morning of the event.

One of Outlaw's signature dishes is Poppy Seed Sandwiches, which she says can be a breakfast item or food for entertaining. The sandwiches are made with sandwich meats, usually ham, cheese, mustard and garlic on poppy-seed bread. Another of her favorite dishes is red velvet cake.

"I do two or three of those during the holidays," Outlaw said.

Outlaw considers herself versatile when it comes to cooking. She likes to try various types of cuisine and will often add her own twist to the dish.

"If someone gives me a recipe, I might add or take

Pumpkin Pie Cake

- 29-ounce can pumpkin
- 1 cup sugar
- 13-ounce can evaporated milk
- 3 eggs
- 1 teaspoon cinnamon
- ½ teaspoon nutmeg
- ½ teaspoon ginger
- 1 box yellow cake mix
- 1 cup chopped nuts
- 2 sticks butter or margarine
- 8-ounce package of cream cheese
- 1 cup powdered sugar
- 8 ounces Cool Whip

Mix the first 7 ingredients. Line a 13-by-9-inch pan with wax paper and pour mixture into pan. Layer one-half box of cake mix, nuts and the other half of the cake mix. Melt butter and drizzle over top. Bake at 350 degrees until done.

After cake cools, turn it out of the pan and pull wax paper off.

Mix cream cheese, powdered sugar and Cool Whip. Spread onto cake and refrigerate.

away to change the texture," she said.

There aren't many dishes Outlaw can't conquer, but there is one she will take the shortcut to prepare — chicken and pastry.

"I despise rolling out the pastry," she said. "I buy my pastry."

Outlaw is a veteran cook, having perfected her craft during her days in high school. Her job at home was to prepare dinner before she could partake in any social events.

"I had to cook supper for my parents every single night when I was in school before I could do anything with my friends," Outlaw said. "I learned some cooking when I lived at home with my parents, then I learned some by trial and error when I got married."

– Jeffery Womble

Southern Caviar

- 1 can (14 ounces) black-eyed peas, drained and rinsed
- 1 can (14 ounces) black beans, drained and rinsed
- 1 can (15 ounces) white hominy, drained and rinsed
- 2 medium tomatoes, seeded and chopped
- 4 green onions, chopped
- 2 garlic cloves, crushed
- 1 medium bell pepper, sweet red or yellow pepper, seeded and chopped
- 1 jalapeno pepper, seeded and minced
- ½ cup chopped onion
- ½ cup chopped fresh cilantro (parsley will work, too)
- 8 ounces of your favorite Italian salad dressing

Combine all ingredients in a medium bowl, mixing well. Chill at least two hours or overnight to blend flavors. Drain before serving. Serve with tortilla chips. (Also does well as a side dish).

Raspberry Delight

- 2 small packages of raspberry Jell-O
- 20-ounce can of crushed pineapple
- 1 cup pineapple juice
- 8-ounce package of cream cheese (softened)
- 9-ounce container of Cool Whip
- 2 tablespoons of flour
- ¾ cup sugar
- 2 eggs, beaten
- Pecans

Prepare Jell-O as directed on box. Allow to jell slightly. Drain pineapple and reserve liquid; add pineapple to Jell-O. Refrigerate until fully congealed. Mix Cool Whip and cream cheese. Spread on top of Jell-O. In saucepan, heat pineapple juice, beaten eggs, sugar and flour to a boil. Let cool and spread on top of cream cheese mixture. Top with nuts.

FTCC Retiree Goes for the Quick-Cooking Recipes

April 7, 2004

Carolyn Shaw

In a countryside of lifelong, country-style cooks, Carolyn Shaw is a bit of an exception.

"I didn't really learn how to cook until about 7 years ago," she said. "You've got so many people who've cooked all their lives. My experience is much more limited."

Don't worry. Shaw's a quick study, and since retiring from Fayetteville Technical Community College, she's making up for lost time.

"I'm a long way from what you'd call an expert cook," she said with a laugh. "I didn't have to cook with my mom around. Then she died suddenly of a massive heart attack. I had to kind of take over."

She began studying old recipes, and she became a faithful reader of quick-cooking magazines.

"I like to cook things that don't take a lot of time," she said.

More recently, she's helped put together a cookbook that combined the best of old country cooking and quick recipes. Her church, Flat Branch Presbyterian, planned to rerelease a congregational cookbook. Thanks to a deluge of contributions, the book grew from about 175 recipes to more than 600. Released last October, the cookbook has generated a lot of community interest.

"It's hard-covered, with a lot of special features," Shaw said. "And at only $12.50, we've had a lot of response.

"It has a little bit of everything. Sometimes you'll find some different recipes for the same thing, but all of them are a little bit different."

One of her favorite recipes in the book is Sesame Chicken Bites. "The sesame chicken is delicious," Shaw said. "It's a big favorite at covered-dish dinners and circle meetings. It came from Marian and Bill Thomas, and people are always looking for it at church functions."

Shaw shows her sweet tooth with a couple of dessert recipes, Snickers Cookies and "Can't-Leave-Alone" Bars. Both, she says, are quick-cookers she found in magazines.

"They're both easy, and they're good," she said. "The 'Can't-Leave-Alone' Bars have a perfect name. Once you start on them, you can't leave them alone.

"The best thing is that anyone can make them. You don't have to be a great cook, but an expert cook can appreciate them."

People interested in ordering a copy of the cookbook can call Flat Branch Presbyterian at 893-8578 from 9 to 11 a.m.

"We may have to reprint the book," Shaw said. "It's been very popular."

– Chick Jacobs

"Can't Leave Alone" Bars

- 1 package (18½ ounces) white cake mix
- 1 can (14 ounces) sweetened condensed milk
- 2 eggs
- ½ cup vegetable oil
- 6 ounces semi-sweet chocolate chips
- ¼ cup butter or margarine, cubed

In a bowl, combine the cake mix, eggs and oil. With floured hands, press ⅔ of the mixture into a greased 13-by-9-by-2-inch baking pan. Set remaining cake mixture aside.

In a microwave-safe bowl, combine the milk, chocolate chips and butter. Microwave uncovered on high for 45 seconds and stir. Microwave another 45 seconds or until the chips and butter are melted. Stir until smooth, and pour over crust.

Drop teaspoons of remaining cake mixture over the top. Bake at 350 degrees for 20 to 25 minutes, or until lightly browned. Cool before cutting.

Snickers Cookies

- 1 tube (18 ounces) refrigerated chocolate chip cookie dough
- 24 to 30 bite-sized Snickers bars

Cut dough into ¼-inch-thick slices. Place a candy bar on top of each slice and wrap dough around it. Place two inches apart on ungreased baking sheet.

Bake at 350 degrees for 8 to 10 minutes or until lightly browned. Cool on wire rack.

Sesame Chicken Bites

- ½ cup dry bread crumbs
- ¼ cup sesame seeds
- 2 teaspoons minced fresh parsley
- ½ cup mayonnaise
- 1 teaspoon onion powder
- ¼ teaspoon pepper
- 1 teaspoon ground mustard
- 1 pound boneless, skinless chicken breast, cut into 1-inch cubes
- 1 to 4 tablespoons vegetable oil

<u>HONEY-MUSTARD:</u>

- ¾ cup mayonnaise
- 4½ teaspoon honey
- 1½ teaspoon Dijon mustard

In a large resealable bag, combine the bread crumbs, sesame seeds and parsley, then set aside. In a small bowl, combine the mayonnaise, onion powder, mustard and pepper. Coat chicken in mayonnaise mixture, then add to crumb mixture a few pieces at a time. Shake to coat.

In a large skillet, saute chicken in oil in batches until juices run clear, adding additional oil as needed.

Honey mustard: in a small bowl, combine sauce ingredients. Serve with the chicken.

Home-Cooked Meals Made Easy

September 19, 2001

Lee Moeller

When Lee Moeller is in a hurry, she has a favorite recipe to fall back on for a quick home-cooked meal.

She used it last week when she had a call at noon that her church, First Presbyterian, was having a special service that evening and wanted the choir to participate. She and her husband, Dr. Arlyn Moeller, both sing in the choir. She's an interior decorator and has been active with boards of civic organizations and a member of a garden club and book club.

"I grabbed a pound of hamburger out of the freezer and got going," she says.

The dish is one she used to make for her family when her children were growing up in Michigan. Arlyn Moeller was in practice in Bay City, Mich., for 23 years. The couple moved to Fayetteville in 1982, when Arlyn accepted a job with Duke University to teach at the former Fayetteville Area Health Education Center. He now practices part time in a family medical group.

The Moellers' son, Mark, is a physician in Colorado. Daughter Laurie lives in Pennsylvania and daughter Lisa lives in Oregon.

"We always tried to have dinner together as a family," Lee Moeller says. She says she cooks at home four or five nights a week now.

The family — now 14 strong — gathers in Ocean Isle each July to give all the young cousins time to know each other, she says.

"I was born and raised in Iowa and we always had a big tradition of Sunday dinners," Lee says.

Aryln Moeller, who grew up in Iowa also, served in the Air Force after medical school. The couple lived in Japan with two babies, about 25 miles outside Tokoyo, for two years.

While in Japan, Lee took some Chinese cooking classes from two American nuns who had lived in a concentration camp in China.

A cookbook the nuns published has been one of Lee's favorites over the years.

"They took Chinese recipes and made them easier for Americans," she says.

— Alice Thrasher

Chinese Fried Rice

See photo in center of book

2 tablespoons oil

1 to 2 cups onions, coarsely chopped

2 cups cold, cooked rice

2 eggs, stirred slightly

1 tablespoon soy sauce

½ teaspoon salt

OPTIONAL:

2 cups chopped, cooked meat (bacon, ham, shrimp, leftovers)

Green peppers

Roasted peanuts, shelled and chopped

Heat skillet. Add the oil and fry the onions until brown. Add the cold, cooked rice and saute.

Add a mixture of two eggs, stirred slightly, soy sauce and salt. Saute until done.

For variety, add chopped meat or green peppers or chopped, roasted peanuts.

When finished with frying rice, pack the mixture gently into a skillet and brown on side. Cut a square in center and sections on the outside ring. Turn one section at a time to brown on the other side.

Note: Dish can be made ahead of time, saving the final browning (with a small amount of oil) until just before serving.

Turkey Buffet Casserole

2 cups cooked turkey, cut up

1 package frozen broccoli

2 cups medium wide or curly noodles

⅓ cup slivered, toasted almonds

1 cup grated cheddar cheese

2 tablespoons butter or margarine

2 tablespoons flour

1 teaspoon salt

¼ teaspoon prepared mustard

¼ teaspoon pepper

2 cups milk

Cook noodles and broccoli separately until just tender. Drain and set aside. In a saucepan, over low heat, melt butter; blend in flour and next four ingredients, stirring constantly until thickened.

Remove from heat; stir in cheese until melted. Dice broccoli (save some flowerettes for top).

Layer noodles, broccoli and turkey in an 8-inch square pan (greased). Pour sauce over all. Arrange broccoli flowerettes on top. Sprinkle almonds over the top. Bake until bubbly, 15 to 25 minutes.

Yield: 4 to 6 servings.

Variation: Substitute chicken or ham for turkey.

Hamburger Stroganoff

- 1 to 1½ pounds lean ground beef
- 1 tablespoon vegetable oil
- 1 medium onion, chopped
- 1 clove garlic, minced
- 1 teaspoon salt
- ¼ teaspoon pepper
- 2 tablespoons flour
- 1 can tomato sauce (8 ounces)
- 1 can mushroom pieces (4 ounces)
- 1 cup sour cream (optional)
- Hot, cooked rice or noodles, for 4 to 5 servings

In a large skillet, brown beef in oil. Add onion, garlic, salt and pepper. Simmer 5 minutes.

Sprinkle flour over meat and stir in.

Pour in tomato sauce and mushrooms. Simmer for another 5 to 10 minutes. Add sour cream just before serving.

Serve over rice or noodles.

Variation: A little red or white wine can be added for subtle flavor, if desired.

Beef with Peppers

- 1½ tablespoons oil
- 1 clove garlic, crushed
- 1 pound beef
- 1 teaspoon salt
- Pepper to taste
- 1 cup soup stock (or 1 beef bouillon cube dissolved in 1 cup hot water)
- 2 tablespoons cornstarch
- 1 tablespoon soy sauce
- 2 tablespoons water
- 1 cup green peppers, sliced lengthwise
- ½ teaspoon fresh ginger, chopped fine
- Rice

Heat skillet or wok. Add oil and the crushed garlic clove. When garlic turns brown, remove and discard. Add the beef, cut in small, thin pieces and fry a few minutes. Season with 1 teaspoon salt. Add pepper to taste. Add 1 cup soup stock (or 1 beef bouillon cube dissolved in 1 cup hot water). Continue to cook a few seconds.

Add a mixture of cornstarch, soy sauce and water.

Cook until sauce thickens, stirring slowly. Add the sliced green peppers and chopped fresh ginger.

Heat thoroughly and serve hot, over rice.

Serves four to six.

Engineer Gets Creative While Cooking

July 4, 2001

Mike Dubnansky

DuPont engineer Mike Dubnansky says he probably is atypical of most engineers.

In his work, he has to be exacting.

In the kitchen, he says he operates more by taste and feel, adjusting recipes and making up new ones as he goes along.

"Cooking is an outlet for my creativity," he says.

"I like to cook and I like going to the grocery store. We spend more, though, when I do the shopping."

That's because he likes to look at all the new things on the market and try them out.

Mike and his wife, Sandy, share the shopping and cooking responsibilities at home for themselves and their children, Michael, 7, and Alexandra, 5.

"Her preference is pastry and breads," Mike says.

Mike says his mother always made home-cooked meals when he was growing up in Baltimore.

"She instilled in me a taste for good food, and food was a big part of my family," he says.

The family moved to Fayetteville from Pennsylvania about five years ago. Sandy has been teaching French at The Fayetteville Academy. They have decided to move back to Pennsylvania to be closer to their families there and in Maryland.

The Dubnanskys are leaving behind good friends in King's Grant and Fayetteville.

"This place, by far, has had the most friendly people of any city we have lived," Mike says.

"We have experienced all kinds of cultures and foods. We have enjoyed having friends over and going to their homes. I wish we could bring them all with us."

Mike says he will miss Eastern North Carolina-style barbecue.

"I came down as a fan of Yankee barbecue and leave as a fan of Eastern North Carolina barbecue," he says.

He also will miss his herb garden. "We like to eat fresh fruits and vegetables and have them still be healthy," he says.

– Alice Thrasher

Grilled, Herbed New Potatoes

1½ pounds new potatoes (red or white)

3 cloves fresh garlic, chopped very fine (food processor preferred)

chopped fresh herbs (thyme, rosemary, parsley and chives are Mike Dubnansky's favorites)

2 to 3 tablespoons olive oil

1 tablespoon butter (can omit, to cut fat and calories)

Kosher salt, to taste

Fresh ground pepper, to taste

Cut new potatoes to desired size, if necessary.

Mix all ingredients together and place into Reynolds aluminum foil bag for grilling.

Cook potatoes on grill, turning bag periodically to prevent burning.

Remove bag from grill and serve.

Serves 4 to 6 adults.

Note: Can also roast potatoes in the oven, if desired.

Green Beans with Garlic

See photo in center of book

1 pound fresh green beans, washed and trimmed

2 cloves fresh garlic, chopped

2 to 3 tablespoons olive oil

1 tablespoon butter (can omit to cut calories and fat)

White wine or water

Kosher salt, to taste

Fresh ground pepper, to taste

Heat pan, then add oil, butter, garlic and green beans.

Stir fry on medium to high heat until garlic begins to turn golden.

Turn down heat slightly, add several tablespoons of white wine and cover.

Cook to desired doneness (check periodically and add more wine if necessary).

Serves 4 to 6 adults.

Fresh Tomato and Mozzarella Salad

See photo in center of book

3 to 4 medium-sized, vine-ripened tomatoes, sliced

6 to 8 ounces fresh mozzarella cheese, sliced

16 to 24 fresh basil leaves

Kosher salt, to taste

Fresh ground pepper, to taste

Slice tomatoes to medium thickness. Slice cheese, thin to medium thickness.

Arrange on a salad plate and top with fresh basil leaves, salt and pepper.

Serve with favorite vinaigrette salad dressing.

Ice Cream with Seasonal Fruit and Berries

- 4 cups fresh, seasonal fruit and berries (whole, chopped or balled)
- 3 tablespoons sugar (can vary according to sweetness of fruit or berry mix)
- 2 tablespoons Grand Marnier liqueur

Combine fruit, sugar and liqueur in covered bowl and chill in refrigerator (overnight preferred).

Serve with vanilla ice cream. Garnish with a thin butter cookie, if desired.

Serves 4 to 6 adults.

Poached Salmon with Horseradish Sauce

- 2 1-pound salmon filets (can use steaks if preferred)
- Juice from half a lemon (if desired)

POACHING LIQUID:

- 3 cups chicken stock (can use water for "meatless" version)
- 1 cup white wine
- Stalk celery, chopped (tops or core with pale colored leaves preferred)
- 1 carrot, chopped
- 2 shallots or onion, chopped
- 2 cloves fresh garlic, chopped
- 4 sprigs thyme, whole
- 2 sprigs fresh parsley, whole
- 10 peppercorns, whole (any or all colors — black, white, green or red)

HORSERADISH SAUCE:

- 8 ounces sour cream (can use light or fat-free to cut fat and calories)
- 4 ounces mayonnaise (Mike Dubnansky prefers Duke's brand)
- ⅓ cup horseradish (more if desired)
- 1 teaspoon Worcestershire sauce
- Dash of ground white pepper
- ¾ to 1 ounce fresh chives, chopped

Wash salmon. If desired, squeeze juice from half a lemon over salmon. Store in the refrigerator.

Combine all ingredients in a large, covered pan. Heat to boil.

Place salmon in pan (fish should not be completely submerged).

Once poaching liquid returns to a boil, turn down heat until poaching liquid just stops boiling. Cover pan.

Maintain poaching liquid below boiling and cook salmon until it achieves desired doneness (medium rare to medium well is preferred).

Remove salmon from poaching liquid and cut to desired serving size.

Serve salmon with horseradish sauce. Garnish with whole or chopped fresh chives if desired.

Serves 4 to 6 adults.

Note: Can retain poaching liquid and freeze for future use, if desired.

HORSERADISH SAUCE:

Combine all ingredients in the food processor and blend.

Hand mix, if preferred.

Chill in refrigerator until ready to serve.

Note: Prepare in advance of meal. Can make up to several days in advance.

Index

Cooks Index